D0392424

ADDICTED TO REFORM

Also by John Merrow

The Influence of Teachers

Declining by Degrees (co-editor)

Choosing Excellence

ADDICTED
TO REFORM

A 12-STEP PROGRAM TO RESCUE
PUBLIC EDUCATION

JOHN MERROW

THE NEW PRESS

25 YEARS

NEW YORK
LONDON

Requests for permission to reproduce selections from this book should be mailed to:
Permissions Department, The New Press, 120 Wall Street, 31st floor, New York,
NY 10005.

Published in the United States by The New Press, New York, 2017
Distributed by Perseus Distribution

ISBN 978-1-62097-241-0 (hc)
ISBN 978-1-62097-243-4 (e-book)
CIP data is available

The New Press publishes books that promote and enrich public discussion and
understanding of the issues vital to our democracy and to a more equitable world.
These books are made possible by the enthusiasm of our readers; the support of a
committed group of donors, large and small; the collaboration of our many partners
in the independent media and the not-for-profit sector; booksellers, who often hand-
sell New Press books; librarians; and above all by our authors.

www.thenewpress.com

Book design and composition by Bookbright Media
This book was set in Janson Text and Gill Sans

Printed in the United States of America

10 9 8 7 6 5 4 3 2 1

For my grandchildren, and yours

Contents

Preface

While pundits and analysts will argue for years about the 2016 election results, left out of the conversation is an astounding fact: *non-voters* vastly outnumbered those who voted for either Donald Trump or Hillary Clinton. Approximately 130 million voters went to the polls in 2016. Clinton received 65,844,954 votes to Trump's 62,979,879, but more than 100 million Americans of voting age did not cast ballots.

In fact, if "not voting" were looked upon as a choice, similar to choosing a candidate, it would have won the popular vote in every presidential election since at least 1916. Americans have a bad habit of not voting. Only three times in the fifteen presidential elections since 1960 have more than 60 percent of the voting age population gone to the polls. The turnout in what we like to believe is the world's greatest democracy generally hovers around 53 to 54 percent. It has dipped *below* 50 percent three times since 1916, most recently in 1996, when only 49.1 percent of the voting age population bothered to vote.[1]

Who are these non-voters? Should we scorn them for their indifference? Don't they understand how many of their fellow Americans have died protecting their freedom and their right to vote? Surely we can agree that their not voting is deplorable behavior.

Not so fast. I have come to believe that most non-voters are behaving rationally. Feeling that they have no stake in our government, they don't vote. And why should they? Schooled to see themselves as insignificant, as adults they keep their heads down, stay uninvolved, and do their best to make ends meet.

Yes, I am holding public schools at least partly responsible for our consistently low voter turnout, because public education, an efficient sorting machine, is undemocratic to its core. Schools sort young children in two basic groups: a minority of "winners" who are placed on a track leading them to elite colleges, prominence, and financial success, and everyone else. While the rest aren't labeled "losers" per se, they are largely left to struggle on their own. That experience leaves many angry, frustrated, and resentful, not to mention largely unprepared for life in a complex, rapidly changing society. Why would they become active participants in the political process, an effort that is almost always led by the now grown-up "winners" from their school days?

Although formal tracking has fallen out of favor, schools have subtle ways of designating winners and losers, often based as much on parental education and income, race, and class as innate ability. By third or fourth grade most kids know, deep down, whether the system sees them as "winners" bound for college or "losers" headed somewhere else.

Ironically, *A Nation at Risk*, the 1983 report that warned of "a rising tide of mediocrity," may have made matters worse. In response, America put its eggs in the basket of student achievement—as measured by student test scores. Believing we were raising academic standards by asking more of students, we were in fact narrowing our expectations. This practice went into high gear with the passage of the No Child Left Behind Act of 2001 and continued throughout the Bush and Obama administrations. What I call "regurgitation education" became the order of the day. This approach rewards parroting back answers, while devaluing intellectual curiosity, cooperative learning, projects, field trips, the arts, physical education, and citizenship.

This fundamentally anti-intellectual approach has failed to produce the results our nation claims to desire. Scores on our National Assessment of Educational Progress (NAEP) have largely remained flat and in some instances have gone down.

What's more, students aren't even retaining what we are demanding they regurgitate. For example, a survey reveals that one-third of Americans cannot name any of the three branches of our government, and half do not know the number of U.S. senators.[2]

Reducing kids to test scores has produced millions of high school graduates whose teachers and curriculum did not help them develop the habits of asking questions, digging deep, or discovering and following their passions. Because of how they were treated in school, many Americans have not grown into curious, socially conscious adults. This is not the fault of their teachers, because decisions about how schools operate are not made in classrooms. It was school boards, politicians, policy makers, and the general public that created schools that value obedience over just about everything else.

But the end result is millions of graduates who were rewarded with diplomas but have never participated in the give-and-take of ordinary citizenship—like voting. Did they graduate from school prepared for life in a democracy, or are they likely to follow blindly the siren song of authoritarians? Can they weigh claims and counterclaims and make decisions based on facts and their family's best interests, or will they give their support to those who play on their emotions?

During the 2016 campaign, Donald Trump welcomed support from those he called "the poorly educated," but that's the incorrect term. These men and women are not "poorly educated," "undereducated," or "uneducated." They have been *miseducated*, an important distinction. Schools have treated them as objects, as empty vessels to pour information into so facts and figures can be regurgitated back on tests.

The sorting process used in schools has another result: it produces elitists (in both political parties) who feel superior to the largely invisible "losers" from their school days. Arguably, those chickens came home to roost in the 2016 presidential election. Candidate Clinton calling her opponent's supporters "a basket of deplorables" was a gaffe that probably cost her the election. But in all likelihood she was speaking her personal truth, because, after all, her schools had identified her as a "winner," one of the elite.

It's perfectly understandable that she would not identify with the people who had been energized by Donald Trump. Most pundits, reporters, pollsters, and politicians fell into the same trap.

Sorting is inevitable, because students try out for teams and plays, apply to colleges, and eventually seek employment, but we must learn to postpone sorting for as long as possible. A new approach to schooling must ask a different question about each young child. Let's stop asking, "How intelligent are you?" Let's ask instead, *"How are you intelligent?"* That may strike some as a steep hill to climb, but it's essentially the question that caring parents, teachers, and other adults ask about individual children. They phrase it differently, asking, "What is Susan interested in?" "What gets George excited?" "What motivates Juan?" or "What does Sharese care about?" Every child has interests, and those can be tapped and nurtured in schools designed to provide opportunities for children to succeed as they pursue paths of their own choosing. Giving children agency over their education—with appropriate guidance and supervision—will produce graduates better equipped to cope with today's changing world. And a larger supply of informed voters.

While the country can survive four—perhaps eight—years of Donald Trump, our democracy must have schools that respect and nurture our children. If we don't change our schools, we will elect a succession of Donald Trumps, and that will be the end of the American experiment.

Memory Lane

It was raining heavily when the departing superintendent picked up his briefcase and left his office for the last time. As he made his way down the hall, a handful of employees clapped, and he smiled in return. Then he popped open his umbrella and went out into the driving rain, his route taking him under the large banner that had heralded his arrival some six years earlier.

Within days, the banner would be gone, an acting superintendent would move into the large office, and the teachers and principals who had resisted change would breath a collective sigh of relief and return to business as usual . . . at least until the next wave of school reform arrived.

Of that they could be certain: a new school reform effort would be announced in short order, because that's how our public education system works.

I've seen this story more times than I can remember: a well-intentioned reformer is hired and arrives with great fanfare, ambitious plans, and an inspiring catchphrase like "A New Start," "Educational Renewal," "Fresh Choices for All," "Children Achieving," or "Putting Children First." In response, those who are comfortable with (or benefiting from) the status quo either hunker down or actively resist the reformer's attempts to change. It may take a few years, but eventually the new leader, worn down from prolonged battles, is forced out or quits in frustration. And business as usual continues.

For decades now, "business as usual" has meant that testing and test scores were in the driver's seat. In my mind's eye, I can see a dozen teachers at Cincinnati's Woodward High School who had worked since September to help their ninth graders adjust to taking responsibility for their own learning, instead of just regurgitating material that had been spoon fed to them.

Although old habits, formed in their first eight years of school, were hard to break, by spring it was finally happening. Then, in May, their principal, who had been supportive of their approach, called them together and ordered them to stop "this new stuff" and start practicing for the Ohio exam, just a month away.[3] They had no choice but to comply.[4]

Did the principal believe that drilling would actually produce better scores, or was he doing what he thought he had to do in order to save his job? Should we condemn his action, or feel his pain? Or do both?

THE NATURE AND PURPOSE OF
"SCHOOL REFORM"

The more I thought about all the well-meaning educators I've encountered over the years, the more I found myself wondering about *the nature and purpose* of most attempts to change schools. The result is this book, which argues that nearly all of our school reform efforts have been directed at *symptoms* like low graduation rates, low test scores, or "the achievement gap."[5] These reforms sound great and may even produce temporary improvements, but they inevitably fail because they are not addressing the root cause of our educational problems: an approach to schooling that is mired in the past and cannot fulfill the needs of the twenty-first century.

It seems to me that our system is sacrificing good, smart, caring people like that superintendent and those teachers and their principal to the false god of school reform: higher scores on tests that measure—at best—"bite-size knowledge." Is it within our power to build a system of schools that allows dedicated educators to be successful, while giving all children opportunities to reach their potential?[6] I believe it is.

The practice in the Bush and Obama administrations was to use scores on standardized tests as the most important measure of a *teacher's value*. Their mantra was that teachers are the key to student learning. "Outstanding teachers give kids the skills and knowledge they need to escape poverty," and so on. To my ears, the people who say this are setting up most teachers (and public schools) to fail because, while that recipe works for a few kids, poverty is a separate problem that those "supporters" seem willing to ignore. And the problem may be worse than most people imagine, because schools rely on a crude measure, eligibility for free or reduced price meals, as the measure of poverty. Unfortunately, that number does not differentiate between poor and "deeply poor" students, who are also identified as "persistently disadvantaged." By eighth grade, disadvantaged students are about two years behind, while persistently disadvantaged are three years behind, two University of Michigan researchers report. "These data also show that persistently disadvantaged children are far less likely than other students to live with two parents or have a college-educated mother or father. Just two percent of persistently disadvantaged children have a parent with a college degree, compared with 24 percent of the occasionally disadvantaged (and 57 percent of those who were never disadvantaged)." More thoughtful interventions are called for, not more rhetoric about how "heroic teachers" can compensate for societal problems.[7]

Our growing income gap ought to embarrass all Americans, and the people who put it on teachers to solve poverty ought to be ashamed. They are, at the end of the day, not friends of teachers, children, or their families.

It is my hope that, even in these sharply polarized times, we can agree that *the purpose of schools is to help grow American citizens.* Consider the four key words: *help, grow, American,* and *citizens.*

"Help": This acknowledges that schools are junior partners in this. They exist to help—not replace—families.

"Grow": Education is a process, sometimes two steps forward, one back. Education is akin to a family business, not a publicly traded stock company that lives and dies by quarterly reports.

"American": *E Pluribus Unum.* We are Americans.

"Citizens": Here we need to put flesh on that term and figure out what we want our children to be as adults. Good parents and neighbors? Thoughtful voters? Reliable workers? And what else?

This is an opportunity for us to talk to each other and to get beyond polarization. Let's continue talking until we decide what we *agree* on. If, for example, we agree that adults should be able to write well, let's acknowledge that the best way for students to learn that skill is to write and rewrite, guided by someone who is knowledgeable.

Do we want to live in communities with adults who can work with others yet also think independently? Then let's acknowledge that children should be working cooperatively in schools, and that they should be making consequential decisions about their own learning. Let's stop pointing fingers at everyone else, take a look in the mirror, and start listening.[8]

A PERSONAL NOTE

I have been tracking school reform for a long time. During my forty-one-year career at National Public Radio[9] and the PBS *NewsHour*, I visited schools and colleges in every U.S. state, France, China, Hong Kong, Thailand, Japan, Spain, and Germany. Along the way, I interviewed every U.S. secretary of education; taught English in high school, a black college, and a federal penitentiary; followed the money trail to reveal how corporate greed created an epidemic of attention deficit disorder; snuck into China in 1977 to report on schooling there; documented the rebuilding of New Orleans schools after Katrina; followed Michelle Rhee in Washington, D.C.,[10] and later exposed her indifference to widespread cheating by adults in her employ; documented the heroic efforts of embattled teachers; made public the low standards of many teacher-training institutions; and tracked the growth of America's obsession with standardized testing, and the subsequent (ongoing) pushback.[11]

In *The Influence of Teachers* (2011) I wrote about the slow pace of change in public education. The digital revolution has transformed virtually every other sector of society, but public schools have been late to the game. In fact, most public schools that have adopted modern technologies use them largely for data management, rather than in support of innovative teaching and learning. Those decisions are not irreversible, as I will explain.

Beyond the basics of reading, writing, and arithmetic, our children need to be comfortable with big ideas, inquiry, and ambiguity. Swimming 24/7 in the sea of information known as the Internet, they need the tools to enable them to distinguish *false* information from *true*. They need the vocabulary—a basic education—to enable them to talk and write about what they know, and to pose questions about what they are uncertain of. Unfortunately, too many school districts seem bent on teaching students trivia—state capitals, the major rivers of the world, and the periodic table—and then testing and retesting them. This approach leaves our children ill equipped to survive and prosper in this era of constant disruption.

The structure of school—children grouped by age—is a barrier to innovative uses of technology, and the Common Core, with its excessive attention to who learns what and when, looks like another barrier. I have a serious issue with the conventional wisdom that detailed national standards are just what we need. Instead, I believe they are pouring concrete around our antiquated, age-segregated approach to learning. Just when modern technologies allow students to move at individual and different speeds, the Common Core standards seem to set in stone the notions of fifth grade, sixth grade, seventh grade, and so on.

I worry that these markers will become stop signs, just as grade demarcations now operate. I recall hearing a school principal complain that he had to tell his ninth graders to "motor down" to get ready for the ninth grade test—because they were doing eleventh grade math. All they will get credit for, naturally, is the ninth grade. Isn't "slow down!" a horrible lesson about the irrationality of the world for those young people to absorb?

Some schools try to bypass age segregation by creating programs for "the gifted," which allows precocious nine-year-olds to do work that's usually for older kids. Sometimes kids skip a grade, but no one seems to question the wisdom of age- and grade-segregation. It's time to do that.

I want to be clear. I am not arguing for "fewer standards," just less specific ones. Rather than perpetuate grade-based learning, could we set standards for age groups? Standards for children ages 6–10 that describe what ten-year-olds are expected to be able to do. Standards for kids ages 11–14 that say, "This is what every fourteen-year-old is expected to be able to do." And graduation standards for those ages 15–18: "This is what every high school senior is expected to be able to do before getting a diploma." Then our system could actually be learner-centered, and not age-segregated.

No doubt some of the twelve steps I am urging communities to take would resonate with Maria Montessori, John Dewey, Abraham Lincoln, Marie Curie, Albert Einstein, and Dr. Martin Luther King Jr. Considered separately, these twelve steps may be neither original nor revolutionary.[12] What *no* school district has done is combine them into an interconnected, interdependent twelve-step program, which is what I believe is necessary if we are to revive public education in America.

My goal is to draw some lessons from a long career immersed in the business of schooling, teaching, and learning, but *Addicted to Reform* is more than a prescription for change. It's also the stories of teachers and students who are engaged in our most important task.

WHY AA?

In adopting Alcoholics Anonymous's twelve-step approach to overcoming addiction as my metaphor for this book, I mean no disrespect to those struggling with addiction or to AA itself; in fact, I believe AA has it right. After many years of covering education and educators, I am convinced that we as a nation are "hooked" on what we hope will be quick fixes for deep systemic problems.

We are in denial.[13] We have deluded ourselves into believing that superficial steps will reform our schools, even though the overwhelming evidence continues to prove otherwise. Whether the drug is alcohol, cocaine, heroin, PCP, or school reform, the "high" soon wears off. Unchecked, addiction kills.

Our addiction to school reform has done and is doing long-term damage. Our current public education system, which tracks and sorts children into "winners" and "losers," is no longer viable, not when our democracy and our economy need more, not fewer, productive, engaged citizens.

Worse yet, we consistently blame the (inevitable) failures of school reform on teachers, students, under-resourced public schools, and sometimes on all three. That's doing serious damage to children's psyches, the teaching profession, and public education generally.

Addicted to Reform spells out the twelve steps that will, I believe, allow us to create a school system that gives every child the opportunity to be a winner. I am hoping that those interested in genuine change will begin in earnest with Step One, "Own the Problem." The steps that follow are interconnected. Every step affects the others, and in each chapter I attempt to identify obstacles that stand in the way.

There will be disruptions and wrangling, but a broad commitment to this twelve-step program should help determined, enlightened communities survive the rough patches. Following this path will, I believe, enable us to create the public schools we need and our children deserve.

Memory Lane

I became an education reporter by combining two jobs I loved, teaching and telling stories. After finishing college, I taught for two years in a public high school, but I had caught the reporting bug earlier, when I took a year off from my studies. Because I had accomplished very little my first two years of college, I told my parents that I would be wasting my time and their money if I stayed in college. With their reluctant blessing, I dropped out of Dartmouth. In my own mind, I would be Jack Kerouac, on the road in search of an identity.

My plan was to spend my year away from college working for a newspaper "out west," which, to this Connecticut Yankee, meant west of the Mississippi River. Once I crossed that mighty river, I would begin my new career.

My job search started in the fall of 1961 with the St. Louis Post-Dispatch, where I confidently approached the personnel office. They politely laughed me out of the room . . . and the city. It couldn't have helped my cause that I had spent the previous night sleeping in my car at a nearby private golf course, although I had brazenly walked in and showered in the men's clubhouse. (I didn't need to shave in those days.)

For the next few weeks I went from town to town, applying at the local weekly (which—hard to believe today—most towns had in 1961). Each time I would introduce myself to the owner or editor in chief: "I'm John Merrow, I'm taking a year off from college, and I would like to write for you." Each time I was sent on my way.

At newspaper number sixteen or seventeen, the Salina *(Kansas)* Journal, *I decided to lie. "Hi, I'm John Merrow," I said to Glenn Williams, the managing editor. "I just graduated from Dartmouth College, and I would like to be a reporter on your fine paper." He hired me.*

I rationalized my lie in this fashion: Once I get my first big scoop, I will go into Mr. Williams's office and tell him the truth. He will be so impressed that he won't object, probably will give me a raise. *That's what I told myself. . . .*

Unfortunately, long before I came close to a scoop, Mr. Williams figured out that I was a callow youth and fired me. Properly suspicious, he called one of my references, Professor David Barker, who was actually my college roommate. In those days, the only phones were in the hall, so I had given my new boss the number for the fourth floor of my dormitory, Gile Hall. I can only imagine the conversation when Mr. Williams asked to speak to Professor Barker. Game over.

He fired me, but he did get me a job with another Kansas paper, the Leavenworth Times. *Leavenworth was (and probably still is) a murky, depressing town whose economy was built on crime. It's the home of four prisons, not just the federal penitentiary made famous by Hollywood. Just outside Leavenworth are the state men's and women's prisons, and nearby Fort Leavenworth is the home of the United States Disciplinary Barracks, the toughest army prison of all. I had the prison beat, a dream.*

Before long I got fired again, although this time it was a badge of honor. It was an open secret that Leavenworth's police chief was on the take. He had to be: he lived in a very expensive home and drove a brand-new Cadillac. Another reporter, who was older and wiser, proposed that we expose this outrage. First we figured out how the scam worked. We staked out the chief's brother-in-law's garbage collection company and discovered that his trucks collected trash only from the town's bars and similar establishments. Those bars were notorious for serving underage soldiers from the fort. Prostitution was a thriving business too, and the pimps and whores were probably paying protection to the chief as well.

It was heady stuff. Byron (his last name lost to memory) and I followed the garbage trucks, took pictures, and schemed about how we could get evidence on tape. Byron was the brains and guts of our effort, and so when the chief and his buddies got wind of what we were up to, they came down hard, and he took the brunt. One night all four tires on his car were slashed, someone threw a brick through his apartment window, and tough guys threatened his wife and children. I got some nasty phone calls, parking and "speeding" tickets, and occasional jostling on the street, but that was all.

I wish I could say that the good guys won and that the chief was exposed, but it didn't happen that way. Byron and I were fired and sent on our way. (I remember that Byron's wife was relieved.) The police chief probably died rich and happy, and as crooked as ever.

I was upset about leaving the girl I had met, but otherwise excited about whatever was coming next. I sold my car and hitchhiked around the country for the next four or five months, stopping to work whenever I ran low on funds. I went to spring training in Florida; spent nights in college fraternities, church-run missions, and even a jail; got propositioned by women and men quite often; turned down a chance to "work" as a gigolo in New Orleans; and went to opening day at the Seattle World's Fair.

As I had promised my parents, I returned to Dartmouth, where I wrote for the campus paper and was a stringer for the New York Times *and* Sports Illustrated. *I graduated in the spring of 1964, one year behind my classmates, but I wouldn't get back to reporting for nearly ten years, when my wandering path ended up at National Public Radio. After graduation I taught high school English for two years, earned my MA in American studies at Indiana University, taught at a black college in Virginia for two years (and at night in the federal penitentiary in the town), received my doctorate from the Harvard Graduate School of Education, and lived on Nantucket Island for nearly two years.*

An education think tank in Washington, D.C., hired me in 1974, and I soon realized that I was not temperamentally suited for sitting around thinking. My boss's reaction was straightforward: "Do something! Start a public forum about education," he said, and told me I could spend up to $10,000 on the effort. When I knocked on NPR's door and said I had ten grand to spend on getting the word out about education, I was all but embraced.

National Public Radio, just three years old, was largely unknown at the time. I had never heard of it before landing in Washington, and, as it turned out, most people were unaware of its existence. NPR had a flagship news program, All Things Considered, *and a couple of strong music programs,* Jazz Alive *and* Voices in the Wind. *It also had a catchall daily series,* Options, *and that's where NPR put my first effort, an in-studio interview with two school finance experts, who explained—in too much detail—how the system worked. Desperate for material to fill the hungry maw, NPR edited the conversation into two programs, each lasting an hour, and so I made my national debut in what must be one of the dullest programs ever recorded.*

Luckily for me, NPR encouraged me to make another program. As I remember it, this time we decided I would go into the field with a tape recorder. Pell Grants were in the news, so I called the office of Senator Claiborne Pell (D-RI) and asked for an interview. "Sure," his press guy said, "just send over the questions you're going to ask." I'm embarrassed to say that I didn't know enough to tell him to take a hike. Instead, I wrote up some questions and sent them over. A few days later I dutifully showed up at the senator's office, introduced myself, set up my tape recorder, and asked my first question.

Senator Pell never even looked up. He just read the answer off a piece of paper he was holding. Question two, same thing. And so on. I remember being bewildered. Only later did I get angry, probably to cover my embarrassment.

I learned my lesson: never again would I submit questions in advance. And, if I could help it, I would avoid career politicians.

After that I went on the road, carrying a small reel-to-reel tape recorder (interestingly enough, the same model that President Nixon used in the Oval Office to secretly record his conversations). I had learned from Senator Pell to get out of Washington, and I did. Down in Kanawha County, West Virginia, parents were burning books, angry that the schools were forcing their children to read about evolution and other issues that challenged their fundamentalist views.

I can still see and hear them belting out John Denver's "Country Roads," their theme song. Rather than mock them for their supposedly "backward" views, I sat in their kitchens and recorded what they had to say. It was a great learning experience for me: most people have stories to tell, and all I had to do was turn on the tape recorder and say "Please, tell me more" or "I'm not sure I understand" every once in a while. Very often I ended up with audio gold.

Book-burners are an easy target, of course. They're easy to depict as "narrow-minded" and "undemocratic." But I discovered they were also real human beings, frustrated by years of being ignored and sneered at. Rather than dismiss them out of hand, I gave them a chance to be heard. I suspect that, because they were religious zealots, they wouldn't have given their opponents—the power elite—a fair shake if they had been in control, but the beauty of NPR was, and is, its commitment to airing diverse points of view. No one had to know how I felt (and no one would have cared anyway).

That polarization and demonization of those holding opposing views is not new, of course, but it does seem to be far worse today than at any time in my memory. I am reminded of the line from W.B. Yeats, "Things fall apart; the center cannot hold." Local public schools were once at the center of our cities, towns, and villages, holding our nation together. What can hold us together now?

INTRODUCTION

Before Entering Treatment

The first task before entering treatment for any addiction is self-assessment. So, what does American education look like? What are its strengths and its weaknesses? For me, American education resembles a figure constructed out of Legos at an all-day family reunion picnic. The result of this disorganized family project (built by random cousins, aunts, and uncles and fueled by laughter and alcohol) would be a huge strange-looking creature, not a monster but a giant that stands tall and is dressed in mismatched, sometimes ill-fitting clothing. If it were alive, this giant would walk with energy but also stumble a lot.[1]

American education is certainly gigantic. We spend about as much on our public schools as we do on national defense, roughly $620 billion a year, but is American education "flush with cash," as Donald Trump asserted in his inaugural address on January 20, 2017?[2]

Actually, some public schools are "flush with cash" while many others are crumbling, because education spending is uneven by geography, race, and social class. The national average per pupil expenditure of about $12,400 masks a wide range, from $29,427 per pupil in Washington, D.C., and $22,587 in New York to $7,650 in Utah and $7,408 in Idaho.[3] Among individual school districts the gaps are even greater, with some districts spending more than $30,000 per student, and others bottoming out at less than $6,000.[4] State governments put up about 46 percent of the money, local communities provide about 45 percent, and the U.S. Congress a mere 9 percent. Much of the federal money is targeted to support economically disadvantaged children through Title I of the 1965 Elementary and Secondary Education Act (known more recently as No Child Left Behind and the Every Student Succeeds Act), but getting actual dollars to poor children has proven to be very difficult. Even today many well-off school districts receive large checks, despite having very few impoverished students.[5] John B. King Jr., who served as secretary of education in 2016–17, made the effort to get those dollars to poor students his signature issue.[6]

Spending on public education has declined since the Great Recession of 2008, largely because many states have cut their budgets. According to the Center on Budget Priorities and Policies, "Thirty-five states provided less *overall* state funding per student in the 2014 school year (the most recent year available) than in the 2008 school year, before the recession took hold," and in twenty-seven states local funding was also cut. Eight states cut funding by 10 percent or more.[7]

Fights about school spending are most often fought at the state level because in 1973 the U.S. Supreme Court ruled that education was not a federally protected right.[8] That case, *Rodriguez v. Texas*, was initially filed in 1968 in San Antonio after hundreds of students at Edgewood High School walked out in protest over insufficient supplies and a lack of qualified teachers. Demetrio Rodriguez, a parent of one of the students, became the lead plaintiff. He lost but didn't give up. Many years later I interviewed Rodriguez, who was then suing the San Antonio school district on behalf of his *grandchildren*!

Plaintiffs seeing equal funding for education often win, but even though their state's supreme court has ruled in favor, that's no guarantee of change. California's *Serrano v. Priest* decision in 1971 ordered the state to equalize funding to bring the lowest- and highest-spending districts to the same level. What did politicians do? They equalized *down*, setting off a spiral of decay. *First to Worst*, my 2004 film for PBS, tells that disappointing story.[9]

We talk as if public education were under local control, but in fact schools are governed by thousands of state and federal laws and statutes. As a consequence, American public education, the Lego giant of my imagination, is a huge and sprawling enterprise: more than 50 million students, 3.1 million teachers, and nearly 100,000 public schools in 13,600 school districts with more than 90,000 school board members.[10]

Schools are at the forefront of demographic change in the United States. While the United States as a whole is not expected to become "majority minority" until the middle of this century, the future has already arrived in American schools, because in 2014 children of color—African American, Hispanic, Native American, and Asian—became the new majority. Over the past twenty years, the number of Hispanic children more than doubled, the number of Asian American children increased by 56 percent, and the population of black and Native American students increased slightly. Over that same time, the white student population in public schools fell by nearly 15 percent. In short, America's future is already here, in our public schools. It's an open question whether the power structure—still predominantly white—can support the changes that must be made in our schools (and whether the still predominantly white power structure will be willing to pay to educate "other people's children," to borrow Lisa Delpit's memorable phrase).

While our public schools seem to be in a perpetual state of reform, the more things have changed, the more they have remained the same.[11] I was an education reporter for forty-one years, and wherever I went, sooner or later someone would ask me to weigh in on a question they were asking themselves: "Is school reform working?"

The blunt answer, I now believe, is that it's not working. For decades now, hardworking and dedicated reformers—most of whom are privileged, white, and upper-middle-class—have been asking the wrong set of questions; they have been attacking the symptoms of our problems, not their root causes.

To be clear, I am not writing off school reform as a failure or a waste. To the contrary, hundreds of thousands—perhaps millions—of children *have benefited from efforts to improve schools.*

Dr. James Comer, E.D. Hirsch Jr., Deborah Meier, Henry Levin, and others built networks of inspiring, child-centered schools with rich curricula. There's been some real progress for individual children. Many children now attend free, high-quality early education programs, go to vibrant magnet schools that focus on the arts or science, are enrolled in public charter schools that aren't obsessed with compliance and test scores, or, because of state and federal grants, attend schools with the latest technology.

But much school reform is short-lived and rarely produces long-lasting structural change. Support for change always seems to evaporate, perhaps because funders and politicians are fickle, because the work proves to be too hard, or because success proves to be disruptive. Often the apparent gains prove to be ephemeral.[12]

Overall, school reform's record is not great. It has not closed what it has long identified as its chief target, the notorious achievement gap between white and African American and Hispanic students, or between affluent and low-income students, according to the National Assessment for Educational Progress (NAEP). Consider just one area, technology and engineering literacy. While about 45 percent of all eighth graders achieved proficiency, there's a 28-point difference between students from low-income families and their more affluent peers. Between racial groups, the disparity is even greater: 56 percent of white students met or exceeded the benchmark for proficiency, compared with just 18 percent of their black peers.[13]

Years of school reform haven't done much for teachers either, nearly half of whom say they would leave teaching if they could. That's the conclusion that emerges in "Listen to Us: Teacher Views and Voices," a 2015 survey that interviewed thousands of teachers and concluded that "public school teachers are concerned and frustrated with shifting policies, over emphasis on student testing, and their lack of voice in decision-making."[14] *USA Today* reported it this way: "About six in 10 are losing enthusiasm for the job, and just as many say they spend too much time prepping students for state-mandated tests. Nearly half say they'd quit teaching now if they could find a higher-paying job."[15]

In fact, many *are* quitting, just when student enrollment is beginning to surge. According to a September 2016 report by the Learning Policy Institute (LPI), "High levels of attrition, estimated to be nearly 8 percent of the workforce annually, are responsible for the largest share of annual demand. The teaching workforce continues to be a leaky bucket, losing hundreds of thousands of teachers each year—the majority of them before retirement age." One could argue that the field is losing the people it needs most: those teaching in schools with high concentrations of poor and minority students and in areas of focus such as special education and English-language learners.

The condition of the replacement pipeline is also a cause for concern. As the Center for American Progress reported in September 2016:

> In almost every state in the country, the supply of new entrants into the teaching profession is waning. Forty-six states and the District of Columbia have experienced declines in teacher preparation program enrollment, but some have been harder hit than others. In eight states—California, Illinois, Indiana, Louisiana, Michigan, Oklahoma, Oregon, and Pennsylvania—total 2013–14 enrollment was less than half of what it was in 2008-09.[16]

Enrollment in Teach for America has also declined dramatically in recent years. Some of the decline may be due to an improved economy, but it's reasonable to assume that the drumbeat of criticism of teachers, a hallmark of the school reform crowd's analysis, is a major factor.

Is it a coincidence that, during recent years of school reform, our public schools have grown *more segregated and less equal*?[17] That depressing news was released by the Government Accountability Office (GAO) on the sixty-second anniversary of the 1954 *Brown v. Board of Education* Supreme Court decision outlawing school segregation. The GAO report noted that poor, African American, and Hispanic students are increasingly isolated from their white and affluent peers. It indicates that the number of high-poverty schools serving primarily African American and Hispanic students (perhaps as many as twenty million students) doubled between 2001 and 2014. "High-poverty, majority-black and Hispanic schools were *less likely* to offer a full range of math and science courses than other schools, for example, and *more likely* to use expulsion and suspension as disciplinary tools, according to the GAO."[18]

In sum, not only has incremental and sporadic school reform been insufficient; it also has damaged the life chances of many young people.

Memory Lane

One evening in the spring of 1979, I was working late on our series commemorating the twenty-fifth anniversary of the Supreme Court's Brown v. Board of Education *decision declaring segregated schools to be unconstitutional. When the phone rang, I picked it up and heard a gravelly voice: "This is Thurgood Marshall. This Merrow?"*

I didn't answer right away, because I assumed it was a co-worker playing tricks.

"Are you John Merrow?" he asked again.

I realized that I was actually talking to the great man himself. I gulped and said I was. He continued, "You know I can't be on your radio program, not while I am on the court. You have any idea how much money the networks are offering me to come on and talk about the Brown *decision?"*

"No, sir," I replied.

"Well, it's a hell of a lot, I'll tell you."

Rather than just give up, I took my best shot. I told him that we had gone back to all five communities that were defendants in the case and that we had interviewed many of the surviving parents and children. We had done interviews not only in Topeka, Kansas, but also in Wilmington, Delaware; Washington, D.C.; Prince Edward County, Virginia; and Clarendon County, South Carolina. All we needed was an interview with the lead lawyer in the case, the man who had stood before the Supreme Court to argue that segregation was per se unconstitutional—that is, Thurgood Marshall himself.

In my attempt to persuade Justice Marshall to give us an interview, I mentioned Gardner Bishop, the courageous Washington, D.C., barber who was one of the plaintiffs. The justice chuckled. "I remember him," he said. "Good man."

And then he rang off.

Prior to the pervasive growth and ubiquity of the Internet, school's objectives were clear and rarely questioned: teach, socialize, and provide custodial care.

Providing access to knowledge is one of three historical justifications for schools. Basically, parents had to send their children to schools because the knowledge was stored there, in textbooks and in the heads of teachers. However, today's young people swim in a sea of information, 24/7. Of course, children need teachers to help them learn to read and master numbers, but beyond that, a new approach is required. Young people must learn how to deal with the flood of information that surrounds them. They need guidance separating wheat from chaff. They need help formulating questions, and they need to develop the habit of seeking answers, not regurgitating them. They should be going to schools where they are expected and encouraged to discover, build, and cooperate. Instead, most of them endure what I call "regurgitation education" in institutions that expect them to memorize the periodic table, the names of all fifty state capitals, and the major rivers of the United States. These "What?" questions must be replaced by "Why?" and "How?" lines of inquiry. After all, the answers to "What?" questions such as "What is the longest river in the world?" are on everyone's tech device. Schools must teach skepticism and encourage curiosity.

Socialization is the second historical justification for sending children to schools. Public school was where boys and girls expanded their worlds beyond family and where young people generally learned about each other.[19] But socialization too has been turned on its head by technology. Today there's an app for just about everything, including ways to communicate with friends and strangers. Today's kids don't need school for socialization in the usual sense of interacting with their peers, because there are literally hundreds of online places for that. Instead, socialization takes on new meanings when kids routinely text with friends they've never met across the continent or even across an ocean. Again, schools must adapt to this new reality and help young people understand two fundamental messages: that digital is forever, and that a new friend who claims to be their age and gender may be a sick stalker or worse. Schools must harness technology to help young people create knowledge out of the flood of information that now surrounds them.

Because technology also isolates, schools need to harness their powers for group activities and projects. They should also create *technology-free* times that provide opportunities for old-fashioned (and essential) face-to-face interaction.

Only custodial care, the third reason we send kids to schools, remains unchanged. Parents still need places to send their children during the workday to keep them safe. So does the larger society, which has long since rejected child labor and does not want kids on the streets. But when schools provide *only* custodial care and a marginal education that denies technology's reach and power, young people—many of whom already battle overwhelming life challenges—walk away, as at least six thousand do every school day, for an annual dropout total of over 1 million.

Tragically, those who *remain* in marginal schools may find themselves in danger, because the youthful energy that ought to be devoted to meaningful learning is inevitably released somewhere. Often it comes out in bullying, cyberbullying, or other forms of child abuse by children.[20] Marginal education that values compliance, sorting by immaterial characteristics, and test scores above all else generally produces dangerous schools.

Unfortunately, those in charge of public education have not been paying attention to these seismic changes. Instead they are warring over teacher competence, test scores, merit pay, and union rules, issues that are fundamentally irrelevant to the world children live in.

And the longer this battle rages and the longer we postpone addressing the real issues, the greater the damage to children and, ultimately, our social structure.[21] The drug of school reform is preventing us from addressing the real issue: *schools that are inappropriate for the twenty-first century*. That is the problem that must be faced head on—and solved.

A NATION AT RISK

When *A Nation at Risk* in 1983 warned us that the "educational foundations of our society are presently being eroded by a rising tide of mediocrity that threatens our very future as a Nation and a people," nearly everyone assumed the report was talking about schools. However, the national commission that wrote *A Nation at Risk* took pains *not* to single out schools.[22] Nevertheless, policy makers and politicians ignored the subtlety and took aim at schools. Ever since, we've been serial reformers and experimenters in public education. We've tried open classrooms, national goals, merit pay, vouchers, charter schools, smaller classes, alternative certification for teachers, student portfolios, and online learning, to name just a handful.

In the beginning, school reform was sporadic. During the Reagan administration, many states raised graduation requirements, but the administration did not push for major initiatives. It wasn't until the first Bush administration, which introduced national goals (through the Goals 2000 initiative), that school reform became a federal priority. Bill Clinton's administration wanted national "opportunity standards," a notion Congress dismissed.

When George W. Bush, a former Texas governor and supposedly a proponent of "states' rights," was inaugurated, he persuaded Democrats to endorse No Child Left Behind. That legislation triggered what became sixteen years of nonstop school reform, guided by "no-nonsense corporate" principles: measure *outputs* (i.e., test scores) and hold the adults responsible. No Child Left Behind evolved into Race to the Top, the Obama administration's version of corporate reform, with states now competing for federal dollars instead of automatically receiving them. Foundations, notably the Bill and Melinda Gates Foundation, jumped in eagerly, and key positions in the U.S. Department of Education were filled with former Gates Foundation officials.[23] School districts did their part, hiring business-minded leaders such as Joel Klein in New York City and ideologues such as Michelle Rhee in Washington, DC

Sixteen years of continual corporate school reform at the federal, state, and local levels has absorbed billions of dollars, but the academic results—measured against the rest of the world—have been disappointing. By contrast, Finland, Japan, and Ontario, Canada, have created coherent systems of education whose students outperform ours on international tests. American students score at or even below the average of all the Organisation for Economic Co-operation and Development (OECD) countries in math, English, and science, which generally means a score of about 500 on the Programme for International Student Assessment (PISA). The Finnish, Japanese, Ontario, and OECD average scores are anywhere from 20 to 104 points higher than the U.S. scores. Moreover, these systems have achieved their results without relying on any of the strategies or fads that we have employed. They've also spent less money; according to McKinsey and Company, the United States comes in dead last in school spending cost-effectiveness, using math scores as a measure, among OECD countries. That is, each point our kids get on PISA costs us more than our competitors spend for their children's points. "Spend more, get less" is not a recipe for success in any line of work.

In those successful school systems, teachers are drawn from the top of the class, are trained carefully, and are paid like other professionals. These systems spend more on the children who are the toughest to educate, they diagnose and intervene at the first sign of trouble, they expect their best teachers to work in the toughest schools, and they expect all students to achieve at high levels. They do not rely heavily on machine-scored multiple-choice tests but are inclined to trust and respect the judgments of teachers. Their curriculum is coherent across the system, which eliminates problems created by students moving around.

Because we have failed to come to grips with schooling's fundamental design flaw, every aspect of our schools falls short:

Funding and governance. With the exception of Hawaii, schools in the United States are locally controlled, with at least 40 percent of the money coming from local sources, usually the property tax. That creates huge within-state disparities that contradict the idea of statewide coherence. School governance is sharply fragmented. The United States has about fourteen thousand school districts, many of which have fewer students than a typical New York City high school.

Teacher training. Most of the roughly 1,400 colleges and universities that train our teachers accept almost everyone that applies. These institutions then provide largely classroom-based training that is not particularly demanding. Because this form of instruction is cheap, for many institutions teacher education is a profit center rather than a well-developed, coherent program.

Entry-level teaching. Our schools pay poor starting salaries (less today in real dollars than starting teachers earned twenty years ago), and so the most ambitious teachers tend to migrate to wealthy districts. Furthermore, most schools provide little assistance to beginning teachers, leaving them to sink or swim on their own. The result is a system in which 12 percent of all teachers are in their first or second year as well as a system-wide attrition rate of perhaps 40 percent in the first five years. Constant churn, which cannot be good for anyone, introduces another element of instability into the lives of needy children.

Teacher shortages. Our fiction is that they don't exist here, but some districts avoid shortages by lowering hiring standards—often to make sure there's a warm body in front of every class. In other words, that man or woman who has been assigned to teach physics may not have ever studied the subject.[24]

Curriculum and instruction. The typical public school curriculum is narrow in two senses: testing occurs in two subjects, math and English language arts (with science sometimes sneaking in), and it's basic to a fault, that is, dumbed down. Our curricula are often out of sync with what's tested. Because of local control, wealthy systems spend more, meaning that the richest kids get even more advantages.

Finally, because systems do not trust the poorly trained and underqualified teachers they've hired, they spend money on "teacher-proof" curricula and then evaluate students based largely or entirely on the results of standardized tests.

Labor and management. In sharp contrast with the high-performing systems and their professional unions, most teachers unions negotiate the smallest details—when teachers have to be in the building in the morning, how soon they can leave after the bell, how many meetings the principal can call before teachers earn overtime, and how many days in advance the principal must notify the teacher before conducting an observation. New York City's union contract runs, with addenda, more than two hundred pages. A professional union's contract, which leaves details to be worked out at the school level, should be no more than twenty pages, perhaps only six to eight, according to those who have studied the issue.

That we are doing poorly is not news. The differences between our approach and those of Finland and the others that are doing well have been spelled out in books such as Pasi Sahlberg's *Finnish Lessons* and reports such as *Standing on the Shoulders of Giants* from the National Center for Education and the Economy (NCEE).[25]

What can be done? The NCEE paper concludes that solutions must be found at the state level, because education is not Washington's responsibility and because local control of funding means that crippling resource disparities within states will continue.

Finding a few states that are tough enough to try to achieve system-wide coherence is a huge challenge. States such as New York are probably too big; others have been in thrall to teachers unions or to the business community, and still others have a strong tradition of local control that is politically impossible to challenge. But any state that meets this long-term challenge should reap great economic benefits, because corporations and other businesses want satisfied employees, and nothing matters more to parents than decent educational opportunities for their children.

However, I believe that real change is more likely to occur at the local school district level, particularly if the Trump administration and Education Secretary Betsy DeVos follow through with their avowed commitment to local control and choice.

ADDICTION BLURS OUR VISION

I believe that years of addiction to school reform are preventing us from coming to grips with a fundamental fact: the old system, which sorts students—whether by ability, income, or any other irrelevant distinction—is flawed beyond repair. We must start anew to create schools that are designed to build on the strengths and potential of every child. And modern technology brings this within our reach. It's time to change. Time to kick the habit of school reform and act instead in the best interests of children, our economy, and our democracy. Beating an addiction is never easy, but we have to act.[26]

The first step is usually the hardest. During my thirties and forties, I was a dedicated runner. Nearly every morning I would roll out of bed, put on my running gear, and go for a run of anywhere from two to fifteen miles. Although I knew from experience that I would *finish* the run feeling energized, I was always reluctant to take that *first* step, from my bed to the floor; it would have been so much easier to roll over and go back to sleep. If a serious runner always dreads taking that first step for something as inconsequential as a morning jog, just imagine how difficult it will be for all of us, collectively, to take the first step on the path to overhauling America's schools.

But we have to do something, because our society has an abuse problem. Not with alcohol, narcotics, or opioids. We are hooked on a *process* called school reform: well-meaning, sporadic, and superficial efforts to fix whatever is perceived—at that moment—to be wrong with our schools. Like drug and alcohol addicts, American education often appears normal and perfectly presentable. Like addicts everywhere, American education swings from highs to lows, often with periods of calm in between. And as with all drug addicts, the only certainties are eruption, disruption, and long-term cumulative damage.

The process of school reform is unquestionably addictive. Its goals—such as improving graduation rates, creating pre-school opportunities, or raising academic standards—always feel good and sound right.[27] Moreover, each reform is narrow enough to be seen as achievable within a reasonable period of time. For these reasons, the hyperfocused reformers, most of whom were and are privileged, white, and upper-middle-class, feel good about themselves and the work they are committed to.[28] Like drug addicts, they get high on the work, their apparent success, and adulation from the media and the public. Unfortunately, as with drug addicts, the high is temporary, lasting only until reality intervenes and it becomes clear that the problem persists.

The twelve-step process starts with Step One, correctly defining the problem—and then owning it.

STEP ONE
Own the Problem

"I'm John, and I am an alcoholic." With those simple words, an addict takes the first step toward a cure. Unfortunately, it's not so simple in education, because before we can own education's problem, we have to define it accurately. That means asking the right question.

Reformers usually ask the *wrong* questions: Is the problem low academic achievement? Is it low standards and expectations? Is it poor teaching? Substandard facilities and outdated books and materials?

- If the problem is *low academic standards*, then let's reform the schools by raising standards. That happened after *A Nation at Risk*, with Goals 2000 and most recently with the Common Core.
- If it's *poor teaching*, then let's reform the system by creating and then supporting the Teacher Corps, Vista, Troops for Teachers, or Teach for America to bring new people into teaching. We've done all that too.
- If it's defined as low-tech facilities, let's pass federal legislation to lower the e-rate and subsidize technology in schools. We're doing that now.

Even if these are genuine issues, they are merely symptoms, the by-products of a school system that has a fundamental flaw—it is a tool for sorting students.[1] Conceiving of schools as mechanisms for sorting "winners" and "losers" rather than as places meant to expand every child's opportunities is the core of our large-scale education problems. In a nutshell, that's the problem that we must acknowledge before we can change our way of educating children.

SCHOOL REFORM'S M.O.

Here's how school reform typically works. A specific educational problem is attacked vigorously until victory can be declared. Then we move on to a new problem and a new reform strategy. But after a decade or so, that first problem reemerges, leading to another reform strategy. It's a never-ending cycle, one that keeps us from confronting and addressing public education's real problem: an outmoded system of schooling that is harming many children and our nation's future.

For an example of the cyclical nature of school reform efforts, consider numerous attempts to raise high school graduation rates. During their tenure, President Barack Obama and Secretary of Education Arne Duncan made improving graduation rates a high priority. They publicly shamed large high schools with low graduation rates, labeling them "dropout factories," and they encouraged strategies such as early intervention with chronically absent students and "credit recovery" programs that relied on technology, often supporting these approaches with federal funds. Many states and districts either joined in or increased their own efforts to boost the numbers and get more students through school.

Some good things did happen. Middle school students with poor attendance records were flagged and given extra attention. Mentoring programs, often involving retired adults, provided one-on-one help for borderline students. Some high school counseling programs were given additional resources. And some districts started small high schools where everyone was known by name, not merely by a number. In late 2016, the Obama administration announced that high school graduation rates had climbed for the fourth year in a row, by nearly one percentage point, reaching 83.2 percent in the 2014–15 school year. As Alyson Klein reported in *Education Week*, "Graduation rates have now risen for students overall from 79 percent in the 2010–11 school year—the first year all states used the same method to calculate graduation rates. But over that same period graduation rates for black students rose even faster, by 7.6 percent. And graduation rates for Hispanic students grew by 6.8 percent. What's more, the rates for English-language learners, students in special education, and disadvantaged students also grew faster than for students overall."[2] The Obama administration and others took bows but also made a point of saying that the battle wasn't won and wouldn't be until everyone graduated.

It wasn't long before holes began appearing in the data. Alabama's graduation rate jumped 17.3 percent in four years, but students there continue to score well below the national averages on most measures, a disconnect that caught the eye of the U.S. Department of Education's auditors. Catherine Gewertz wrote about it in *Education Week* in late 2016:

> The Alabama department of education has admitted that its high school graduation rate is inflated, and that it's taking steps to crack down on how credits and diplomas are awarded.
>
> Thursday's announcement, reported by the news site AL.com, came in the wake of an audit by the U.S. Department of Education's Office of the Inspector General. Alabama's top education brass issued a statement of admission and regret.
>
> The state department of education "has determined, after completing an initial audit, that the graduation rate was misstated to the people of Alabama—policymakers, educators, parents, students, all citizens—and to the [U.S. Department of Education]," the statement said.

California's rapid improvement was also being audited by the U.S. Department of Education, perhaps because so many graduates in the Golden State qualified for diplomas by taking online "credit recovery" classes. As Maureen Magee of the *San Diego Tribune* reported in late 2016, "Like other districts, San Diego Unified has expanded online 'credit-recovery' courses to help students meet new graduation standards. Last school year, 1,381 twelfth-graders—more than one in five—enrolled in an online class to earn a diploma, with about 91.5 percent of them passing the courses they had previously earned a D in or failed."[3]

Those with long memories greeted the good news with skepticism because, as Yogi Berra observed, it seemed to be "déjà vu all over again." It turns out that earlier generations of reformers also adopted the cause of increasing high school graduation rates. It was a hot issue in the early 1990s, when a confidential source sent us student transcripts from an Oakland, California, high school. The transcripts revealed that some administrators, in their zeal to raise their graduation rate, were giving students course credit for delivering messages, while other students "earned" credits toward graduation in classes they never took. Teachers told us that they made their own compromises; they flunked students who never came to class but awarded a D to a student who showed up occasionally and a C- to a student who didn't cause any trouble. In other words, students could do *no work whatsoever* and receive a passing grade—as long as they didn't make waves. Come graduation day, these students, and the ones who actually did the academic work, would all receive the same diploma! *Failing Forward*, a twenty-minute film I produced for PBS, called public attention to the practice and help to stop it (at least for a while).[4]

Florida made a big push to raise its high school graduation rates during Jeb Bush's eight years as governor (1999–2007), and some school administrators, eager to satisfy his demand for higher metrics, cut corners. Some low-performing students were "counseled out"—advised to leave school and instead enroll in a General Educational Development (GED) program. That qualified as a transfer, not a dropout, which meant a bump in the school's graduation rates, but the school leaders did *nothing* to help the departing students enroll in GED programs, nor did they check with the GED programs to see whether the students actually enrolled. Out of sight, out of mind!

Unfortunately, the practice continues in Florida. The Orlando public school system is sending low-achieving students to a for-profit charter school, as Pro Publica reported in February 2017.

> Sunshine takes in cast-offs from Olympia and oth-er Orlando high schools in a mutually beneficial arrangement. Olympia keeps its graduation rate above 90 percent—and its rating an "A" under Florida's all-important grading system for schools—partly by ship-ping its worst achievers to Sunshine. Sunshine collects enough school district money to cover costs and pay its management firm, Accelerated Learning Solutions (ALS), a more than $1.5 million-a-year "management fee," 2015 financial records show—more than what the school spends on instruction.
>
> But students lose out, a ProPublica investigation found. Once enrolled at Sunshine, hundreds of them exit quickly with no degree and limited prospects. The departures expose a practice in which officials in the nation's tenth-largest school district have for years quietly funneled thousands of disadvantaged students—some say against their wishes—into alter-native charter schools that allow them to disappear without counting as dropouts.[5]

However, when the focus was put on individual students instead of metrics, the results proved to be impressive. In July 2012, *PBS NewsHour* carried my two-part report about a successful and innovative effort in the Pharr–San Juan–Alamo school district in Texas.[6] Superintendent Daniel King reached out to hundreds of former students, all dropouts, and persuaded them to reenroll in high school. The attraction? The opportunity to take college-level courses along with their high school classes. It worked. At graduation, dozens of former dropouts received their high school diplomas and either a community college degree or a vocational certificate at the same time!

By contrast, reform efforts that focused on raising graduation percentages and not on individual students often proved deeply flawed. We documented Florida's and California's misbehaviors, noted above. That's not the full list of deceptions:

1. In some schools and districts, standards were lowered, allowing unqualified students to get their diplomas.[7]
2. Students actually received credit for courses they never took.[8]
3. Administrators changed grades.[9]
4. Students received full credit for semester-long courses in just one week, pushing buttons on computers in so-called credit recovery sessions.[10] These online courses boost graduation rates but have been shown to be fundamentally flawed in that many of the students who passed them were unable to demonstrate proficiency on subsequent tests. Consider Georgia, where 20,700 students took these online courses in 2015. "About 90 percent of Georgia students who took one of these courses last year in subjects covered by state tests passed the course itself. But an *Atlanta Journal-Constitution* analysis of results of the state-required tests found only about 10 percent of them were proficient in the subject." The newspaper's report is damning: "The courses have little state regulation. There's no requirement they be taught by a teacher, much less a teacher certified in the subject. Districts are free to place students who bombed a subject on their first try in teacherless online courses and hope for the best. There are no state rules that limit how quickly students can finish courses or to prevent cheating on most parts of the courses."[11]

But they do boost those all-important graduation rates. So who cares if the young people are receiving diplomas that are close to worthless?

Unfortunately, illegal and unethical acts have been shown to be all too common in "reform" efforts to boost graduation rates. As with addiction to drugs and other substances, self-deception and an unwillingness to face the past are classic behaviors.

The problem with reforms focused on numbers proves Campbell's law: "The more any quantitative social indicator is used for social decision-making, the more subject it will be to corruption pressures and the more apt it will be to distort and corrupt the social processes it is intended to monitor."[12] In other words, those who live by numbers will die by numbers.

School reform since the passage of No Child Left Behind in 2001 has advertised itself as "evidence-based," with leaders such as former District of Columbia schools chancellor Michelle Rhee boasting about their "data-driven decision-making." These school reforms rely heavily on some simple metric such as graduation percentages or student scores on machine-scored multiple-choice tests as the measure of educational accomplishment. That policy has invited deception, cheating, and even criminal behavior. In every case, students are the losers because they are being lied to about their level of accomplishment.

GETTING "BUSINESSLIKE"

A new twist on school reform emerged a few years after the passage of No Child Left Behind: using "business practices" to turn around failing schools. This approach turns out to be just as ineffective and perhaps even more superficial than most dropout prevention programs. Like the latter efforts, school turnarounds sacrifice students on the altar of high test scores. And despite a clear record of failure, the notion attracted attention and money during the Bush and Obama administrations.[13] In 2009, the Obama administration allocated $3.9 billion for three years of what it called School Improvement Grants; applicants were required to choose one of four federally approved models for turning around failing schools, of which there were about five thousand nationwide. Secretary Duncan made it clear that he was going to favor applicants who promised either to fire most of a school's staff or to convert to a charter school. States and districts complained about the rules, but because it was the Great Recession, they still lined up to apply for the money.

Turning around schools happens to be a school reform I have some familiarity with because I followed one school's effort for an entire year, back when the trend was just developing. Thomas C. Boushall Middle School, with 735 students, was the ideal candidate for a school turnaround. An urban, high-poverty school in Richmond, Virginia, that had had three principals in seven years, Boushall was generally understood to be both "out of control" and "failing" and had been placed on the state's dreaded warning list. In 2004–5 Boushall students were written up for 2,500 "misconduct" infractions, and 50 percent of its students had scored "below basic" on the state's reading test and even lower on the math test. The student body was nearly 100 percent African American, and one-quarter of its students were labeled as having special educational needs, three times the national average.

Enter Parker Land, a thirty-one-year veteran school leader in his mid-fifties, as Boushall's next principal. Tall, well-mannered, and seemingly unflappable, Land had not lost his idealism. "I truly believe—I take this seriously—I truly believe that if we don't solve the problems of inner-city schools, our democracy is going to suffer."

He had given up the principalship of a high school in an affluent Virginia suburb and taken a pay cut to enroll in the state's brand-new School Turnaround Specialist program, which at the time was the hot new school reform idea. The aim of the program was to create "rapid response teams" of school leaders who would be trained in principles of effective business management, and then send them to the state's toughest schools. Training for this challenge consisted of nine days at the Darden School of Business at the University of Virginia, in partnership with the School of Education.[14]

Land was confident. "It's not a huge mystery as to how to turn schools around. It's leadership, establishing a basic understanding of respect among all parties, and that includes students," he told me. "And somebody had to do it. I mean, it's really—I don't want to say—one of the things I really don't want to sound like is a missionary. I do not want to sound like a missionary. But I have a mission."

He began the year brimming with optimism: "I see a school that sparkles. I see student work everywhere, everywhere. I see smiles. I hear joy." And he had a straightforward view of the problem: poorly prepared teachers. "So much of misbehavior is a result of teachers just being poorly planned. You can preclude a lot of student misbehavior with a good lesson plan."

I was shocked. "Do you really believe that bad behavior is a consequence of bad teaching? Do you have any doubts about whether you're doing the right thing here?"

"None, no doubt. If you're going to raise the building, you have to push, push, push on those teachers who are dragging their feet."

Not surprisingly, most teachers did not react well to being blamed. After three months the school remained chaotic, and Land abandoned the strategy he'd announced at the beginning of the school year, that good instruction was the solution to bad behavior. Now he had a new plan: "Solid rules, solid consequences, solid rewards. That's a program."

He admitted he was learning: "I have lots of experience with kids who have real tough environments and abusive environments, and, you know, those emotional issues, and those kind of needs that prevent them from learning. But it's the sheer number that's here; that was something I wasn't prepared for."

Land had hoped to move away from the disciplinary practices of his predecessors, but that didn't happen. Just as they had done, he issued in-school suspensions to disruptive students and then isolated them in a trailer behind the school, used for years to keep troublemakers out of the way. At Boushall this program was known, without irony, as "Choices."

But by early April, Land's new message—"We will never be where we need to be until everybody is looking for problems and trying to find solutions"—seemed to be taking hold. Though slow, progress was visible. Teachers had agreed to monitor the hallways between classes, and the number of disciplinary problems was going down. Students who behaved were being rewarded with dances and ice cream sundae parties after school.

Although most clocks still weren't running, most water fountains weren't working, and the major repairs hadn't taken place, Land wasn't discouraged. He jokingly agreed when I suggested that he was a "gradual turnaround specialist." He said, "I'm looking for little victories that you win on a daily basis."

Then came a rude awakening. His superintendent, Deborah Jewell-Sherman, made clear that as far as she was concerned, "turnaround" meant only higher test scores. "We're going to need to look at your plan for remediation recovery because if you look at your writing scores, they were not good. We're going to have to be on it, and we're going to have to be very vigilant; we see things that are not going in the direction we want them to go," she told him behind closed doors.

Although Land seemed reluctant, he went along. "My vision is that there's so much more. We can be—you know, there's so much more to these kids that needs to be developed. But, you know, the educational world is one that says, 'Show me academic test scores.' That's life now. So that's the way it's going to be."

And that's the way it was in classrooms. "A lot of time is being spent on how to take tests, what kinds of questions are on tests, how to read test questions, the facts that are needed to answer questions on a test," veteran English teacher Madieth Malone told me. "We usually spend time reading novels. I would love to do that, but now I need to spend my time focused on the bare necessities, those absolute things that I know will be tested."

Land organized rallies, balloons, music, and cheerleading, telling the students, "You're just as bright as any students I've ever worked with. There's no question about that, your ability, none. My gut tells me that we'll probably cross the hurdles." If they crossed the hurdles on Virginia's Standards of Learning exams, Boushall would get off the warning list and Land would receive an $8,000 bonus for having turned around the school.

All summer long, Land, Jewell-Sherman, and Boushall waited for the results. There would be no celebration. The scores dropped, to a 55 percent pass rate in English and a 46 percent pass rate in math. No bonus for Land. And for Boushall, another year on the warning list.

Jewell-Sherman reacted calmly. "We'll analyze it and move from there. That's part of public education in these United States. But did he have a plan when a problem emerged? Absolutely. He and that team did all that they could."

Madieth Malone felt differently: "The bottom line, that's what everybody looks at. They don't see the small successes; that's what I look at. I have to look at kids who were not coming to school who are coming, kids who were not working who are working. Kids who are smiling more, who are enjoying school more."

Land had a measured response: "I think the school year has improved. I'm not going to say I've seen a big change, a drastic change, 180-degree turnaround, you know, but I have seen improvement." When I asked him if he thought he had failed, he replied, "I wouldn't feel personally that I've failed. I've learned an awful lot. I've learned that our kids, a significant number of those kids are in crisis. And there's a level of support that's needed that we just haven't realized yet."

There was more disappointment to come. Land had promised Boushall students he would be there for three years, his full commitment to the state's turnaround program, but before the school year ended, the superintendent made him principal of one of Richmond's high schools.

And so in the fall Boushall Middle School had its fifth principal in nine years.[19] "A lot of people are feeling abandoned, and this is not the first time that this has happened to our staff," Malone told me, adding that it was worse for the students. "A lot of our kids are disappointed. Many of them have very inconsistent environments. The school is one place that they can come and be assured that things will be consistent. Instability, once again, is being created in a school where our kids are so fragile they don't need that instability."

The superintendent dismissed Malone's concerns. "I think that our students are a lot more resilient than you're giving them credit for. Parker Land is not their father; he's their principal. His successor will be out there greeting them every day."

Land hewed to the company line when he said goodbye to Boushall students: "I think we're right there on the doorstep, and I hope that when we get our scores back, you invite me back to celebrate, because it's going to be a nice celebration. It's going to be a really special, sweet celebration when we make those federal standards and those state standards."

Parker Land wasn't the only turnaround specialist in the Virginia program who struggled. Fourteen of the program's twenty-one principals failed to meet federal standards for improvement at their schools. Although Land and the other turnaround specialists had made three-year commitments to their schools, more than half either changed schools or left the program after just one year.

As for Deborah Jewell-Sherman, the chaos and failure at Boushall did not interfere with her own career trajectory. She soon left Richmond to take a position at her alma mater, the Harvard Graduate School of Education, where she teaches future leaders the intricacies of urban school reform.[16]

If you're wondering whether subsequent principals managed to turn around Boushall Middle School, here are some numbers. In 2015, 49 percent of eighth graders scored "proficient" in math and 52 percent scored "proficient" in reading, a small but significant improvement since 2006. However, the wild swings of the test scores indicate just how unreliable the measuring stick is. In reading, 85 percent of sixth graders were proficient in 2012; the next year, as seventh graders, only 49 percent were proficient; that number went up slightly the following year, when they were eighth graders. The variation in math scores was even more pronounced: as sixth graders in 2012, 62 percent were proficient, but as seventh graders their proficiency rate fell to just 18 percent; it rose to 33 percent when those kids were eighth graders.

Even assuming the effect on scores of some students leaving and others transferring in, who in their right mind would label a school "failing" or make policy decisions based on those test scores?

We never did find out how much state, federal, and foundation money went into Virginia's school turnaround program, but it had to have been many millions of dollars. No doubt much of it went to the University of Virginia's Darden Business School and School of Education, as well as the Richmond Public Schools central office. It's clear that few dollars, if any, were spent on teachers and students.

The lessons were ignored. As Andy Smarick wrote in "The Turnaround Fallacy" in 2010:

> For as long as there have been struggling schools in America's cities, there have been efforts to turn them around. The lure of dramatic improvement runs through Morgan Freeman's big-screen portrayal of bat-wielding principal Joe Clark, philanthropic initiatives like the Gates Foundation's "small schools" project, and No Child Left Behind (NCLB)'s restructuring mandate. The Obama administration hopes to extend this thread even further, making school turnarounds a top priority.
>
> But overall, school turnaround efforts have consistently fallen far short of hopes and expectations. Quite simply, turnarounds are not a scalable strategy for fixing America's troubled urban school systems.[17]

However, the Obama administration wholeheartedly and enthusiastically adopted the school turnaround strategy, clearly benefiting companies such as Blueprint, consultants, and academics but not necessarily many children or teachers. The failure of this approach was confirmed in January 2017, when the department's own comprehensive study of School Improvement Grants (SIG) reported that more than $3 billion had produced negligible results. Basically, SIG failed, the evaluation concluded:

- Overall, across all grades, we found that implementing any SIG-funded model had no significant impacts on math or reading test scores, high school graduation, or college enrollment.

- When we compared student achievement gains from different models in elementary grades (2nd through 5th), we found no evidence that one model was associated with larger gains than another. For higher grades (6th through 12th), the turnaround model was associated with larger student achievement gains in math than the transformation model.[18]

WE NEEDED A WAKE-UP CALL

Our addiction to school reform is not a new problem. One could argue that we got hooked in the mid-1980s, after the report *A Nation at Risk* warned that our educational foundations were being eroded by "a rising tide of mediocrity."[19] The call for action was supported by evidence: soft academic standards that allowed some students to earn high school diplomas without taking any serious math courses, crumbling school facilities, a sclerotic system that promoted teachers based solely on years on the job. That report made reform of our public schools an urgent national priority, and we have been reforming ever since.

We've had plenty of wake-up calls since 1983. Take, for example, *For Each and Every Child*, the 2012 report of the Equity and Excellence Commission (created by Congress but appointed by education secretary Arne Duncan). In a section labeled "An Unfinished Reform Agenda," it looked back.

> In 1983, *A Nation at Risk* famously spoke of the "rising tide of mediocrity" that threatened our schools. Nearly 30 years later, the tide has come in—and we're drowning. Since that landmark report, we've had five "education presidents" and dozens of "education governors" who have championed higher standards, innovative schools, better teaching, rigorous curricula, tougher testing and other education reforms. And, to be sure, there has been important progress. Reading and math performance levels in our elementary schools, for example, have improved in recent

years, as has mathematics performance in our middle schools.[20]

Owning up to the current problem doesn't require condemning or rejecting the past or denying all the good that public schools have done. The schools that our grandparents, parents, and we ourselves went to were, for the most part and for most children, adequate for times when good jobs were available to those without a diploma. Those schools educated generations of citizens who went on to live productive lives, they Americanized generations of immigrants, and they provided employment for millions of adults.

SCHOOL REFORM, PERSONIFIED

For me, the enduring image of school reform as practiced during the Bush and Obama administrations is Michelle Rhee, the charismatic and tireless young chancellor of the Washington, D.C., public schools from 2007 to 2010.[21] I see her staring at the spreadsheet open before her on a round table in her office. Directly across from Rhee is one of her hundred-plus school principals, all of whom will be summoned to meet with her early in the school year. I sat in on four of these meetings, and the conversations followed a pattern. First the Chancellor would summarize the school's performance over time—generally flat-line and poor—on the District's standardized test, the D.C. Comprehensive Assessment System (DC CAS). Was the principal satisfied? she would then ask. The question had only one acceptable answer, and the principals dutifully responded with some version of "We can do better."

The trap set, Rhee would then ask, "How much better?" Her tone signaled that she was asking for a hard number, a *guarantee* of increased scores. Whatever number the principal offered, Rhee negotiated it up, much the way a car dealership owner might set monthly sales quotas for the salespeople on the floor.

By the time their meetings ended, the principals had promised their boss that their DC CAS scores would go up five, ten, fifteen, even twenty points. When she ended the meetings, Rhee made it clear that their futures depended on their students coming through on the DC CAS.

Blindly worshiping test scores is always a bad idea, but with the DC CAS, it was an open invitation to disaster. It's a low-stakes test whose results did not impact students in any way at all—not their promotion or retention, not their class standing. Students had *zero* incentive for trying to do well on the test whose scores would determine the adults' futures.

Honorable teachers and administrators jumped through hoops—even offering cash—to try to persuade students to take the test seriously. (Later you will read about the District of Columbia principal who told his students they could choose a tattoo for him if they passed the DC CAS.)

Less than honorable (or just desperate) educators took matters into their own hands. They helped students during the test, they gave out "practice tests" that included questions from the actual exam, and even held "erasure parties" after school—before sending the exams to be graded.

Cheating on the DC CAS exams was a piece of cake, because the security system basically put the fox in charge of the henhouse: the exams were distributed to the schools about a week in advance, and the principals were expected to keep them secure.

Nationally, for school reformers such as Michelle Rhee, Beverly Hall in Atlanta, Joel Klein in New York City, Chris Cerf in New Jersey, superintendents in El Paso, Texas, and Columbus, Ohio, Deborah Gist in Rhode Island, and U.S. Secretaries of Education Rod Paige, Margaret Spellings, Arne Duncan, and John King, higher test scores were the holy grail.[22]

No, not the holy grail. Test scores are their addiction, the equivalent of crack cocaine, oxycodone, or crystal meth.

Speaking of tests, here's one for you, a simple multiple-choice question.

> American students are the most tested kids in the world.
> Which of these events is most likely to slow down the billion-dollar testing industry?

a. Citing budget problems, public school boards vote to eliminate about half of their standardized tests.

b. Led by their unions, teachers in many parts of the country go on strike over the increasing amount of class time that is devoted to "test prep," teaching students how to fill in bubbles, and monitoring exams.

c. Many of the men and women who write test questions quit their jobs, citing burnout from the pressure of having to create so many new tests every year. Some change careers and take lower stress jobs as Navy Seals, air traffic controllers, or press secretaries.

d. Millions of students, with the approval of their parents, simply refuse to take the tests.

You will find the answer later.

IGNORING THE DRIP, DRIP, DRIP OF BAD NEWS

When bad news comes in slow drips, it's easier to choose to ignore it and look the other way. As I was working on this book, the National Assessment of Educational Progress released scores, and the news was once again bad. The scores of high school seniors went down in math and flat-lined in reading on NAEP, known as "the nation's report card."

The students who took that NAEP test had been through twelve years of schooling under No Child Left Behind and Race to the Top, federal programs that were supposed to improve achievement. No doubt many were in schools that had been "reformed," and yet their scores went down again. Are we slow learners? If you ate a certain food for breakfast every morning and it made you feel sick, how long would you keep eating that food? If you put regular gas in your fancy car all the time and it developed engine knock and lost power, how long would it take you to switch to high-test?

The NAEP results were actually worse than the headlines indicated, because the scores of the lowest performers declined the most. That's significant, because those are the kids our schools drill in test-taking. In fact, the NAEP analysis noted that students who said they had *not* been prepped for state tests scored a 291 on the NAEP reading test, while those who said they had prepped for state assessments "to a great extent" scored 282. Drill not only doesn't improve scores; it makes them go down.[23]

However, as *Education Week*'s Liana Heitlin noted, reactions from the establishment were "mostly tempered."[24] Secretary of Education John King "acknowledged that teacher practices have changed in recent years, and simply said, 'we need to be patient—but not passive—in continuing to pursue the goal of preparing all students for success after high school.'" In other words, let's "keep on keepin' on" with incremental reform, even though the most recent NAEP scores of fourth and eighth graders also declined.

King wasn't the only one who urged us to stay the course. Again quoting *Education Week*'s Heitlin, "The declines, particularly among the low performers, provide 'evidence that is corroborated by all kinds of other evidence that we need to do a better job of supporting in particular our most vulnerable kids,' said Daria Hall, the vice president for government affairs and communications at The Education Trust."

And apparently the best way to support them is to spend lots of time practicing test-taking. Denial continues to be the order of the day among those at the top of the pyramid. They have too much at stake to admit that school reform has failed. Calls for change are not going to come from the top.

But even if the establishment were to admit that it's addicted to school reform, would that mean change? Sadly, it probably doesn't work that way. At least in education, significant change seems to occur only after people realize they've hit bottom and can no longer tolerate the status quo. We haven't hit bottom in public education because a lot of us feel that our schools are at least "good enough."[25] We have gotten so accustomed to mediocrity that we don't realize the situation we are in. Some in positions of power know that significant changes would produce disruption and create losers, including education schools and testing companies. Doing nothing is easier.

If you need more convincing that school reform has not worked and is not working, consider following the money in order to determine its costs . . . and to see who is benefiting from mediocrity.

Memory Lane

Options in Education, *my weekly series, became a fixture on NPR, and we managed to raise money from the Ford Foundation and a couple of other places. With my own weekly one-hour NPR program and a mandate to report on education, I had a pretty big tent to operate in, which I did for eight wonderful years, from 1974 to 1982.*

I took full advantage of my freedom. I snuck into China with a group of Canadians in early 1977, the first NPR reporter to get into that vast country. In 1981 I spent nearly three months in juvenile institutions (which we were not supposed to call "prisons," although many were) in several states, a transformative experience that taught me to distrust bureaucracies. I discovered that once a state had opened a juvenile facility, its highest priority was keeping it full of young offenders, in order to justify employing all those adults who ran it. And so they did. When the juvenile crime rate went down, the system criminalized behavior that, in times of high juvenile crime, drew a slap on the wrist or a call to the parents. So, for example, with the juvenile crime rate down in 1981, Minnesota began locking up kids who ran away from home, a practice that kept the joint full and the adults working.[26]

In 1982 I took a big gamble, leaving NPR and Options in Education *to try my hand at television. I wanted to document American attitudes toward children, not just in schools but in all aspects of society, and I thought I could raise the money and make the films in a year or so. It took nearly four years and left me broke.*

And so in early 1985 I was unemployed and, to put it mildly, nervous about my future. The seven-part documentary series I had spent two and a half years working on, Your Children, Our Children, *had not resulted in a flood of job offers for me, but it had won an Ohio State Achievement of Merit Award. Although the judges erroneously categorized* Your Children, Our Children *as a program for children, they did say they considered it "excellent with regard to significance, authoritativeness and uniqueness" and praised its "quality research, well-crafted script, flawless pacing and high technical standards." That I went all the way to Columbus on my own dime to pick up the prize certificate shows how desperate I was.*

It all worked out, because of a friend who, luckily for me, was close to seven feet tall. Doug Bodwell, then director of education at the Corporation for Public Broadcasting, the umbrella organization over both PBS and NPR, noticed me hanging out by the wall in a large room full of journalists. I happened to see him standing in the center of the room, motioning with one hand to me to come over, and with his other hand signaling to someone else. I made my way through the crowd, and Doug introduced me to the other person he had been beckoning: Linda Winslow, then deputy executive producer of PBS NewsHour. *"Linda, John should be reporting for you," Doug said. Linda asked me if I had some story ideas. I didn't, but of course I said that I did. She asked me to send them to her, which—once I came up with some—I did. She hired me for two pieces, basically my tryout. My debut piece was a story about public school teachers and their summer jobs in delis, hardware stores, and fast-food restaurants in McMinnville, Oregon. I was accustomed to holding the radio equipment, not standing in front of camera, and so I had to borrow producer Mike Joseloff's blue knit necktie for my first TV stand-up.*

Before long I had a half-time job, which within a few months turned into a full-time job, and a great one at that. I have often wondered how my career would have turned out if Doug Bodwell had been five foot ten, not six foot ten.[27]

STEP TWO

Calculate the Cost of Reform

Because school reform is big business—and often very profitable—let's take some time and follow the money. But be warned: this chapter may raise your blood pressure.

The school reform "industry" gets a good chunk of the $620 billion federal and state education dollars, plus millions more from foundations, businesses, and wealthy individuals. Publicly funded charter schools, a prominent school reform, receive hundreds of millions of dollars in donations every year. Mark Zuckerberg gave the Newark, New Jersey, schools $100 million to support charter-driven school reform. The Bill and Melinda Gates Foundation, the Eli and Edythe Broad Foundation, and the Walton Foundation have handed out millions to expand the influence and reach of charter schools.[1]

Where is the money going? Lots of it goes to individuals, because school reform can pay well. For example, the top three executives at Teach for America collectively are paid more than $900,000. The highly regarded KIPP charter network, whose schools are ostensibly public schools, pays its three top executives collectively well over $1.3 million annually, and the KIPP organization has managed to accumulate "reserves" (cash assets) of at least $70 million.[2] In New York City, the honchos of at least twenty charter schools earn far more than the chancellor of New York City's public schools, who has responsibility for more than 1 million students. The founder and CEO of just *two* charter schools with a few hundred students (and poor academic results to boot) pulls down over $500,000 a year.

The school reform crowd believes in widespread testing, and so a lot of money—billions and billions—goes to testing. In 2012 the Brookings Institution estimated that testing contracts with vendors such as Pearson come to at least $1.7 billion a year.[3] But that dollar figure does not consider test prep materials, state personnel to manage contracts, the costs of technology (i.e., computers) for administering the test, and the huge amount of teacher and administrator time spent in preparing for tests, administering the tests, and analyzing test results. FairTest, an organization that opposes excessive reliance on testing, believes the full cost is "tens of billions of dollars annually."[4]

Can money buy support for school reform or mute criticism? Foundations would seem to think so, if their grant-making is any indicator, because their largesse in support of school reform is mind-boggling. For example, from roughly 2009 to 2015, the Bill and Melinda Gates Foundation handed out $135,425,600 to just eight organizations, usually in the category of "advocacy." Two right-leaning organizations, the American Enterprise Institute and the Thomas B. Fordham Institute, received $5,634,000 and $3,497,000, respectively. Two teachers unions, the National Education Association (NEA), through its foundation, and the American Federation of Teachers (AFT), pulled in $9,227,000 and $11,189,000. The National Alliance for Public Charter Schools received nearly $17,000,000. Editorial Projects in Education, publisher of *Education Week*, received $10,730,000.[5] An ostensibly independent consulting group, Bellwether, received just over $7,000,000; its founder, Andrew Rotherham, who writes a weekly column for *Time* magazine, has been roundly criticized for failing to disclose his sources of support. But the grand prize goes to the Council of Chief State School Officers (CCSSO), an openly enthusiastic supporter of the Common Core, which has received $71,162,000 in Gates support.

The U.S. Department of Education has devoted hundreds of millions to the two highly questionable school reforms I discussed in Step One, dropout prevention and school turnarounds.[6]

Foundations support education reporting at *Education Week* and the *Hechinger Report*, often for coverage of specific school reform efforts.[7] Foundation and government school reform dollars have kept (and are keeping) hundreds of professors such as Harvard's Thomas Kane and writers like Rick Hess of the American Enterprise Institute busy and presumably comfortable. (It's what one wit has labeled "the leisure of the theory class.")

WHERE DOES ALL THAT MONEY GO?

Unfortunately, it's difficult to pinpoint exactly where education dollars are going or what we're getting in return, because education spending is rarely transparent. As noted, it's a $620 billion business affecting about fifty million students, which averages out to about $12,400 per kid.

Actual spending per student, however, is wildly uneven.[8] In the nation's one hundred largest school districts in fiscal year 2014, spending per student ranged from a low of $5,634 in Alpine School District, Utah, to a high of $21,567 in Boston Public Schools and $21,154 in New York City. Nationally, and without any geographic cost adjustment, median spending per student was $9,506 in cities, $10,668 in rural areas, $11,344 in the suburbs, and $9,214 in towns. Local funds—mostly from property taxes—accounted for 36.7 percent of education spending, $230.6 billion. The federal government provided about 9 percent, although the feds make a lot of the rules.[9]

If schools really did spend a little over $12,000 per pupil, it would mean that a classroom with twenty-five students has a theoretical "classroom dollars" total of $300,000. The teacher might be absorbing, in salary, benefits, and pension, about $100,000. Where does the remaining $200,000 go?[10] That's tough to know.

However, most states and districts do not claim a 25:1 pupil/teacher ratio. New Jersey, for example, pegs its statewide pupil/teacher ratio at 12.6:1, adding that districts on average have just one "support person" for every 78.8 students and one administrator for every 169.5 students.[11] Most school districts have worked hard to increase the last ratio to demonstrate that they do not have a bloated central office, often called "the Blob."[12]

Spending in charter schools is much harder to follow because charter schools, as I will explain, have been allowed to change the rules of the game, even though they're spending taxpayer dollars. Even nonprofit charter schools are independent and rarely subject to scrutiny until their charters (usually five years) come up for renewal. Often the public then discovers that the charter operators have done strange, indefensible, and sometimes illegal things with public money, by which time the money is long gone.

Memory Lane

"The Blob," Secretary of Education William Bennett's epithet for bloated school bureaucracies, came from a report I did for NewsHour *back in 1985 or 1986. For an examination of the growth of school bureaucracies nationwide, producer Tim Smith and I chose to focus on Alexandria, Virginia. We took viewers through the district's list of top administrators, noting that high school principals (arguably the most crucial job of all) did not even make the list, although someone in charge of air-conditioning did. At some point, a person I was interviewing said that districts always add programs and positions but rarely if ever eliminate either. He added, "It's like a blob—it just keeps growing." Bingo! My mind went immediately to that old Steve McQueen movie,* The Blob, *a black-and-white film with really tacky special effects. The Blob, an alien invader from outer space, resembled a huge garbage bag as it flowed through vents and enveloped people. Tim figured out how to get the rights to use scenes from the film, and we were off and running.*

Our piece opened with the film's Blob coming through a window or vent and burying someone; then it cut to me outside somewhere, and I said something like, "That's only a movie, but chances are there's a Blob in your hometown right now . . . in your schools. . ."

The night the piece aired, Secretary Bennett called me at home with his congratulations, and told me he was going to use the term from then on. I knew him a little bit because I had done a profile of the new secretary for NewsHour. *He was, at the time, a refreshing fellow to be around.*

I took grief from other reporters, many of whom did not tilt right, for giving Secretary Bennett ammunition.

THE BIGGEST HYPOCRITES

To me, the biggest hypocrites in the world of education are the advocates of school reform who preach that "poverty can never be offered as an excuse" for poor student performance but then do *nothing* to alleviate poverty and its attendant conditions. What they are saying, bottom line, is that it's the teachers' fault when kids in poverty-ridden schools do poorly on tests or fail to graduate.

These preachers disguise their mendacity with words of praise for teachers, calling them "heroes whose brave work changes the lives of their fortunate students." Sounds great, but when it comes from those who discount all the other factors that affect outcomes, it's hypocrisy. They're setting up teachers and schools to be blamed. How satisfying and convenient to have a simple, easy-to-grasp analysis. And profitable on the lecture circuit, by the way. Former District of Columbia chancellor Michelle Rhee's fee is a reported $50,000, although she once discounted it to $35,000 for a university during the Great Recession. As Valerie Strauss reported in the *Washington Post*:

> In these tough economic times, when education budgets are being slashed, Rhee signed a contract with Kent State University at Stark to be paid $35,000 to speak to about 600 people, plus expenses of not more than $5,000 that the school was to provide, including:
> —first-class airfare
> —a VIP hotel suite
> —meals and "all reasonable incidentals"

—town car and driver for ride from Rhee's home to
the airport, airport to the hotel, hotel to the engagement "or any combination thereof"[13]

Rhee reportedly made more than 150 public presentations during her short tenure as head of Students First, the political lobbying organization she started after leaving Washington.[14]

Michelle Rhee is not the only preacher, just the most prominent one. And of course poverty is not an *excuse*, but surely Rhee
and others understand that substandard housing, inadequate
health care, poor nutrition, abuse, and abandonment (all of which
are more likely in high poverty areas) are *factors* in poor academic performance. So why are these hypocrites either standing
by silently or actively opposing efforts to alleviate poverty and
thereby improve the lives of students outside of school? As J.D.
Vance writes in his brilliant *Hillbilly Elegy*, "We can build policies based on a better understanding of what stands in the way of
kids . . . But, I add, only if we are honest about social conditions
in America.[15]

Even if these so-called thought leaders genuinely believe that
poverty is not an excuse, shouldn't they be outraged that most
states are actively making things *worse* for poor kids?[16] At least
thirty states are systematically shortchanging poor areas when
they distribute education dollars, as Jill Barshay of the *Hechinger
Report* made clear: "The richest 25 percent of school districts
receive 15.6 percent more funds from state and local governments
per student than the poorest 25 percent of school districts, the
federal Department of Education pointed out last month. That's
a national funding gap of $1,500 per student."[17]

A report by the centrist-right Alliance for Excellent Education
demonstrates the clear link between poverty, race, and academic
outcomes. According to the Alliance's report, there are more than
twelve hundred high schools with graduation rates at or below
67 percent, and they can be found in nearly every state.[18]

These high schools predominantly, and dispropor-
tionately, enroll traditionally underserved students.

In Michigan, for example, African American students represent only 18.4 percent of K-12 students in the state, but they account for 69.1 percent of the student population in the lowest-performing high schools. In Massachusetts, Hispanic students represent 16.4 percent of K-12 students, but they account for 51.3 percent of the student population in the lowest-performing high schools.

Nationally, of the more than 1.1 million students attending these low-graduation-rate high schools,

- 40 percent of students are African American, even though African American students make up less than 15.7 percent of the overall K-12 public school student population;
- only 26 percent of students are white, even though white students make up 51 percent of the overall K-12 public school student population; and
- 70 percent are students from low-income families, even though students from low-income families make up 50 percent of the overall K-12 public school student population.

So let's ask, who benefits? Whose lives would be disrupted the most if the status quo were to change and we stopped underserving so many poor kids and so many nonwhite kids? Or, to ask it another way, who is benefiting from the prevailing mediocrity? To answer those questions, follow the money.

We might want to start the investigation with charter schools, both the for-profit and the nonprofit varieties (because, when it comes to money, they're almost indistinguishable). Rarely do they disclose how they spend their public tax dollars, and their political enablers don't demand it. Marian Wang's reporting on this issue for ProPublica documented how some charter operators are laughing all the way to the bank, putting our public dollars right in their accounts.[19]

However distasteful you may find the notion of adults diverting dollars from the education of kids to their own personal use, what they're doing is *legal*. Politicians and charter authorizers have made it legal, and we ought to ask why they don't demand transparency. The scandals just seem to keep on coming in Charter World. Which state has the worst track record when it comes to keeping crooks and charlatans from wallowing in the public money trough? Candidates would include Ohio, where there has been scandal after scandal; Pennsylvania, where the auditor general, Eugene DePasquale, has labeled his state's charter school law the "worst" in the nation; and Michigan, where the clear majority of charter schools are run for profit. All could easily be awarded the crown "Worst of the Worst."

Then I looked into California, the state with more charter schools (1,230) and more charter school students (370,000) than any other. Valerie Strauss of the *Washington Post* explored the situation recently:

> There is a never-ending stream of charter scandals coming from California. For example, a report released recently (by the ACLU SoCal and Public Advocates, a nonprofit law firm and advocacy group) found that more than 20 percent of all California charter schools have enrollment policies that violate state and federal law. A *Mercury News* investigation published in April revealed how the state's online charter schools run by Virginia-based K12 Inc., the largest for-profit charter operator in the country, have "a dismal record of academic achievement" but have won more than $310 million in state funding over the past dozen years.[20]

Carol Burris, former educator of the year and high school principal of the year in New York, is writing a book about charter school practices. Here's what she's written about just one California city, San Diego:

> One of the largest independent learning charters, The Charter High School of San Diego, had 756 stu-

dents due to graduate in 2015. Only 32 percent actually made it. The Diego Valley Charter School, part of the mysterious Learn4Life chain, tells prospective students that they "are only required to be at their resource center for one appointment per week (from 1–3 hours), so it's not like having a daily commute!" The Diego Valley cohort graduation rate in 2015 was 10.8 percent, with a drop out rate of 45 percent. The San Diego School District's graduation rate was 89 percent.[21]

When president-elect Donald Trump selected Betsy DeVos to be his secretary of education, her home state, Michigan, found itself in the glare of the spotlight, and suddenly there was a new contender for least efficient and most wasteful charter schools. It turns out that most charter schools in Michigan score lower than traditional public schools, 80 percent are for-profit, and—because of DeVos's lobbying and cash contributions to lawmakers—all are essentially exempt from public scrutiny. A highly regarded reporter, Steven Henderson of the *Detroit Free Press*, provided stomach-turning details in "Betsy DeVos and the Twilight of Public Education."[22] His lead: "In Detroit, parents of school-age children have plenty of choices, thanks to the nation's largest urban network of charter schools. What remains in short supply is quality." Henderson then provides example after example of perfectly awful charter schools that have been allowed to remain open and to expand.

> This deeply dysfunctional educational landscape —where failure is rewarded with opportunities for expansion and "choice" means the opposite for tens of thousands of children—is no accident. It was created by an ideological lobby that has zealously championed free-market education reform for decades, with little regard for the outcome.

And at the center of that lobby is Betsy DeVos, the west Michigan advocate whose family has contributed millions of dollars to the cause of school choice and unregulated charter expansion throughout Michigan.

Follow the money, if you have the stomach for it. In charter world, it seems that greedy, unscrupulous school reform crooks are everywhere.

Memory Lane

I have a strong personal interest in the charter school movement because I served as moderator of the historic 1988 meeting at the headwaters of the Mississippi River where the fledgling notion of "chartered schools" took shape. The idea had been floated by teachers union leader Albert Shanker and veteran educator Ray Budde a few years earlier, and in 1988 the Minneapolis Foundation convened several dozen thought leaders, many of whom remain active.[23]

From that meeting came draft legislation that, after much haggling, was passed by Minnesota's legislature and signed into law. In 1992 the nation's first charter school opened in St. Paul.[24]

What I remember most clearly was the widespread optimism that every school district—we had well over fifteen thousand then—would open its own charter school as a "laboratory." Because everyone at these charter schools—teachers, students, and administrators—was there by choice, new ideas and approaches could be tried out. The results, both successes and failures, would be shared across the district, thus allowing all schools to improve.

Sadly, that never happened. School boards opposed charter schools because they wanted to maintain control. Teachers unions saw charter schools as a threat to their own power (and Shanker himself was one of the first to come to that conclusion). Meanwhile, voucher advocates embraced charter schools as "a step in the right direction" toward ending the monopoly of what they call "government schools," while some liberals seized on charter schools as a way of having their own "private" school paid for with public dollars.

I did a fair amount of reporting about charter schools over the years, numerous pieces for the NewsHour *and two documentaries:* Education's Big Gamble *in 1997 (which looked at charter schools in Arizona, California, and Minnesota) and* Rebirth: New Orleans *in 2013.[25]*

Today, the term charter school *is virtually meaningless. Those two words on the door of a building tell you nothing about what goes on inside, just as the word* restaurant *reveals nothing about the quality or kind of food being served.[26] Enrolling a child in a school just because it's a charter, Ted Kolderie (a founder of the movement) has observed, would be like buying a car based on its color.*

Sadly, "buyer beware" is the best phrase to attach to charters these days—a disappointing state of affairs for a movement that began with such high hopes.

QUESTIONABLE LEADERSHIP

It seems to me that the leadership of the charter school movement ought to be held responsible for *not* strongly supporting transparency in all financial matters. I put the question to Nina Rees, the executive director of the National Alliance for Public Charter Schools, in June, 2014. Here's the relevant part of my letter:

What I wonder is how many Charter Management Organizations [CMOs] are playing fast and loose with the system.[27] Here's one case in point: We are looking into a CMO that is growing; its records indicate that its President owns the building his charter schools operate in, and so he billed the CMO for rent—a hefty sum. The CMO pays him a salary, a 16% management fee and an additional 7% or so for "professional development" for the staff. In recent years he has added categories, notably "back office & support" for nearly $300,000 and "miscellaneous equipment rent"

for $317,000. In FY 2008 he billed for $2.6M, but in
FY 2012 the number climbed to $4.1M. His 5-year
total is $15.8M . . . and he's a CMO, not an EMO.

We have a number of other examples, which
prompts my questions: who's minding the store, and
whose responsibility is it? Is it the role of national
organizations like yours to set standards for transparency? State politicians? I have no idea but would love
to hear your thoughts.

She responded almost immediately: "I would say it's the authorizers more than anyone else—if they fail, the state lawmakers.
We are here to shine a light and guide though, so if you think
there is a systemic problem, it's important for us to know."

She seems to be saying that her national organization bears
no responsibility for policing the charter movement, for pushing states to write tighter rules, or for calling out the profiteers.
That's someone else's job.[28]

However, even Arne Duncan, the former U.S. secretary of education, has now concluded that charter operators and supporters
have to take responsibility for calling out those who are exploit-
ing the system. In the foreword to Richard Whitmire's profile of
successful charter schools, Duncan wrote that charter schools are
not exempt from "a responsibility to promote better accountability for charters. Fairly or unfairly, the bad actors in the charter
sector reflect unfavorably on all charters. Learning from the best,
and culling out the worst, is a shared responsibility that shouldn't
be ignored."[29]

Duncan's phrase "the bad actors" makes me wonder how many
are out there in Charter World. Those who believe that charter
schools are a vital engine for positive change have a responsibility
for calling out the bad actors and for supporting laws and regulations that make cheating, stealing and other frauds difficult to
hide. If they're not supporting transparency, then they are align-
ing themselves with the bad actors.

JESSE JAMES WOULD BE ENVIOUS

Suppose Jesse James were to return to earth today. Would he pick up where he left off, robbing banks and trains, or would he find a better way to try to make money? Would he give up crime and go straight?[30] If I were a gambler, I'd bet that Jesse would abandon his native Missouri and move to North Carolina. There's money to be made there—legally—and not just in tobacco, textiles, and hogs, but also in public not-for-profit charter schools!

Jesse James, meet Baker Mitchell, who runs charter schools in North Carolina. Of course you've heard of the notorious criminal Jesse James, but you may not be familiar with Baker Mitchell. He's a businessman who has figured out a completely legal way to extract millions of dollars in payment from North Carolina for his public charter schools.[31]

In his early seventies Mitchell moved from Texas to North Carolina and opened some charter schools to help children. He now has four and has been talking about opening more. Even though none of his publicly funded schools was set up as a nonprofit institution, about $19 million of the $55 million he has received in public funds has gone to his own for-profit businesses, which manage many aspects of the schools.[32] *ProPublica* reported that Mitchell's Roger Bacon Academy—the for-profit management company that runs the schools' day-to-day operations from top to bottom—rents land, buildings, and equipment from Coastal Habitat Conservancy LLC, which Mitchell also owns. Until last year, he also sat on the charter school board of trustees.

At first he billed his own charter schools for only two line items, "building and equipment rental" and "management fees," for a total of just $2,600,878 in FY 2008 and $2,325,881 in FY 2009. But apparently he was learning how the system works. In FY 2010 he added an innocuous-sounding line item, "allocated costs," for which he billed $739,893, cracking the $3 million barrier.

The next year he added more line items:

Staff development and supervision: $549,626
Back office and support: $169,357

Building rent, classrooms: $965,740
Building rent, administration offices: $82,740
Miscellaneous equipment rent: $317,898

The grand total for FY 2011 was $3,712,946. (If Jesse James were alive today, he might be dying from envy.) Mitchell broke the $4 million barrier in FY 2012, when the same line items totaled $4,137,382. And in 2013 Mitchell's companies received $6,313,924, as follows:

16 percent management fee: $2,047,873
Administrative support: $2,796,943
Building and equipment rental: $1,474,108

Dig into the audited statements and you get some idea of where the $6,313,924 did *not* go.[33] For example, the schools spent only $16,319 on staff development, which works out to less than three-tenths of 1 percent.[34] They report spending just $28,060 on computers and technology, which is also about three-tenths of 1 percent.

I am sure you have figured out where all this money comes from. Mitchell's schools collected nearly $9 million from North Carolina and the federal government in fiscal year 2013. Local school districts paid Mr. Mitchell's schools anywhere from $4,095 to $1,712,328, depending upon the number of students from that district.

The entire sum his schools took in, roughly $15 million, was not all profit; surely there were legitimate expenses, such as building maintenance, insurance, utilities, and so forth. That's a logical leap, but we have to infer here since charter school operators do not have to disclose spending. These are public dollars, but the public *has no legal right to know* how its money is being spent because Mitchell's charter schools aren't actually spending the money; his for-profit businesses are. Nondisclosure is fine with him.

Mitchell has also expressed frustration with a state law passed this summer that requires charter schools to comply with public records laws. Still, the new law does not apply to charter management companies such as Mitchell's. The board of Mitchell's charter schools has repeatedly tangled with local news outlets that have made public records requests seeking salaries and other financial details from the schools. In September 2014 the *StarNews* of Wilmington, North Carolina, filed a lawsuit against the schools' nonprofit board, alleging that it has violated the state public records law.[35] (The board chair for Charter Day School, Inc., John Ferrante, did not respond to the newspaper's requests for comment.)

Mitchell himself has taken a hard line against disclosures of financial information concerning his for-profit companies. For private corporations, he wrote on his blog in July, "the need for transparency is superfluous" and is simply a mechanism for the media to "intrude and spin their agenda."[36] In fact, he aggressively defended the lack of transparency:

> We must be careful to distinguish between unfettered *government inspection* and unlimited *public disclosure*. The government, in its role issuing contracts and grants, requires the right to inspect and audit the records of its contractors and grantees. . . .
>
> So when a politician says that private corporations must be subject to the same public disclosure and transparency as government entities, he is effectively saying that government is not capable of properly exercising its oversight duties.

But when he says we can rely on government inspection, Mitchell must know that he's in no danger. In North Carolina and elsewhere, agencies with supervisory authority over charter schools are often staffed and led by staunch charter school advocates, who are rarely willing to hold charter schools accountable to the public.

How the great state of North Carolina, once known for its prochild education policies under the leadership of former governor James B. Hunt Jr., became a playground for canny profit seekers is carefully explained in sharp detail by Ted Fiske, the former education editor for the *New York Times*, and Duke professor Helen Ladd. Their study confirms that Mitchell is operating within the law.[37]

Mitchell's story is not an isolated case. Evidence of financial sleight of hand and skullduggery by charter schools, both for-profit and not-for-profit, is piling up. But with charter school supporters in positions of great power and the dollars flowing from charter school advocates to legislators, turning this tide will not be easy.

THE "VIRTUAL LEARNING" FIASCO

If brick-and-mortar charter schools are problematic, the evidence of *academic* failure among online or "virtual" for-profit charter schools has become impossible to ignore. Even the right-leaning, cautious National Alliance of Public Charter Schools has been moved to chastise virtual charter schools. More significantly, so has one of the country's most generous supporters of charter schools, the Walton Foundation. In a paid column in *Education Week* in January 2016, the foundation, which spends $10 million annually for research on charter school impact (including a study by Stanford University's CREDO, the Center for Research on Education Outcomes), called for "rethinking" online learning, writing, in part:

> The results are, in a word, sobering. The CREDO study found that over the course of a school year, the students in virtual charters learned the equivalent of 180 fewer days in math and 72 fewer days in reading than their peers in traditional charter schools, on average.
>
> This is stark evidence that most online charters have a negative impact on students' academic achievement. The results are particularly significant because of the reach and scope of online charters: They currently enroll some 200,000 children in 200 schools

operating across 26 states. If virtual charters were grouped together and ranked as a single school district, it would be the ninth-largest in the country and among the worst-performing.

(More than 50 percent of virtual charter students are in just three states, Ohio, Pennsylvania, and California.)

The Walton Foundation called for greater scrutiny and immediate action.[38] However, the foundation did not propose banning for-profit virtual charter schools from doing business. It concluded instead, "Online education must be reimagined. Ignoring the problem—or worse, replicating failures—serves nobody." That's not enough. I believe that preventive action should include an outright ban of all for-profit charter schools and complete financial transparency for public charter schools, so that their fiscal behavior can be scrutinized. After all, the CREDO report the Walton Foundation cites concludes that "academic benefits from online charter schools are currently the exception rather than the rule."[39]

Just nine months after the Walton column appeared, *Education Week* published a remarkable investigative series, "Rewarding Failure," that illuminates the depths of greed and inside dealings of the online for-profit charter school industry. *Education Week* reported that virtual charter schools receive more than $1 billion a year in taxpayer funds and are rarely shut down, despite their widespread failure to educate the vast majority of their clients. In some schools most students rarely even logged on, and their academic performance lagged months behind that of peers in traditional public schools. As the series notes,

> Online charters have proven to be a lucrative venture for K12 Inc. and the other for-profit companies that manage the schools, which are set up through nonprofit boards.
>
> K12 Inc., which also has other education-related businesses, brought in nearly $873 million in revenue last fiscal year, over 80 percent of which came from

schools it managed, according to its most recent filing
with the Securities and Exchange Commission. Connections Education, another major player, is owned
by Pearson, an international education company that
posted $5.5 billion in sales last fiscal year. (Pearson
officials would not disclose how much revenue is gen-
erated by Connections.)

It's a business model fueled largely by public dollars.
Nearly all of the state and federal money allocated to
an online charter school may go to the management
company, depending upon the contract and how much
of the school's operations are run by the company. In
many cases, the management company provides curriculum, technology services, administration staff,
and teachers to the schools.[40]

The charter school movement, a favorite of those leading
school reform, seems to have the system wired, starting at the
very top of the pyramid with the U.S. Department of Education. Before he resigned in late 2015, Secretary of Education
Arne Duncan steered a two-year award of $249 million to char-
ter schools, this despite his own inspector general's 2012 report
finding serious deficiencies in the program's administration.
Remarkably, $71 million went to Ohio, the state with one of the
worst charter school track records, leading former governor Ted
Strickland (also a Democrat) to ask Duncan to reconsider the
award.[41]

How bad are things in Ohio? The *Akron Beacon-Journal*
reported:

> No sector—not local governments, school dis-
> tricts, court systems, public universities or hospitals
> —misspends tax dollars like charter schools in Ohio.
>
> A *Beacon Journal* review of 4,263 audits released
> last year by State Auditor Dave Yost's office indicates
> charter schools misspend public money nearly four

times more often than any other type of taxpayer-funded agency.

Since 2001, state auditors have uncovered $27.3 million improperly spent by charter schools, many run by for-profit companies, enrolling thousands of children and producing academic results that rival the worst in the nation.[42]

The U.S. Department of Education has not rescinded or modified its grant to Ohio.

Even the 74 Million, a right-leaning organization that is firmly in the school reform camp, is appalled by what's happening in Ohio. Its report opens this way:

> "A national embarrassment," is how Stephen Dyer, a former Ohio state legislator and current education fellow at progressive think tank Innovation Ohio, describes his state's charter sector.
>
> Greg Harris, the director of StudentsFirst Ohio, a pro-charter group, seems to agree: "We think charters have a role in the education base, but we also think most of the charters in Ohio stink."[43]

Yet, despite the hard facts and the public spotlight, virtual charters continue to proliferate, enriching a handful of already rich people and blighting the lives of thousands of children. This is the bed that school reform has made.

YOUR TAX DOLLARS AT WORK

To help pull the country out of the Great Recession of 2008, Congress appropriated $100 billion for education, including an unprecedented $4.35 billion in discretionary money, dollars that Secretary Duncan could spend as he saw fit.[44] He and his advisors (most from the school reform camp and many from the Gates Foundation) decided to hold a competition, which they named Race to the Top.

Desperate for dollars, most states applied, promising to do Duncan's bidding.[45] One of his four qualifying criteria was, essentially, "more charter schools." States had to agree to make it easier for new charter schools to open. Congress has also done its part, with appropriations and legislation supporting charter schools.

Studies of the effectiveness of charter schools have been mixed but largely unflattering. The most reputable studies have been done by CREDO. In studies in 2009 and 2013, CREDO found that the vast majority of charter schools in the United States are no better than traditional public schools. In 2009, 83 percent of charters were the same or worse than public schools, and in 2013 about 71–75 percent were the same or worse; furthermore, CREDO noted that students at new charter schools had lower math and reading gains than students at traditional public schools. CREDO concluded that "the charter sector is getting better on average, but not because existing schools are getting dramatically better; it is largely driven by the closure of bad schools."[46] Charter schools that outperform traditional public schools—KIPP, Achievement First, and Uncommon Schools—seem to spend between 20 and 30 percent more per student than the traditional schools in their respective districts.[47]

What CREDO and other research have in common is a reliance on standardized test scores as the sole determinant of school quality. That simple measure is easiest to manipulate in schools that are largely free from scrutiny. As I and many others have reported, many charter schools turn away or drive out students who are likely to do poorly on these tests, practices which make the schools appear more effective. Even with this advantage, charter schools, for the most part, rarely do better than traditional public schools. Aware of the damage that rote education does to poor and minority children, in 2016 the NAACP called for a moratorium on charter school expansion, a controversial move that alarmed the school reform community and its supporters. The editorial boards of the *New York Times* and the *Washington Post*, along with many other school reform supporters, reacted with alarm, calling the NAACP's position "misguided," but the nation's oldest civil rights organization stood its ground.[48]

WHO'S CLEANING UP?

Want to know who else is benefiting from school reform? Let's compare the pay pulled down by public school superintendents with the money paid to the CEOs of some charter school networks. Before you read on, write down your hunch: who is raking in the most on a per-student basis?

Let's begin with Chicago, where the public school enrollment (including public charter schools) has dipped to 392,000 students. The leader of Chicago Public Schools (called the CEO) is paid $250,000, or 64 cents per pupil. Factor out the 61,000 students in charter schools, and his wages go up to 76 cents per kid.

One of Chicago's leading charter networks, the nationally recognized Noble Network of Charter Schools (NNCS), paid its CEO and founder, Michael Milkie, a salary of $209,520 and a bonus of $20,000. NNCS, which received the Broad Prize for Charter Schools in 2014, enrolls 11,000 students, meaning that Milkie is paid $21.00 per student.

Now let's turn our attention to New York City, where Chancellor Carmen Fariña presides over a school system with 1.1 million students and is paid $227,727 per year. That comes to 20 cents per child. But she also receives a retirement annuity of $208,506, so if we factor that in, she's pulling down a whopping 40 cents per child.

New York's most prominent charter school operator is Eva Moskowitz, the founder and CEO of Success Academies. She has received a significant pay raise and now makes $567,000 a year, as Ben Chapman reported in the New York *Daily News*.[49] Success Academies enrolls 11,000 students, the same number who are in Chicago's Noble Network. So Moskowitz is earning $51.35 per student, nearly two and a half times what Milkie is paid per student. If Carmen Fariña were running Success Academies instead of the nation's largest school district, at her current pay rate of 40 cents per student she'd be earning $4,400 a year! Put another way, Moskowitz is being paid about 128 times more per student than Fariña.

However, Eva Moskowitz doesn't come close to claiming the

crown for highest-paid charter school CEO, because New York City is also home to a charter network that enrolls only 1,400 students and pays its leader in the neighborhood of $525,000 per year. (I write "in the neighborhood" because the most recent salary isn't available, so this number is based on earlier years and the pattern of annual increases.) So this CEO is raking in $375 per student.

This charter network's leader must not have a "pay for performance" contract. The network is notorious for losing students. In one school, 126 students were enrolled in full-day kindergarten, but there were only 36 students in twelfth grade; it seems pretty clear what happens year after year. In another school in the same network, there were 119 kindergarteners but only 33 high school seniors. The common argument for charter schools is that they are "life-changing," but just *one* of that year's graduates from this school headed off to college, while the others reported "plans unknown." In a third school, one senior was headed for a four-year college, three said they would be attending two-year institutions, and the remaining twenty-eight reported "plans unknown."

Like Eva Moskowitz's Success Academies,[50] this network loses a lot of students, but, unlike Success Academies, the students who stay perform poorly. Here's the percentage of students in one school in the network who scored at the "proficient" level in English language arts, by grade: fifth grade, 8 percent; sixth grade, 12 percent; seventh grade, 11 percent; and eighth grade, 28 percent. In another school in the network, the figures were 4 percent, 20 percent, 17 percent, and 30 percent. In math in that first school, 6 percent of fifth graders scored "proficient," as did 36 percent of sixth graders, 52 percent of seventh graders, and 48 percent of eighth graders. In the second school, the corresponding figures were 27 percent, 37 percent, 39 percent, and 34 percent.

But those relatively high math scores may be illusory. Scores on the NAEP, the National Assessment of Educational Progress, were unimpressive. In fourth grade, 36 percent scored "proficient" in reading and 35 percent did so in math. In eighth grade, 33 percent scored "proficient" in reading and 31 percent achieved that score in math. In another of this CEO's schools, the respective numbers are 36 percent, 35 percent, 33 percent, and 31 percent.

This same charter network has famously high turnover rates among teachers. In the most recent report, 38 percent of teachers departed—nearly four out of every ten teachers. In another school, 31 percent left. One thing that students in high-poverty schools need is continuity, which they apparently do not get in this network.

Oh, by the way, the CEO who makes all that money also has her own car and driver, according to Ben Chapman of the *Daily News*.

I am referring to Dr. Deborah Kenny, the founder of Harlem Village Academies, a network of just five schools and fourteen hundred students. I suspect Kenny is happy to have Eva Moskowitz taking all the flak in the media about harsh discipline and high turnover rates, because that means her network's performance is not being scrutinized and she can fly under the radar.[51] But there's no question that Deborah Kenny takes home the blue ribbon in any "Earns Most, Does Least" competition.

FAILURE PAYS, DIRECTLY AND INDIRECTLY

"Remedial education" is another school reform money pit. Follow the money, and you will discover that big bucks are being spent on remedial education at every level. And while some kids get "remediated," the overall situation never changes: the adults in charge may be wonderful, likable human beings, but their jobs depend on a steady stream of failed students, meaning that they do not have a stake in fixing the system.

Keep following the money. How much of the $100 million Mark Zuckerberg donated to "fix" Newark's public schools has gone to consultants? How much money goes into the trough labeled "professional development" and is never seen again? How much are school systems spending on highly paid central office staff (with salaries of more than $100,000 per year) whose job it is to go watch teachers they don't trust to do their jobs?

The money trail also leads to Big Pharma, because sales of medications used to treat attention deficit disorder (ADD) or attention deficit hyperactivity disorder (ADHD) now amount to $9 billion, up from $4 billion in 2007. It may not come as a surprise to learn that Big Pharma has two feet firmly planted in the federal trough on this—taxpayers are footing the bill for children covered by Medicaid, and the rate of ADD diagnosed in that group of children, the *New York Times* reports, turn out to be about one-third higher than the rest of the population.

Some of the effects of school reform are indirect, which means that its beneficiaries are more difficult to identify. For example, the school reform movement often blames teachers for school shortcomings, in order to justify policies that narrow the curriculum, increase testing, and remove teachers based on student scores. The resulting churn hurts the field, damages morale, and brings added uncertainty into the lives of students.

But not everyone loses when teachers leave in droves. Reporters ask "Who benefits?" because *someone always does.* Even the most complex stories involve both winners and losers; even in the worst of situations, somebody ends up benefiting. For example, while all drivers lose when roads are not maintained, those potholes also mean that auto repair shops make more money. And while all residents suffer in a city with inadequate or unsafe drinking water, such as Flint, Michigan, those who bottle and sell water make money. So when reporters dig deeper, they may find that the beneficiaries of disasters are also the major obstacles to remedying unfair situations. So let's ask that all-important question about the exceptionally high rate of churn in our teaching force: who benefits from teacher turnover?

Precise numbers are hard to come by, but perhaps 40 percent of all new teachers leave the profession within their first five years. Turnover is not evenly or randomly distributed: teachers in low-income neighborhoods leave in much larger numbers. Minority teachers, who've been aggressively recruited, leave faster than their white peers, generally because they've been assigned to the toughest high-poverty schools.[52] I've been in schools with turnover rates of 25–35 percent every year.

Turnover is not inherently bad, of course. When older teachers retire, they are replaced. Alternative certification programs such as Teach for America operate from the premise that most of their "graduates" will not make a career out of teaching but will move on at the end of their two-year commitment. Some new teachers turn out to be pretty bad and are let go, and others discover that teaching is a lot harder than they expected and look for greener pastures.

Whatever its causes, churn has had a profound impact on our teaching force. As recently as 1987, when schools enrolled 45 million kids, about 65,000 new teachers were hired each year. Thirty years later, schools now enroll 53 million students, and they are hiring 200,000 new teachers every year. In percentage terms, the number of students increased about 9 percent, while new teacher hires grew by nearly 200 percent. Today 12 percent of all public school teachers are in their first or second year. According to *Education Week*, in eight states 15 percent of the teachers are new. Within states, however, the percentages vary, meaning that in some districts the percentage of rookies may be much higher:

> According to *Education Week*'s analysis of the OCR data, Florida reported the highest proportion of novice teachers in the country, with about a quarter of its teachers in their first or second years. The District of Columbia and Colorado, both with nearly 18 percent of their teaching forces qualifying as new, also came in at the top of the list.[53]

Nationally, one-quarter of our teachers have less than five years of experience. By contrast, in 1987 the modal teacher had fifteen years of experience—that is, we had more teachers with fifteen years of teaching experience than with any other amount of experience. Today the modal teacher is in her first or second year.[54]

Churn hurts students. Researchers from Stanford, the University of Michigan, and the University of Virginia come to that conclusion in their study "How Teacher Turnover Harms Student Achievement," which found that "turnover affects morale and the professional culture at a school. It weakens the knowledge base of the staff about students and the community. It weakens collegiality, professional support and trust that teachers depend on in their efforts to improve achievement."[55]

When schools have to find replacements for so many teachers every year, it would seem that school boards (and taxpayers) benefit, because green teachers are cheaper than veterans. Payments into retirement plans are lower, because those dollars are a function of salaries, and new teachers earn less. Of course, if school boards help new teachers succeed by mentoring them as they learn classroom management and other tricks of the trade (assistance that costs money), then churn is not a way to save money. However, my experience as a reporter has been that many, perhaps most, school systems are content to let new teachers sink or swim on their own.[56]

I nominate schools of education as the primary beneficiaries of churn. After all, someone has to train the replacements. Consider one state, Illinois: In 2012, its institutions of higher education graduated more than 43,000 education majors, presumably the majority of them trained to be teachers. The largest producer of teachers, Illinois State University (ISU), has more than five thousand would-be teachers enrolled, and its website reports that one of four new teachers hired in Illinois between 2008 and 2011 was an ISU graduate. Illinois K-12 schools employ about 145,000 teachers. If 20 percent leave in a given year, that creates 29,000 vacancies—that is, jobs for 29,000 replacements. If 10 percent opt out, the K-12 schools need 14,500 trained replacements. However, if only 5 percent of Illinois's teachers left every year, there would be just 7,250 job openings for the state's 43,000 graduates who majored in education.

But why pick on Illinois? Teacher turnover is also high in California, which, according to the highly regarded education website EdSource, has among the highest student-to-staff (teachers, counselors, librarians, and administrators) ratios in the nation. Having the responsibility for thirty-five to forty-five high school students who face severe poverty and trauma makes teaching beyond challenging. But many teachers have more than two hundred students each day. Is it possible to teach science or English (including writing) to two hundred students?

Every institution in America that prepares teachers is on the horns of a dilemma. They want classroom teaching to be seen as an attractive career option so that undergraduates will choose to major in education. But, on the other hand, they benefit when teaching jobs are plentiful, because an exodus of teachers from the classroom means their enrollment will not go down. But if teachers stay, then the need for new teachers drops, and enrollment at teacher-training institutions falls. Follow the money!

If I am right about schools of education and school boards being the primary beneficiaries of churn, then it follows that neither of them can be entrusted with the responsibility for making teaching a genuine profession. In fact, it may turn out that schools of education and school boards have been (and will continue to be) *obstacles* to genuine change. Instead, we ought to be taking a hard look at school reform policies that create or exacerbate turmoil in teaching.

For schools to prosper, we have to (1) follow the money, (2) call out hypocrites, (3) prosecute crooks, and (4) demand transparency.[57] Education spending should be transparent and open for inspection and debate. The money trail should be easy to follow.

Our addiction to school reform has cost us more than dollars. As Step Three will show, we have also paid a steep price in terms of collateral damage.

Memory Lane

I came thisclose *to becoming President George H.W. Bush's education advisor. Sometime late in 1989 I got a phone call from a person with close connections to the White House, who wanted to know if I had any interest in advising the president on education.*

Who, me?

Of course, there was a backstory to the offer. The administration's first choice, John Chubb, told a few people that he would soon be in the White House, riding herd on Lauro Cavazos, the elegant but supposedly ineffectual secretary of education. When that gossip showed up in the newspapers, Secretary Cavazos made it clear to the White House that if Chubb got the job, he would resign. Apparently the secretary had enough juice to get Chubb booted out before he even got to move in.

The administration's second choice was Joe Nathan of Minnesota, who had come to its attention because of his work for the National Governors Association. However, Joe turned down the job because he wanted to stay in his home state with his wife and young children. I knew this because Joe had asked my advice about the job, life in Washington, schools for his kids, and so on. (And I later learned that it was Joe who threw my hat into the ring.)

I assumed that I was being considered because of my report on school choice in District Four in New York City, *a lovely* NewsHour *piece that celebrated that school district's truly remarkable but under-the-radar accomplishments. As we had reported, District Four was dead last among the city's thirty-two districts when the leadership (Anthony Alvarado and Sy Fliegel) decided to scrap all District Four's junior high schools. They invited staff to submit proposals for unique schools organized around themes. In the end Alvarado and Fliegel approved some interesting themed schools; fine arts, back-to-basics, and maritime junior highs were among those that got to open. Then parents and their children were told, "Take your pick."*

School choice was a huge success, and within a few years District Four had climbed from last place to seventeenth place among the thirty-two districts in academic achievement. Parents from outside that district were doing whatever they could to get their children in the schools there. And if some schools were not chosen by enough parents, they went out of business and were soon replaced by new approaches dreamed up by education entrepreneurs. Republicans and other conservatives loved the story, and the piece—with me in it—was shown all over the place, including the White House.

I assumed that someone in the administration connected the dots (erroneously): "Gee, he reported favorably on school choice, so he must be one of us." I was wined and dined by some fancy financial types in penthouse dining rooms and beautiful estates. Then I got a letter asking me to come to the White House for an interview with the president's domestic policy advisor, Dr. Roger Porter.

But first I wanted advice from Robin MacNeil and Jim Lehrer. Could I go over to the other side for a while, I asked, without destroying my future credibility as a reporter? Sure, both assured me, as long as I didn't stay too long.

So I trotted off to the White House for a meeting with Porter. You may remember that George H.W. Bush was our self-styled "education president." He had called the first-ever National Education Summit, an event held with great fanfare in Charlottesville, Virginia, in 1989. Out of that meeting, which forty-nine of the country's fifty governors attended, had emerged a commitment to national education goals, which I assumed the education advisor would help create.

The idea of helping set our public schools on a strong path was heady stuff, and the lure of the inner circle was strong. After all, I had been around in 1983 when A Nation at Risk *warned about the "rising tide of mediocrity," and now we had a president who seemed genuinely committed to public education in ways that his immediate predecessor, Ronald Reagan, had not been. I knew public schools pretty well and told Porter that I felt I could help shape the goals in ways that would make them sensible and achievable.*

"That's not the job," he told me. "We've already written the goals. They were pretty much in place before Charlottesville. Your job will be to sell them." These were to be called Goals 2000, with 2000 representing the year they were to be achieved; today the eight goals seem almost quaint—and still out of reach:

1. *All children in America will start school ready to learn.[58]*
2. *The high school graduation rate will increase to at least 90 percent.*
3. *All students will leave grades 4, 8, and 12 having*

*demonstrated competency over challenging subject matter
including English, mathematics, science, foreign languages,
civics and government, economics, the arts, history, and geography, and every school in America will ensure that all students learn to use their minds well, so they may be prepared
for responsible citizenship, further learning, and productive
employment in our nation's modern economy.*

4. *United States students will be first in the world in mathematics and science achievement.*

5. *Every adult American will be literate and will possess the
knowledge and skills necessary to compete in a global economy
and exercise the rights and responsibilities of citizenship.*

6. *Every school in the United States will be free of drugs, violence, and the unauthorized presence of firearms and alcohol and will offer a disciplined environment conducive to
learning.*

7. *The nation's teaching force will have access to programs for
the continued improvement of their professional skills and
the opportunity to acquire the knowledge and skills needed
to instruct and prepare all American students for the next
century.*

8. *Every school will promote partnerships that will increase
parental involvement and participation in promoting the
social, emotional, and academic growth of children.*[59]

*I gulped and said okay. I remember telling him that the best way
for me to do that would be to write opinion pieces and speeches, and
I could do some of that from New York, where I was living.*

*"Not our way," Porter said. And he told me that I would be
expected to be in the office early and to stay late, making it clear
that brownie points went to those who put in the longest days. "Oh,
and another thing," he said. "Education is just half of the job. Your
portfolio will also include transportation."*

Wait a minute—the education advisor to our "education

president" is supposed to spend only half *of his or her time on edu-cation? What's wrong with this picture?*

We agreed to disagree, and I turned down the job before it was ever offered to me.

I was beginning to suspect that hypocrisy in the nation's capital was widespread and bipartisan. Could it be that almost everyone in Washington was focused on images, politics, and elections, and that kids and schools would get the scraps that were left over, no matter who was in charge?

STEP THREE
Don't Pay the Price

Children, teachers, schools, and society have paid a price for school reform, however well-meaning some reformers may have been. Our addiction to school reform has caused significant collateral damage: a narrowed curriculum, thousands of hours spent on testing and test prep, a demoralized teaching force, the resignations of effective teachers fed up with excessive testing, time and money spent recruiting those teachers' replacements, huge cuts and occasional bankruptcy proceedings in school districts because of dollars diverted to online for-profit charter schools, and the cumulative negative effects on the public's view of schools caused by the drumbeat of criticism.

Step Two provided dollar figures. Here I want to tell you stories about women, men, and children affected by school reform. My argument in this book is that because we have become addicted to the *process* of largely superficial school reform, we have lost sight of our children's best interests and our nation's future. Caught up in the minutiae and the political skirmishes, we have lost our way.

What is the (non-cash) price of school reform? I've often seen it up close. Take P.S. 1 in the South Bronx, a low-income part of New York City. It serves about seven hundred students, pre-K through fifth grade, most of whom qualify for free or reduced-price lunch. Nationally, only 33 percent of fourth graders read at grade level, but at P.S. 1 just 18 percent of fourth graders were at grade level.

Brenda Cartagena spends a lot of her time teaching her South Bronx fourth graders how to take reading tests, instead of having them read. A veteran, she's begun to think she may have made a mistake devoting her life to teaching. "The system takes the fun out of reading. I want them to read for enjoyment. I want them to grab that book because it's fun. I tell them, 'Reading, you travel, you meet new friends, you learn how to do new things,'" she told me. "But it's very difficult, you know? They take the joy out. And it's hard to infuse it back."

Because we are addicted to school reform, those test scores will be the primary evidence used by politicians, policy makers, and realtors (who use high test scores to market homes) and real estate agencies to determine whether she and her colleagues are doing a good job. Her colleague Michelle Alpert was equally perplexed and frustrated: "I don't know what the better solution is. But I do think obviously that this puts way too much value on test scores. There has to be some sort of—you know, something else taken into account if you really want to measure a school's success, a teacher's success, a student's success."

The real victims of school reform and its insistence on high test scores are the kids, many of whom become convinced that they aren't worth much. Even though they had learned to read in first grade, by fourth grade they "knew" they couldn't read, because they couldn't pass that damn reading test.[1] They are the living embodiment of the price we are paying for school reform.

Memory Lane

I know most first graders can read with comprehension because I've seen it, time and again, in first-grade classrooms all over the country. Often I would ask a first-grade teacher if I could take over the class. Then I'd ask the kids to cover their eyes and then would write some nonsense sentences on the blackboard. Something like "The blue pancake went swimming in the lake and ate a fish."

When I gave the kids permission to look, many would gaze at the board and then start smiling, their faces telling me that they understood what they were reading.

When I asked what the kids thought of my story, at first most were reluctant to answer, either because they were being polite or because they weren't sure if it really was okay to tell an adult that his story was stupid. When I phrased the question differently, how- ever, the floodgates opened.

MERROW: *Is there anything wrong with that story?*
STUDENTS *(in unison): Yes.*
MERROW: *What's wrong with that story?*
STUDENT 1: *There's no such thing as a blue pancake.*
MERROW: *There's no such thing as a blue pancake. All right. Is there anything else wrong with that story?*
STUDENT 2: *Pancakes don't have a mouth.*
STUDENT 3: *A pancake can't eat anything because they don't have a mouth.*
MERROW: *Pancakes don't have a mouth. Anything else?*
STUDENT 4: *They don't swim.*
STUDENT 5: *It doesn't make sense because a pancake can't swim.*
MERROW: *They can't swim. Okay. So maybe it's not a very good story.*

Here's the tragic news: by fourth grade, most of those kids will fail their reading tests. Why? Perhaps they've decided they would rather draw than read, or perhaps they have lost their innocence and are now aware of some harsh truths: their mother is incarcer- ated, or their family is on the verge of being evicted (again), or there's not enough money for groceries.

It must be painfully clear that any kind of school reform that defines reading as "passing a reading test" makes matters worse.

SCHOOL REFORM IS INTENSELY POLITICAL

Although school reform is often presented by its supporters as nonpolitical, nonideological, and nonpartisan, it is not. Although No Child Left Behind passed with bipartisan support, its impact on schools was decidedly tilted toward the business-oriented, bottom-line model favored by school reform. As Charles Kerchner of the Claremont Graduate School has written, "The rhetoric of school reform treats portfolio creators as free of political interests in contrast to rapacious teachers unions and self-protecting school administrators." Reformers, he notes, always claim to be above politics and thus able to "innovate and adapt rapidly, outpacing the sluggish pace of incremental reforms within traditional school districts."

He continues:

> The foundations, philanthropists, and civic elites . . . want something. They want dominance over public education. They want to rebrand the word "public" as something other than the delivery of schooling by a government agency called a school district.
>
> In order to do this, they need to take away resources controlled by that system: jobs held by teachers, access to school building and property, control over the means of training and hiring . . .
>
> So, when someone comes to your town with the promise that they can change your failed urban schools, do it quickly, and make an end run around urban politics, don't believe them.[2]

As Kerchner points out, in the past fifteen or twenty years school reform has become intensely politicized. The Bill and Melinda Gates Foundation, the Broad Foundation, the Walton Foundation, and other foundations have invested billions in support of school reform.[3] Critics of these efforts, led by bloggers Diane Ravitch, Mercedes Schneider, Anthony Cody, and a handful of other effective activists, believe corporate reformers want to destroy public education (and perhaps make fortunes in the process), not improve it.[4] They characterize these efforts as "education deform."

TEACHERS UNIONS

"Teachers unions: threat or menace?"[5] That's the sort of "debate" I can imagine taking place in the school reform movement, particularly those organizations that bankroll efforts to increase the number of charter schools or end tenure and seniority provisions in union contracts. The Walton Foundation stands out, but the group also includes the Broad Foundation and a large handful of wealthy hedge fund operators.

It may be that the Walton Foundation is opposed to all unions, not just teachers unions, because the foundation's parent company, Walmart, has a track record of opposing unionization, and many of the Walton family heirs are personally contributing to efforts that teachers unions oppose.

Some of the strongest (and financially most generous) opposition to teachers unions comes from places where those unions have a powerful grip on the legislative and political process and use that power to protect jobs at all costs. California is a prime example because in that state the California Teachers Association (CTA) pretty much gets what it wants from the state legislature and usually from the governor as well, no matter the latter's political affiliation. Because of the CTA's chokehold, teachers in California get tenure after just two years, a ridiculous notion if ever there was one. (That really means that a principal must make his or her recommendation early in a teacher's second year, because the process takes time.) The CTA, which encompasses members of both national unions—the National Education Association and the American Federation of Teachers—also steadfastly defends seniority, the policy known as "last hired, first fired." This is old-line trade unionism that does not acknowledge the complexity of teaching or the importance of teamwork.

School reformers spent millions challenging California's rules on seniority and tenure in a case known as *Vergara v. California*.[6] The reformers won the first round but ultimately lost in August 2016 when the California Supreme Court declined to review an appeals court ruling that upheld the state's (and the CTA's) positions.

School reformers in New York City work with a tough, protectionist teachers union and have the scars to prove it. Not surprisingly, many in the nation's financial capital are willing to write big checks to charter school organizations such as Success Academies, whose nonunion workforce appeals to billionaires Daniel Loeb, John Paulson, and others.

But there's *no correlation* between strong teachers unions and poor schools, none at all. To the contrary, states with the most effective school systems, such as Massachusetts, have strong teachers unions. That evidence does not seem to count with school reformers, however, because, as noted, they're choosing between "threat" and "menace."

Memory Lane

I cut my teeth, journalistically speaking, with a protectionist teachers union, the Philadelphia Federation of Teachers (PFT), when I spent six years chronicling the efforts of an idealistic new superintendent to improve that city's public schools. The resulting film, Toughest Job in America, *is one of my personal favorites.[7] In it you meet and get to know some very tough union leaders, including a shop steward at one high school who basically says he'd defend seniority to the death and a union vice president, Jack Steinberg, who maintains that it's impossible to hold teachers responsible for student learning.*

Here's the conversation I had with Steinberg:

JOHN MERROW: If I'm a teacher, and I set out to teach the kids long division, and they all learn long division, did I do a good job?

JACK STEINBERG: Yes. (Pause) Now what if they didn't . . .

MERROW: Wait . . . Okay . . .

STEINBERG: What if they didn't learn long division?

MERROW: Did I do a bad job?

STEINBERG: Let's say you teach three classes. And in one class they could do it, and one class they couldn't. Are you doing a good job or a bad job? Or are . . .

MERROW: How about a good job in one class and a bad job in the other?

STEINBERG: But you did the same job in both classes. What's wrong? (Pause) And if you're asking, can you evaluate a teacher on the performance of the students . . .

MERROW: Yes. Yes or no?

STEINBERG: No, you cannot.

MERROW: You cannot evaluate a teacher on the performance of his or her students?

STEINBERG: Right. Right.

MERROW: I just want to know where you draw the line. If I set out to teach long division . . .

STEINBERG: All right.

MERROW: . . . and not a single kid learns long division—it's the right age to teach long division and learn it—not a single kid learns long division, did I do a bad job?

STEINBERG: (Pause) I don't know. I really don't know because there are too many variables.

After that back-and-forth appeared on national television, Steinberg was muzzled by his union, but the PFT never wavered from its protectionist positions. Albert Shanker, then the president of the PFT's national union, the American Federation of Teachers, told me that he found the PFT impossible to deal with. He may even have called them dinosaurs.

It's both my hope and my strong belief that some teachers unions will help create the schools our nation needs, but let's not pretend that dinosaurs no longer roam the earth.

THE COST IN HUMILIATION

Teachers and principals are also paying a high price for school reform. Consider Brian Betts, the principal of a "failing" middle school in Washington, D.C., during Michelle Rhee's tenure as chancellor. Under intense pressure from Rhee to get test scores up, Betts offered $100 to every student who answered every question on the test, whether they got them right or wrong.

But he went even further in his effort to get his students over the passing bar, as one student told me:

STUDENT 1: He said that he is going to get a tattoo.

MERROW: What was your reaction?

STUDENT 1: I mean, I was surprised. I don't know if he's really going to do it.

STUDENT 2: I don't think he's going to get it. I mean, that's just crazy.

But Betts said he was serious. The kids could choose the tattoo, but he would choose its location on his body. Other school leaders held huge pep rallies before the tests and offered ice cream sundae parties to students after the tests were over.

All of this bizarre behavior was a direct consequence of school reform. Teachers and principals were being judged—sometimes fired—based on scores on a test that meant nothing to students. These tests were designed to measure the health of a system, but results-obsessed leaders such as Atlanta's Beverly Hall, Joel Klein of New York City, Eva Moskowitz of Success Academies, and Michelle Rhee of Washington, D.C., were misusing the scores to promote, demote, and dismiss personnel.

In the end, Betts did not have to get a tattoo. Neither cash inducements nor the promise of a tattoo were enough to get his kids over the bar.

THE GREEKS SHOULD HAVE A WORD FOR IT

Because cheating by adults is part of the price we are paying for School Reform, I've coined a word for it: *edugenesis*. My new word has a counterpart in medicine, *iatrogenesis*, meaning "doctor-caused problems." It's a big deal: according to the *Journal of American Medicine* in 2000, somewhere between 44,000 and 98,000 people die every year because of problems inadvertently caused by medical care. So I give you *edugenesis*, my term for adults artificially and dishonestly raising student scores by various forms of cheating.

It's also a big deal: some educators have had "erasure parties," others obtained the actual tests in advance so they could—literally—teach the test, and still others helped students by pointing to correct answers. All this cheating—by a *minority* of principals and teachers—was the direct result of school reform's intense pressure to raise scores on standardized tests, and threats of dire consequences if scores did not go up. Take your pick of cities where some principals and teachers have cheated to raise student scores; in each case I think you will find that the "doctor" at the top put intense pressure on his or her minions to "perform or else."

Atlanta, where eleven educators ended up with prison terms for their part in a massive cheating scandal, remains the poster child, but the cheating was just as widespread in Washington, D.C., when Michelle Rhee was chancellor. If Washington had courageous political leadership and a strong newspaper like the *Atlanta Journal-Constitution*, I have no doubt that the District of Columbia students whose scores were falsely inflated would be getting an apology and perhaps some remedial instruction as compensation. My colleagues at Learning Matters and I carefully documented Michelle Rhee's "reign of error" there. In other cities (Columbus, Ohio; Baltimore; El Paso, Texas, among them), adults have been caught systematically breaking the rules. Unlike iatrogenesis, edugenesis doesn't literally kill people. All it does is ruin careers and blight lives.

On a positive note, I sense the tide is turning. The backlash against excessive testing seems stronger than ever, and many knowledgeable people are recognizing that our system is almost alone in using standardized tests to evaluate teachers, while other countries use them to assess students (which is precisely what they were designed to do).

Let's look instead at the idea of grading schools. We need an accountability system that measures quality and effort, not poverty or some characteristics that an ideologue might love or hate. Let's not insist on (or settle for) a single letter grade; students get marks in English, social studies, algebra, and so forth, so why shouldn't a school get multiple grades?

Now ask yourself what a school should be graded on. How important are scores on fill-in-the-bubble tests? How much should graduation rates count? Should we pay attention to rates of attendance and truancy?

What else counts? How about hours of recess per week, hours of art and music, and time devoted to project-based learning? (For all three, more is better.) How about counting hours spent on test prep and teacher turnover? (Here, less is better.) Before we're through, we have to answer all those questions.

Memory Lane

When I was eight years old, my morning chores included collecting the eggs of the thirty to forty chickens on our farm. I'd bring them to the kitchen, then wash my hands and walk to school with my older sister. It was a simple four-step process: collect the eggs, deliver them to the kitchen, wash up, and head off to school.

Unfortunately, I sometimes forgot the third step, washing my hands, meaning that I might have had some chicken poop under my fingernails when I entered my third-grade classroom. Unfortunately for me, my teacher that year was a hygiene fanatic who required us to line up and approach her desk, breathe into her face so that she could determine whether we had brushed our teeth, and show her our hands so she could see if we had washed. I always brushed my teeth after breakfast, so I never failed the halitosis test, but she got me on the "clean hands" exam quite a few times.

Each time the punishment was a black star next to my name on the wall chart that was prominently displayed near the classroom door. She started the chart on day one of the school year, and I got quite a few of those unforgettable black stars during the year. It was humiliating, but I still made the mistake of not washing up quite a few times—after all, I was only eight, and then there were the times when we were running late . . .

What brings this to mind is the practice in some benighted school systems of posting students' scores on state exams on a "data wall" in each classroom, so that every kid can see how he or she did . . . and how everyone else did. That's supposed to make kids work harder. But does it?

In a thoughtful essay about this trend, teacher Launa Hall wrote that she resisted the requirement at first but eventually gave in and created her own "data wall," a decision she regretted as soon as she saw her students looking at the scores.

> *My third-graders tumbled into the classroom, and one child I'd especially been watching for—I need to protect her privacy, so I'll call her Janie—immediately noticed the two poster-size charts I'd hung low on the wall. Still wearing her jacket, she let her backpack drop to the floor and raised one finger to touch her name on the math achievement chart. Slowly, she traced the row of dots representing her scores for each state standard on the latest practice test. Red, red, yellow, red, green, red, red. Janie is a child capable of much drama, but that morning she just lowered her gaze to the floor and shuffled to her chair. . . .*
>
> *I regretted those data walls immediately. Even an adult faced with a row of red dots after her name for all her peers to see would have to dig deep into her hard-won sense of self to put into context what those red dots meant in her life and what she would do about them. An 8-year-old just feels shame.[8]*

Like her students, I was eight. I felt ashamed whenever I received a black star and whenever I looked at the wall chart, a constant reminder of my failure. I got teased, of course, and even now, at age seventy-five, my dominant memory of third grade is the teacher's morning physical exam, not projects I may have worked on, books we read, or playground games. I survived my literal chickenshit education, though, probably because it was only one misguided teacher who just wanted to teach hygiene who was embarrassing me, not official policy across a school district.

Some districts use numbers in place of names on their mandatory "data walls," but of course it doesn't take long for kids to figure out who is who. Whether such systems use numbers or names, it is a disgrace for entire school systems to endorse public shaming of their students. This excess, the offspring of school reform's misguided obsession with test scores, rarely if ever works. It's a chickenshit policy that will further turn people against public education, at least the 50 percent who are below average. Will pleasant memories of school overshadow their shame at being publicly humiliated? How supportive are they likely to be as adults when they are asked to vote for school funding or to defend teachers against unwarranted attacks?

Could some educators be adopting public shaming as a way of driving some kids away? In a system obsessed with test scores, it's easy to imagine that some charter school operators would go to extreme lengths to get low-performing students to transfer out.

I have reported and written about Eva Moskowitz and her Success Academies charter school network, where policies have been created to drive away students who are not obedient or good at test-taking. Shaming is built into the very structure of these "no excuses" schools, the darlings of many in the school reform movement.

And that's pure chickenshit.

SCHOOL REFORM CAUSES ROT AT THE CORE

Although most parents report being satisfied with the particular schools their own children attend, in Gallup polls they regularly give the entire system a grade of C- and sometimes worse. Because of the widespread acceptance of standardized test scores as the measure of quality, many have come to equate learning with testing, and the curriculum has paid a price. The arts, science, physical education, and many important extracurricular activities have been minimized or even eliminated. Because they aren't tested, they aren't taught. When the only goal is higher test scores, anything that gets in the way has got to go.

We have driven teachers to "teach to the test," something that might be okay if the tests were legitimate assessments of deep learning. Because school reform demands that students pass tests, we tell teachers how to teach, with scripted curricula that tell them what to say and when. Teachers are robbed of autonomy but held accountable for results. And we wonder why so many excellent teachers cannot wait to get out!

The school reform crowd loves the notion that it can measure precisely just how much an individual teacher adds to an individual student's learning. This might work in baseball, which endorses a statistic called "wins above replacement" to indicate how much value a given player adds, but teaching is more complex than hitting a baseball.

Nevertheless, "value added" has become a cornerstone of school reform, largely based on work funded by the Gates Foundation and done by Eric Hanushek of the Hoover Institution at Stanford and Thomas Kane of the Harvard Graduate School of Education. Convinced that three years with a good teacher solves most problems, they have models that invite politicians and policy makers to figure out ways to get rid of "low-performing" teachers, using student test scores as the determinant. Although reputable economists have debunked the idea of a direct connection between one teacher's quality and his or her students' scores, it persists, adding to the price we pay for our addiction to school reform.[9]

Going forward, we have to write rules and create procedures to prevent money from being misspent or wasted. Reporters are trained to ask "Who benefits?" and to follow the money, but the system of schools that we are designing cannot be built on the *hope* that reporters will uncover scandals.[10] Transparency and double-checks have to be built into the system at every juncture. The goal is to design a system that discourages or prevents bad behavior, eliminating temptation wherever possible, because, given the chance, some people will do the wrong thing.

I draw three conclusions from the failure of school reform:

1. A fundamental redesign is required because tinkering cannot solve what ails schools.
2. The education establishment—state, local, and federal—is *not* going to come to the rescue.
3. It's on *you and others like you* to make change happen. If *you* agree that the problem is not low graduation rates, high dropout rates, an achievement gap, or any other issue school reform focuses on, *you* now own the problem. If *you* agree that it's no longer practical or ethical to ask "How intelligent is this child?" and that we must create schools that identify *each* child's interests and potential, then *you* are prepared for the challenges inherent in redesigning schools. You are ready to do the right thing, which means asking the *right question*.

STEP FOUR

Ask the Right Question

We've acknowledged that our schools and their dominant pedagogy are inappropriate for the twenty-first century and have to be replaced. *But what will replace them?* The answers become clear when we ask the right question about each and every child.

Remember, today's schools have evolved into a sorting mechanism to identify and label children from a very young age. Even though tracking has long since fallen out of favor, many (perhaps most) schools have subtle, or not-so-subtle, tracking systems. By third or fourth grade most kids know, deep down, whether the system sees them as "winners" bound for college or "losers" headed somewhere else. Economics reinforces tracking as well. Because school characteristics are nearly always a function of a community's wealth, some of our schools are decrepit to the point of being unsafe, which has the effect of "tracking" those students downward. Schools in wealthy communities have modern facilities, the most experienced teachers, the latest technology, and perhaps even climbing walls in the gym. That is the track for "winners."

Essentially, our current system examines each child and demands to know, in a variety of ways, "How intelligent are you?" Standardized, machine-scored tests are the "objective" instruments most commonly used to determine the answer to what is, today, the *wrong* question.

A new system of schools must ask a different question about

each child: "*How* are you intelligent?" That may strike you as a steep hill to climb, but it's my version of the questions that caring parents, teachers, and other adults ask about individual children. They phrase it differently: "What is Susan interested in?" "What turns George on?" "What motivates Juan?" or "What does Sharese care about?" Or one can pay attention to young children at play to find out what makes them tick; as Yogi Berra may have said, "You can observe a lot just by watching." Every child has interests, and those can be tapped and nurtured in schools that are designed to provide opportunities for children to succeed as they pursue paths of their own choosing. Giving children agency over their own education—with appropriate guidance and supervision—will produce a generation that is better equipped to cope with today's changing world.

Like most of the changes required to remake public education, this shift—close to a 180-degree change—will not be easy. Some policies, procedures, and attitudes will have to change, and people who refuse to adapt will have to be moved out. The current education system works on a medical model, diagnosing what's "wrong" with children and then putting them in one ward or another for "treatment." The approach I put forth in this book is, by contrast, a health model, identifying children's strengths and interests and then developing a course of action that builds on those assets while also taking care to see that children master basic skills such as literacy and numeracy.

DIAGNOSING ADD: BITTER FRUIT

The medical model of education may also help explain the epidemic of attention deficit disorder diagnoses among our youth. Begin with high pressure, test-centric schools promoting intense competition that only a few can win. Add to that mix ambitious parents who need an explanation for their children's "failure" that doesn't fault their parenting. Solution: a diagnosis of ADD, which absolves the schools and the parents.[1] Instead, it's a medical problem that drugs can solve.

The current rise in ADD diagnoses is "déjà vu all over again," but with a twist. My colleague John Tulenko and I reported this story in 1995 in *ADD: A Dubious Diagnosis?* for PBS.[2] We exposed the greed and venality of pharmaceutical company Ciba-Geigy (then the maker of Ritalin) and the advocacy group CHADD (Children and Adults with Attention-Deficit/Hyperactivity Disorder), as well as the naiveté of the U.S. Department of Education, which had been snookered by CHADD into endorsing the use of Ritalin.

Our reporting and the subsequent furor slowed down the rush to medicate, but not for long. The *New York Times* reported in 2013 that 6.4 million children ages four to seventeen had received an ADD diagnosis at some point, a 16 percent increase since 2007 and a 53 percent increase over the previous ten years.[3] Two-thirds of these kids get medicated with Ritalin, Adderall, or some other stimulant, which, if nothing else, guarantees that we lead the world in consumption of amphetamines. Roughly one out of every five high school boys is being labeled as having ADD, and one out of ten is taking medication.

It's going to get worse if the American Psychological Association relaxes the definition of ADD, which will make it easier for children to be labeled. Under the new definition, losing your cellphone or losing your focus while doing homework may be enough to get the label. If this behavior "impacts" your life, you could have ADD. The current wording requires that a behavior "cause impairment."

Even doctors and others whose overly relaxed attitude about ADD contributed to the explosion in diagnoses are upset by what's happening now. Dr. Ned Hallowell, who famously once told parents that some stimulants were "safer than aspirin," now says, "I regret the analogy." He told the *Times*, "That we have kids out there getting these drugs to use as mental steroids—that's dangerous, and I hate to think that I had a hand in creating that problem."

Certainly ADD exists, but the epidemic—past and current—is man-made. In the 1990s it was created largely by greedy pharmaceutical manufacturers, abetted by teachers who wanted tightly controlled classrooms and parents who were looking to explain why their sons didn't seem to be on track to get into Harvard. In fact, recent research also suggests that overly demanding parents are a cause of persistent ADD. "The finding here is that children with ADHD whose parents regularly expressed high levels of criticism over time were less likely to experience [a] decline in symptoms," said Erica Musser, an assistant professor of psychology at Florida International University and lead author of a study on the condition published in the *Journal of Abnormal Psychology*.[4]

Today? As noted earlier, the money trail again leads to Big Pharma, because sales of ADD medications now amount to $9 billion, up from $4 billion in 2007. In his remarkable book *ADHD Nation*, Alan Schwartz (a *New York Times* reporter) provides stunning evidence:

> Fifteen percent of youngsters in the United States—three times the consensus estimate—are getting diagnosed with ADHD. That's millions of extra kids being told they have something wrong with their brains, with most of them then placed on serious medications. The rate among boys nationwide is a stunning 20 percent. In southern states such as Mississippi, South Carolina, and Arkansas, it's 30 percent of all boys, almost one in three. (Boys tend to be more hyperactive and impulsive than girls, whose ADHD can manifest itself more as an inability to concentrate.) Some Louisiana counties are approaching half—*half*—of boys in third through fifth grades taking ADHD medications.
>
> ADHD has become, by far, the most misdiagnosed condition in American medicine.[5]

Two veteran educators alerted me to another factor in the current epidemic: test score pressures. Students with special needs, such as ADD, are allowed to take important exams, including the SAT and the ACT untimed, and nobody's the wiser. The admissions committees at Harvard, Amherst, Stanford, et cetera are not told that Elizabeth or David had all the time in the world. That is why, these educators said, some parents don't mind at all when their children get the ADD label—and may even seek it out. It is, one said, "a win-win situation, or so parents believe."

But there's no free lunch. If the kids take the medication, their bodies change. They're also learning an unintended (and inaccurate) lesson: there's a pill for all their problems. And if they don't take the pills, they may sell them, because there's a strong market for the stimulants, which are "uppers" for kids who don't actually need to be calmed down. James Swanson of Florida International University told the *New York Times* that 30 percent of the pills are sold or passed around.[6]

As Dr. Richard Friedman observed in the *Times*, "I think another social factor that, in part, may be driving the 'epidemic' of A.D.H.D. has gone unnoticed: the increasingly stark contrast between the regimented and demanding school environment and the highly stimulating digital world, where young people spend their time outside school."[7]

Real work is something that young people won't forget. And meaningful work teaches young people the insights and skill sets that will serve them well as adults.

Oh, and those kids will probably do just fine on whatever standardized tests the system throws their way.

Memory Lane

Investigating attention deficit disorder was a surreal experience in many ways. Both PBS and my producing station in South Carolina were extremely nervous about taking on a powerful drug company. They delayed the broadcast for months, made us double our insurance, and insisted that we add a question mark to the program's title.[8] We knew we had proved that ADD was often a dubious diagnosis and that the current epidemic was man-made, a product of greed, but the powers that be were just plain scared.

The program stepped on a lot of powerful parental toes, including those of some in my industry. We reported that many parents actively sought a diagnosis of attention deficit disorder as a way of "explaining" why their child wasn't on track to get into Harvard or Princeton. In other words, drugging a child was preferable to raising questions about their own parenting or their child's abilities and interests.

But the investigative process itself is what I remember best. When we followed the money trail, we discovered that Ritalin's manufacturer was secretly funding a supposedly neutral parents group, CHADD. We also learned that CHADD had secretly infiltrated the U.S. Department of Education and was lobbying to loosen the restrictions on Ritalin to make it even easier to get (at a time when the United States was already consuming more than 80 percent of the world's supply).

Drug company Ciba-Geigy, the manufacturer of Ritalin, knew that we knew what was going on, and when we went to interview representatives of the company, we were escorted by (seemingly armed) guards into a large room where the drug company had already set up its own cameras to record everything. Despite their advance warning, the Ciba-Geigy spokesperson admitted that the company was getting huge benefits by covertly funding the supposedly neutral nonprofit CHADD, which in turn was endorsing Ritalin. CHADD was a messenger, he said.

CHADD's co-founder, Dr. Harvey Parker, seemingly accustomed to accolades from parents and to the high life, told us that he felt no guilt about endorsing Ritalin or keeping Ciba-Geigy's funding of the organization secret. Parker told me that Ciba-Geigy owed CHADD because the group was helping so many children by introducing them to Ritalin. And he had no qualms about his nonprofit's efforts to lobby Congress and the government agency that regulated drugs either, even though nonprofits are strictly prohibited from lobbying.

Furthermore, no one at CHADD or Ciba-Geigy expressed any remorse about duping the U.S. Department of Education either. Department funds had paid for a series of glossy public service announcements (PSAs) in which "ordinary" parents sang the praises of Ritalin. The department withdrew the PSAs when we reported that all the parents were officials of CHADD.

Katie Couric invited me to debate the issue on the Today *show with the unctuous Parker and a "neutral" university professor. My colleague John Tulenko had done his homework, however, and told me that the professor's work was supported by Ciba-Geigy, something the* Today *show did not know. So when Katie asked the professor to weigh in on whether the ADD epidemic was man-made, as we asserted, the professor attacked me. When Couric gave me the opportunity to respond, I had the great pleasure of asking the professor whether she had told the* Today *show that Ciba-Geigy was paying for her "research." Her only response was stunned silence.*

I also wrote an op-ed for the New York Times *and appeared on some cable and NPR shows to discuss our findings. We managed to derail the ADD express for a while, but it's back with a vengeance. As the Bible warns, "Love of money is the root of all evil."*

We often say that schools cannot do it alone, but what do we mean by "it"? What exactly is the purpose of schooling? Young people swim in a 24/7 stream of data. In that world of information overload, young people need to learn the *habits* of challenging, asking questions, doubting, and digging. I believe they ought to be doing that in their classrooms, guided by skillful teachers who are comfortable with giving students greater control over their own learning.

The absence of individual responsibility for learning is high school's "deep, pervasive, insidious flaw," according to Samuel Levin, a student who actually started his own high school.

> Because when I realized that, from the ages of fourteen to eighteen, teenagers have almost no real responsibility in school, I was genuinely shocked. How can we expect kids to emerge from high school as responsible

adults if they never experience real responsibility in school?

What's more, isn't one of the key goals of an education system to prepare the next generation to inherit the earth? Isn't the goal to cultivate stewards so that, in the future, the planet and society are in better hands than they were in the previous generation? But how can high school cultivate stewards if it never lets them practice stewardship? For four years, I realized, we steward high schoolers, like a flock of sheep, when we should be slowly handing them the reins.[9]

Technology floods our world with information, but the human brain can develop ways of weighing and sorting information to separate the wheat from the chaff. We need to encourage—and model—choosing the wheat. Some schools do this. "What do you know?" Deborah Meier, the great educator and a founder of the modern small schools movement, would ask of students. "And how do you know that you know it?" At the best schools, the "it" of education moved away from regurgitation and toward inquiry a long time ago.

But most education policies reinforce an unimaginative vision of education, a business model with a bottom line of standardized-test results. Ironically, many forward-thinking business leaders have discarded that narrow view and instead support schools whose graduates can think critically, make sense out of contradictory information, and work well with people of every age, race, gender, religion, and sexual identity.

Unlike its rhyming barnyard relative, "it" does *not* just happen. These are choices that *we* make.

REDEFINING INTELLIGENCE AND ABILITY

If schools begin to ask how each child is intelligent, the greatest beneficiaries will be children with special needs, because for years most schools didn't even ask whether these kids possessed measurable intelligence.

The Education of All Handicapped Children Act of 1975 (PL 94-142) and its successors forced educators to consider the question "How is this child with *special needs* intelligent?"— something rarely, if ever, asked by most educators prior to 1975.[10] The bill passed because Congress had become aware that, out of the estimated eight million children with disabilities, one million were receiving no formal education at all; some were kept at home, while others, abandoned by their families, were doomed to spend their lives in institutions. Although the vote in the House and Senate had made it veto-proof, the 1975 act was not universally popular. In a break with tradition, President Gerald Ford refused to allow photographers into the room when he signed the bill. He was upset and angry about the precedent the law was setting—requiring services but not providing the money. He predicted—correctly—that this "unfunded mandate" would become a financial albatross around the necks of school boards because it mandated services but did not pay for them.[11]

In direct response to widespread failure of educators to provide services, the new law empowered parents, creating a legal entitlement for their children. It created an adversarial relationship, parent versus school, with the law on the parent's side. Parents could demand a diagnosis (and challenge the results). Every child who was diagnosed and labeled would then be provided with an Individualized Education Plan (IEP), which would serve as a very specific road map for their education. The new law also created, almost overnight, a new area of specialization for teachers and a growth industry for schools of education.[12] To this day, it's easier to find a job in special education than in any other area of teaching.

The law required that students with disabilities be educated in the "least restrictive environment," a reaction to the widespread practice of isolating and segregating these students. However, the practice of "mainstreaming" in regular classrooms has created its own issues, and many teachers continue to complain that they have not been adequately trained to work with this population of students.

Complaints and problems aside, the act and its successors

improved the lives of millions of children.[13] Because the 1975 law allowed states to phase in their compliance, I was able to visit a few states *before* they began providing services. I reported on how these unfortunate children were dealt with by public schools. It was a nightmare—no other word suffices. In New Mexico, for example, severely physically disabled children were locked up with little or no consideration for their mental capacity. Some desperate families kept these children at home, rather than condemn them to life in an institution.

Before passage of the act, schools did not have to make any special effort to educate children with disabilities, and I remember visiting middle school and high school classrooms where disabled children were simply assigned to draw pictures or weave bracelets while the other kids studied American history or French. Those days are over, or should be anyway. The Education of All Handicapped Children Act and its successors also created opportunities for those *without* disabilities to learn about differences and to learn empathy.[14] That's no small thing.[15]

Memory Lane

In my mind's eye, I can still picture the vast, dimly lit room. About half the size of a football field, it was filled with men, women, and children strapped into wheelchairs or otherwise restrained. If I close my eyes, I can hear the wailing and moaning, rising and falling, mixed with a cacophony of animal sounds that I never would have imagined humans were capable of making. This snake pit was in New Mexico's main facility for handicapped children and adults, the Las Lunas Hospital and Training School, still open and still accepting children more than four years after Congress passed PL 94-142.

Curious about this, I had gone to New Mexico in the spring of 1979. My guide led me toward the distant corner where the "retarded" children were kept. Along the way she stopped to point out a man in his mid-twenties in a wheelchair, his arms and legs restrained. His neck was puffed up like two softballs, one on each side, the grotesque growths expanding and contracting as he breathed.

My guide explained: "If you watch him, he's pulling air in through his mouth into a cavity that he's probably created over the years between his carotid arteries and his skin . . . It's very self-stimulatory, and this has evolved over the years. This fellow's been institutionalized ever since he was a young infant, and I guess in earlier days he was considered to have no potential for anything at all. People just left him to his own devices, and he began to self-stimulate."

I asked her how children ended up in such a horrible place. Sometimes, she told me, babies and infants were left on the doorstep during the night, abandoned by parents who couldn't cope. When she saw my skeptical look, she told me about the Christmas cards. The institution sent holiday cards to the parents or guardians of all the residents every Christmas, and every year at least half of them came back marked "Addressee Moved, Left No Forwarding Address."

In the children's corner, she introduced me to Bill, a young man in a wheelchair. He was twenty-one, a quadriplegic who could not speak, the result of cerebral palsy. But he could move his head, and he smiled as we were introduced. He was wearing a miner's helmet with a lamp, and on the front of his wheelchair was a blackboard with common words such as feel, need, hungry, love, and pronouns in boxes. Around the edges of the blackboard were the letters of the alphabet and numbers, and in opposite corners at the top, the words yes and no. On the bottom were the days of the week. Using his lamp to shine on words and letters, Bill could communicate with others.

Bill was clearly not mentally retarded, but there he was in the state hospital that housed the mentally retarded. I asked the guide how this could have happened. "There are certain tests that they run through these children or adults that, because he was handicapped, he couldn't do certain testing," she replied. "And so therefore they just diagnosed him at lower functioning."

What she was saying, basically, is that the people running the institution just assumed that physically *disabled individuals were* also mentally *disabled, meaning they received minimal care, and no education to speak of. Bill had gotten lucky, because one day an attendant thought she saw a light in his eyes, more than just a glimmer of intelligence, and so she and others improvised ways to teach him to read and compose messages. He had learned rapidly, she told me, and now he could carry on a conversation. "He's very aware of everything. He can be pretty conniving. He's got us all jumping. I think that, if Bill would have been given the educational opportunities, he could be at a very, very high level."*

Then I interviewed Bill, saying aloud into the tape recorder what he signaled with his headlamp. He told me that would rather be on television than just plain old radio, smiling as he wrote those words. Here's the end of that interview:

MERROW: *"What do you do on Sundays?"*
BILL: *C-H-U-R-C-H*
MERROW: *"Church. You go to church on Sundays?"*
BILL: *YES*
MERROW: *"Do you believe in God?"*
BILL: *YES*
MERROW: *"How many years have you been going to church?"*
BILL: *TWO*
MERROW: *"Two years. Got it. Thank you, Bill."*
BILL: *GOODBYE. I LOVE YOU.*

I shed tears of joy, because this young man's life demonstrated that the human spirit is unquenchable. But I cried tears of sorrow at the same time, because his life, like so many other young lives, has been wasted because society was unable to see beyond physical and mental differences.

GETTING DOWN TO BASICS

You are deep into a book about education and have taken only one test. How on earth did this happen? Well, the free ride is over. Here's your second test, consisting of just two forced-choice questions.

1. The primary purpose of public schools is to produce:

   a. Educated students
   b. Knowledge

2. Which more accurately describes the structure of public schools?

   a. Teachers are "labor," and administrators are "management"
   b. Students are "labor," and teachers are "management"

My hunch is that most American business leaders would select A as the correct answer to both questions. After all, that's the traditional model of school, in which teachers teach and students learn. It's often known, pejoratively, as the "factory model": teachers (the workers) teach facts and figures to students, who emerge from this assembly line after twelve years as "educated."

That's a paradox, because for years American business has expressed its unhappiness with schools and has devoted lots of money and energy to reforming them. Yes, like the rest of us, the business sector is addicted to school reform.

What America's business leaders are doing is akin to buying faster ponies for the Pony Express. But in the twenty-first century, faster ponies won't get the mail delivered on time, and schools adopting current reforms won't provide the workforce that business needs. Nor will those schools produce the healthy citizenry our nation needs.

Studies indicate that many public school graduates do not possess the skills and capabilities that matter to the CEOs of GE,

DuPont, Xerox, Amazon, JPMorgan Chase, and about a hundred other leading companies surveyed by the Business Council and the Conference Board. As a consequence, these companies say they are having difficulty finding the skilled workers they need. By some estimates, at least 40 percent of corporations are leaving positions unfilled or are exporting the jobs they cannot fill at home.

For nine out of ten CEOs, the most important skills and attributes are work ethic, teamwork, decision-making, critical thinking, and computer literacy. Only the last is included in some school curricula. In all, the more than one hundred CEOs surveyed were asked to rank-order thirteen skills and attributes. The traditional school subjects, "basic reading and math" and "writing and communications" ranked sixth and seventh, while "physical/health readiness" ranked twelfth. What are often dismissed by pundits and critics as "soft skills" actually mattered *most* to business leaders.[16]

What about the basics? How well do the schools teach reading, writing, math, and communication? Not very, the CEOs reported. Asked to rate the capability of their current workforce, just 23 percent rated it as "very capable" in basic reading and math; for writing and communication, the "very capable" proportion drops to 15.5 percent. In other words, schools are not emphasizing most of the skills businesses need, *and* they are not doing a good job of teaching the ones that they do stress. I am not arguing that schools should do whatever business wants, only that employers are part of public education's constituency and must be listened to.[17]

Why haven't our schools been teaching more of what business wants? It's not as if American business hasn't been involved in, and generally supportive of, public education at the local and national levels for years. In the last part of the twentieth century, "school-business partnerships" were in vogue. These locally driven efforts often involved volunteers from businesses helping out in the schools, while their companies donated equipment and materials. When "partnerships" fell out of favor—probably because the results weren't clear—they were often replaced by internship programs that put young people into "the world of work."

Today many business leaders and wealthy hedge fund tycoons, impatient for results, are likely to support "no excuses" charter organizations that stress academic results. Others have put their prestige and dollars behind Teach for America, a program that seeks to upend the teaching profession.[18]

The imprint of business is clearly visible at the national level. Although only two business leaders and one small businessman (a dentist) served on the eighteen-member commission that produced the report *A Nation at Risk* in 1983, its language and message could easily have been written by the U.S. Chamber of Commerce. Its warning about "a rising tide of mediocrity" sparked the school reform movement that continues today. And while President George H.W. Bush hosted the inaugural National Summit on Education in 1989, business soon took over. The second and third summits were convened by IBM CEO Louis Gerstner at IBM headquarters in Armonk, New York, with President Bill Clinton attending as an invited guest. Those meetings and subsequent national commissions coalesced around a central theme: the failure of schools to produce enough high-caliber graduates was threatening our country's economic leadership.

To businesses' way of thinking, graduates were the "product" in a straightforward factory model paradigm: teachers were given raw material—kids—to turn into productive, capable young adults. In that factory model, teachers are the workers, so it's not surprising that business leaders, who are the management, have not been natural allies of teachers unions.

However, if schools are going to improve dramatically, everyone, and especially the business community, needs to realize is that the old factory model is no longer valid. Because of the information revolution, students—not teachers—must be the workforce. They must become "knowledge workers," and their "product" is knowledge. In this new paradigm, teachers are now part of management, a concept that some people may have difficulty dealing with.

MEASUREMENT MATTERS

Asking "How is a child intelligent?" does not mean ignoring measures of the overall performance of all students, the schools, and their teachers, but it does require moving away from sorting. From the earliest days, school systems have been sorting students, and that's a habit that will be hard to break.[19] The bigger problem is that the current crop of school reformers is heavily invested in *improving* the sorting mechanism. They have spent billions to make sorting fairer and more efficient, so that the poor and minorities are not automatically shunted aside. They support the growth of charter schools, for example, as a way of thwarting the public school monopoly, which they see as a root cause of the educational system's inefficiency. From my perspective, these (mostly) well-meaning people are trying to make the Pony Express faster by adding horses. Though they obviously do not see it that way, only time will tell whether they will be willing to examine their strongly held views. Of course sorting will still occur, certainly in the college admissions and job-hunting/hiring processes. Sorting isn't inherently wrong. Our mistake is to sort too early, before giving all children the opportunities we want for our own kids.

If you are now willing to commit to building schools that ask the right question—"How are you intelligent?"—of each child, congratulations. You've attained a basic understanding of the current school reform landscape and accept that we are in dire need of a different and more sane way going forward. Now it's time to dig into what should be going on in our schools. Step Five, and all the steps that follow, are guideposts for redesigning American education.

STEP FIVE
Make Connections

"Only connect," urges one of E.M. Forster's central characters in his novel *Howard's End*. Forster wasn't writing about adolescents and children, but he could have been. Because most children don't care how much you know until they know how much you care, making connections with them is essential. Children need nurturing and support, and when they don't feel connected to their school and the adults therein, they will look elsewhere. As Erika Christakis notes in *The Importance of Being Little*, "It's really very simple: young children need to know and to be known."[1] Angela Duckworth, author of *Grit: The Power of Passion and Perseverance*, adds, "When adults demonstrate that they care and that they believe in you, much is possible."[2] Carol Dweck makes similar points in *Mindset: The New Psychology of Growth.*[3]

As a practical matter, Step Five calls for schools that are small enough so that every student can be well known to at least a couple of adults in the building. That's the critical piece often missing in public education, where teachers are sometimes responsible for 150 or more students. As the late educator Ted Sizer said, "That's not teaching; that's crowd control." Those conditions make it extremely difficult for caring adults to connect with all the needy children they come in contact with on a daily basis.

Of course, a small school doesn't guarantee connecting, because what matters far more is a caring attitude and philosophy. Adults need to learn to see the world from kids' level, from the ground up and not from the top down. There is good news: lots of schools and communities are embracing this idea. Today, it's usually under the label of "social and emotional learning."[4] The modern roots of this approach are in the work of Dr. James Comer, M.D., whose Comer School Development Program pioneered the idea that schools must nurture first and teach second.[5] Beginning in the late 1960s in New Haven, Connecticut, the tireless Dr. Comer built a network of more than eleven hundred public elementary schools organized around a core belief: when children feel supported, their academic performance, their life skills, and their outlook on life improve.[6] What came to be known as the Comer Process holds principals, administrators, teachers, and parents—essentially every adult associated with the school—responsible for making academic and social decisions collaboratively, but always in the best interests of children. "This holistic strategy links children's academic growth with their emotional wellness and social and moral development in a collaborative school culture congenial to learning."[7]

AFFECTION DEFICIT DISORDER, THE NEW ADD

Often children and adolescents who appear disconnected from or resistant to schools are diagnosed with attention deficit disorder, with medication following the diagnosis. As noted in Step Four, greedy and opportunistic adults created the ADD epidemic in the 1990s. Now it seems to me that we have a *new* ADD: *affection deficit disorder*. That's the term I use for the disconnected world we are creating for young people.

When kids cannot connect at school, they leave—in droves.[8] About one million young people drop out of school every year. A disturbingly large and growing number of adolescents choose to end their lives. Getting tough, being more rigorous, or adopting the Common Core won't change this situation and may make things worse. But there's a lot we can do.

Affection deficit disorder is more apparent in upper-income families. All too often, wealthy kids get lots of "stuff" from their parents—their own credit cards, cell phones, and computers, high-definition TVs in their rooms, and a fancy car when they get their driver's license. From early on, they're scheduled to the max, with private lessons in ballet, skiing, piano, French, and martial arts. That sort of attention—private tutors and all the stuff you can charge—is no substitute for affection.

But it's not just the wealthy. All children crave and need attention. In February 2007, when the United States was bogged down in two wars with our all-volunteer military doing the heavy lifting, the news routinely reported about men and women doing their fourth, fifth, or sixth tour of duty in Afghanistan or Iraq. I started wondering about their children. What must life be like for them, these "children of the surge," with one parent or the other constantly away from home—and in what is euphemistically called "harm's way"? So off we went to an elementary school at Fort Bragg, North Carolina, where I expected to find an atmosphere of "hop to" or "suck it up, kid." Instead I discovered what most of our schools could—and should—be: warm, welcoming places without any signs of affection deficit disorder.

I spent most of my time with Nancy Welsh, a veteran kindergarten teacher, and Gary Wieland, a military veteran who had been teaching for sixteen years. Their demeanors couldn't have been more different. Welsh was tender and loving, while Wieland was gruff. Welsh welcomed us (five adults and our equipment) into her classroom, while Wieland made it clear he was tolerating us only because his principal had ordered it. Both were, however, totally focused on their students and keenly attuned to their needs.[9]

Early one morning, we observed Corey and Scarlette Keeling and their three children as Corey, a medic, boarded a military plane to leave for his third deployment. Scarlette later described the sudden emptiness: "Everything leaves—his clothes, you know, his shoes, the laundry's gone. It's like he was here and everything was great. And we argued and pinched and poked and drove each other crazy, you know, and it's like, 'Oh! If I could just have one more day of that.'"

Expecting that her kids would want to go home after this, Scarlette had rented movies and bought popcorn. But five-year-old

Austin insisted on going to school. When they arrived, principal Tim Howle, a retired major in the Army's Special Forces, greeted them cheerfully with a high five for each child. "My job is to take care of these kids, take care of the families, and take care of the teachers," he said. "We're the consistency in the lives of these kids."

McNair Elementary School is located in the middle of Fort Bragg. It's one of about two hundred schools (with 8,700 educators and approximately 84,000 students) run by the Department of Defense. At the time of my visit, 40 percent of the 372 students at McNair had a parent serving in Iraq or Afghanistan. These kids were scared, sometimes angry, and often confused, but the adults—big, tough military men and women—understood the importance of affection, a hug, or a high five. They didn't lie and say, "Your dad or mom is going to be fine," because they didn't know if that was true. But they made school a safe place, a place where kids were allowed to be needy. Scarlette Keeler said it well: "Our children are already strong. They don't need somebody else to tell them to be strong. They need somebody to let them know that being sad is okay, being angry is okay, and being confused is okay." In other words, affection is the key.

At McNair Elementary School, we discovered children's well-being to be a top priority. When Austin arrived at his kindergarten class that February day, teacher Nancy Welsh kept a close eye on him. "He's pretty agitated right now, his emotions bother him," she told me. "He's also tired, because it's been a big week for him." Welsh encouraged him to talk about his feelings; Austin told her he was sad. She responded by giving him a fun assignment: to draw a picture of a happy dream with his dad, which they worked on together as he talked about it.

"This is their security zone," Welsh said. "This is where they can be a kid. I let them be sad and I tell them it's okay to be sad. I say things like 'I would be sad too if my daddy was far away' or 'I'm sad that your mommy's not here.' So it's okay to be sad, but I'll say, 'Let's try to feel better now.'" (If only this kind of response were encouraged—even expected—in most public schools, instead of disturbances being automatic triggers for punishment!)

Austin was not the only kid in class with that situation; in fact, fourteen out of Welsh's seventeen students had a parent on active duty overseas that day, and another parent was scheduled to leave in two days. While I was watching, a young boy came up and gave Welsh a hug. "Kenyon just came up to me and said, 'I miss Mommy,'" she explained later. "He just had a very sad look on his face, and I said, 'I'm sorry, I know you do' and I gave him a hug. He hugged me back and held on. I try to do for every single child whatever they need. And they don't always need the same thing either."

But they all need to keep on learning, and Welsh never lost sight of that. Nor did her principal, Tim Howle. "I have made it a point to be personally involved with all the kids," he told me. "I know what caring and nurturing can do in education. I see it every day."

At that point, I asked him whether nurturing could get in the way of learning. "No," he said, hitting my softball question out of the park. "You can't separate education and relationships. If you want a great educational environment, you have to have a personal relationship with the kids. If we just comforted children all day, we would never get to the standards that we have to teach. And it wouldn't help the parents to have a child who is not learning what they have to learn. No, we don't lose sight of the academics at all."

Nancy Welsh told me that nearly half of her students were beginning to read simple sentences. (Keep in mind that our national goal is to have children reading by the end of third grade.) When I checked back with her at the end of the year, she told me that nearly all of her kindergarteners were reading.

With the wars in Iraq and Afghanistan raging, I tried to find out her politics. She wouldn't tell me, no matter how hard I tried. "My position is to teach the children, to love the children," she said. "I'm not a politician, and I'm not someone who expresses opinions about whether we should be in Afghanistan or Iraq or Korea or anyplace else for that matter. I have such an influence on kindergarteners, and I am very, very careful about what I say."

"But do you have a position?"

"Sure," she said, with a small smile.

"Do you feel strongly?"

"I definitely do."

"Would you tell me?" I pressed.

"No," she laughed. "I will not."

Across the hall in Gary Wieland's third-grade class, there was no ambiguity about the ongoing wars. "Our policy for being over there is right," he told me. "And these kids hear that from me." Wieland had been teaching at McNair for sixteen years; before that, he served in the military for thirty. Wounded in Vietnam, he received a Silver Star and a Bronze Star. A staunch conservative and self-identified "Fox News guy," he strongly mistrusted what he called "the liberal media"—and he obviously put my employer, *PBS NewsHour*, squarely in that group. Before the day was through, he and I had bonded, but it wasn't a walk in the park.

When we entered his classroom he was teaching about Iraq, asking his students for a working definition. "How do you like this so far—'a desert country in the Middle East'? Does this cover what you been saying?" He looked at the definition written on the board, and then turned back to his students. "Now, why are your mom and dad there? Why did they go there? Why are they in Afghanistan? What are they bringing?" He waited. "Freedom," called out several children before long.

"Freedom?" Wieland asked, writing the word in large letters on the blackboard. "Yes!"

Later I asked him about what struck me as political indoctrination. "I didn't make that definition up," he replied, bristling. "Students gave me that definition."

"But do you agree with it?"

"Yes, sure I do."

"Would it be okay if a teacher took the opposite position and defined Iraq as a country where America was wasting $2 billion a week?" I asked.

Wieland glared at me. "I spent a career in the military on foreign soil so that those people could say that." His look indicated that I was one of "those people." "It's not all about the ABC's," he continued. "They know I'm a safe haven for them when something is wrong. They know they can come to the old man and talk to me about it." Principal Howle supported Wieland, saying, "I really don't care about their politics. As long as they love the kids and do the right thing by the kids—what's more important?"

Gary Wieland loved his kids, even as he pushed and teased some while hugging others. "It's about when a kid leaves here, what does he look like compared to when he walked in the door. Can he think independently? Can he solve problems? My kids blew the doors off the standardized tests that we took last year. I mean, with reading scores, the entire class was in the 95th percentile on national norms, 93rd percentile for math," he told me.

On that day in February, seven of Wieland's seventeen students had a parent in Iraq or Afghanistan. "I've become their surrogate dad," he said. "They really know that I have a relationship with them and that I'm going to stand in the gap." Every time a McNair parent was about to leave for a combat zone, Mr. Wieland would invite the parent to the classroom; in front of everyone, he would take a dollar from his wallet and give it to the parent.

He described what happened when Tedrick's dad left for Iraq. "His father came in the classroom and I said, 'Tedrick, stand up,' and I handed the dad a dollar and I said, 'When you get back you owe me that.'" Then I said to Tedrick, 'You know, you're now my kid, little boy.'" And I told Tedrick's dad, 'If you take care of my country, I'll take care of your son.'"

Later I asked Tedrick's mother, Renee Philyaw, where the dollar was. "Here in the wallet," she said. "He has it in his will that if something happens to him, Tedrick gets that dollar."

Wieland stays in touch with parents he's entered into "contracts" with. He started giving out the dollars during the Clinton era, with U.S. interventions in Bosnia and other areas. Although he hasn't kept a record, he guesses that he's given out about $100 to parents over the years. (Tedrick's dad came home safely a year later.)

I pressed both teachers and the principal with questions about death and danger. Their answers differed, but their level of support for the kids was the same.

"If a kid asks the tough questions—'Is my dad going to die? Is Mom going to get killed?'—what do you say?" I asked.

Wieland answered: "I tell them, 'I didn't. Been there, done that. You know, they hurt me, but here I am to annoy you. Your dad is the best-trained soldier in the world. The folks around him are as good as he is. What's to worry about?'"

"We had a child here," said Welsh, "not in my class, but another kindergarten class last year, whose daddy did not come back, so I do not want to tell them 'Your daddy's going to be fine' or 'Your mommy's going to be fine,' because I don't know that."

Tim Howle added: "I can't tell you I'm going to be here tomorrow. I can't tell them 'Mom's going to be here tomorrow,' but I'm going to tell you, 'No matter what, there's someone here to take care of you.' These kids are resilient. They come into this building every day doing what they have to, learning and going on with their life. They feel safe. They feel like someone cares."

And it wasn't just "someone" who cared. Everyone at that school seemed to care about every child. And because there was no affection deficit at that school, the kids paid attention. Because there was no affection deficit, there was time and space to focus on learning, and much of it was joyful. As noted earlier, the third and fourth graders at McNair excelled on standardized tests, with scores in the 80th and 90th percentiles.

Parents are in the front lines in the fight against affection deficit disorder—not with a credit card, the newest iPhone, unlimited texting, or medication, but with hugs and thoughtful listening. Government can also be part of the solution. Government at all levels could act to end the affection deficit by restoring art, music, physical education, recess, and field trips to our schools. And public school teachers could adopt the health model of schooling: Teach to strengths. Build on strengths. Show students that you care deeply about them personally and academically.

We need to change because the new ADD is leaving kids behind. It's leaving them insufficiently skilled and without a sense of public purpose, and it's leaving them confused or angry. The new ADD is sowing seeds of social destruction. A split society of haves and have-nots, with everyone disconnected, will eventually pull us all down, and there's no wall high enough to protect us if we don't recommit to a decent opportunity for all.

Memory Lane

When there's affection deficit disorder in troubled families, children are likely to pay a heavy price. Because I was free to report on anything involving children and youth on my weekly NPR series, in 1978 I decided to report on mental health services for kids.[10] And so I spent six weeks visiting facilities in Maryland, Texas, and a few other states. What I learned is now old news: Rich kids get therapy; poor kids get powerful drugs. Rich kids are treated for as long as necessary; poor kids are put out on the street when they reach the (limited) number of days that will be covered by insurance.

The series I produced on that subject was controversial because of the tough issues and because of occasional profanity. In Texas at a state institution for young children with mental problems, I interviewed children for several days. Lisa is the child I remember best. She was only nine and had already lived in "thirteen or sixteen" foster homes, she said. We were alone in a fairly large room, sitting on a couch, talking about whatever was on her mind. At the end of our long conversation, I gave her an impromptu spelling test.

merrow: How do you spell sugar?
LISA: Sugar. S-H-U-G-E-R.
merrow: How do you spell couch?
LISA: Ooo! Couch. C—No. K-A-O-W-C-H.
merrow: How do you spell soda?
LISA: S-O-A-D.

Lisa was a charmer. At one point she asked me what I was going to do with the recording. When I told her it was for a radio program, she exclaimed, "Oh, yuck." She paused and then added, "Don't put it on AM. Put it on FM."

I took the bait. "Why?" I asked

I could hear the laughter in her voice as she answered. "We don't even listen to FM," she said. "We only listen to AM."

Her doctor told me that Lisa had been abandoned at age two by her natural parents. They left her with some relatives, who in turn gave her to other friends, who then left her on someone's doorstep; those people eventually brought her to the Department of Human Resources, leading to a long line of foster homes.

At the end of the conversation, Lisa suddenly stood up in front of me, smiled, and asked, "Do you like me?"

"Yes, of course I do," I told her.

"But do you really like me?" She smiled again when I said yes. Then she did an awkward curtsey and lifted her dress up over her head, showing me her underpants. "Now do you like me?"

I was dumbfounded. I ended the interview right there because I didn't know what to do or say. A nine-year-old girl, desperate for affection, was offering me her body. What sorts of awful things must have been done to her by adults, and for how many years, for her to have learned this behavior?

And how does one treat the mental problems caused by that abuse? As a patient in a state institution, she was entitled to a few weeks of treatment, but because the state didn't have enough counselors, the default treatment was drugs.

Later a doctor told me that sexual behavior like that was part of her sad history, a survival tactic she had learned early. The doctor told me that she would go to school without any underwear and would do cartwheels in the playground. She was, he said, simply looking for affection—albeit in the most inappropriate way.

What would Lisa's life be like when she was a teenager? I may have seen her future when I interviewed Mary, who had been recommitted to a Texas state institution for older children for the third time.

> *Sometimes I feel so down at heart*
> *I feel like I might fall apart*
> *But then these words come back to me,*
> *"Just take your time, and you'll be free."*

Mary wrote that song, which she sang for my tape recorder. She talked about wanting to escape and hitchhike home to Houston, even though her previous hitchhiking trips had ended badly, one in a multiple rape.

She told me that she had not informed her doctor about being raped, but I learned that he was aware of her sexual activity. "I know that she has had some—she's quite flirtatious with some of the guys back on the ward. I don't have any personal knowledge of her having had sexual activity with anybody around here, while she's here. But it might have happened," the doctor said.

At one point Mary said someone—meaning me—needed to massage her "sore" shoulder. Later she asked me to come closer to tell her if she had "sleep in her eyes." I declined both invitations.

Music mattered very much to Mary, who broke into song during our conversation, including this song she made up on the spot to end the interview.

> *This is the last song I'll ever sing for you.*
> *It's the last time I'll tell you*
> *Just how much I really care.*
> *This is the last song—*
> *But I'll sing more later on.*
> *Right now it's time for lunch*
> *And I think I'm gonna be gone.*

Mary, who was smart and aware, didn't hold back when talking about the dark side of her life, the drug use and sexual abuse. She told me what had happened when her allotted weeks of treatment ran out the last time. "They gave me a few dollars and opened the gate and told me to go," she said. She had no family members who would take her home, she said. "I had to hitchhike home. It was a hot day, and a convertible of boys came by and stopped to give me a ride. I got in, but they wouldn't take me home until I gave them all blow jobs, so I did."[11]

And then there was Roy, eighteen years old. Like Mary, Roy was an involuntary patient at a Texas mental hospital for adolescents.

ROY: *I smoke, and I'm eighteen. Can't read. Can't read or write*

MERROW: Not at all?

ROY: *No, I can't read or write at all.*

MERROW: How about those words up there on the board? Can you read any of those?

ROY: *No, just too hard for me. Really, I can't read those.*

MERROW: There's a word up there. Can you read that one?

ROY: *B-E?*

MERROW: Yeah, what does that say?

ROY: Be?

MERROW: That's right. How about the word that comes before it, T-O?

ROY: *T-O? To? I think it's to. Yeah. (Laughs)*

A few years earlier Roy had been arrested and jailed in Austin for a minor offense. In jail he attempted suicide. When the police later found him living in a park ("like an animal," his doctor said), he was confined to the mental hospital, where he had not caused any problems.

MERROW: How about the word that comes before that, H-O-W?

ROY: Tah?

merrow: No, it's an H.

ROY: Who? *I don't know. I can't really do it right. I ain't much in reading.*

MERROW: How about O-W? O-W is what you say when some-body punches you.

ROY: Ow. *(Laughs)*

merrow: So, now put the H in front of it. What have you got?

ROY: Um, how? How!

MERROW: Yes. You could read those three words in a row. Go ahead.

ROY: Uh, "how to be."

Psychotropic drugs such as Thorazine, Mellaril, Prolixin, Hal-dol and Moban (and sometimes electroshock) were the normal treatments in Roy's institution and in most public mental health facilities at the time. Roy's daily dose was 800 mg of Thorazine, a drug whose side effects include dizziness, drowsiness, anxiety, sleep problems, and constipation.

At one point in our conversation Roy yawned and asked me if we were almost done.

MERROW: *Ready to stop?*
ROY: *Yeah, I think I am.*
MERROW: *Okay, thanks a lot.*
ROY: *Okay.*

He paused, and I waited. After a short time, the words spilled out.

I mean, I didn't tell you the whole story. Um, when I was nine years old, my stepdad and my mom met each other and, well, they used to knock me around all the time, my stepdad did.

When he turned fourteen, Roy finally felt big and strong enough to turn on his abusive stepfather. He defended himself with a baseball bat . . . and he ended up in a juvenile institution, based, he said, on the testimony of his stepfather.

When we said goodbye, Roy assured me that he wasn't going to attempt suicide again.

ROY: *I think I can make it.*
MERROW: *Want to shake on that?*
ROY (laughs): *Yes.*
MERROW: *Okay.*
ROY: *I guess that's all I can say now. Bye.*

One of the children I talked to was nine, one eighteen, and the other nineteen, but the three conversations are eerily and sadly similar: a strong need to be heard, to feel a connection—and their shocking histories of mistreatment by those closest to them. Sexual, physical, and emotional abuse is another tie that binds them. My heart went out to all three, but especially to young Lisa, who seemed destined to travel the awful road that Mary was on.

I met Lisa, Mary, and Roy in 1978.[12] If they survived, they would be in their fifties or sixties. Their doctors were not optimistic. Lisa's doctor feared she would end up as a prostitute or in serial, abusive marriages. Roy's best bet, his doctor said, was vocational remedial education and, perhaps, a job as a janitor or greenhouse worker. Mary's future was even darker because of her apparent addiction to street drugs.

Could any school have saved Lisa, Mary, and Roy? Would feeling connected to some caring teachers have been enough to counteract sexual and physical abuse, abandonment and more? Perhaps not, but they deserved a chance. We can't rewrite the past, but we can build schools where making and maintaining connections is the first priority.

THE MOST DISCONNECTED OF ALL

In the 1970s and 1980s, gay and lesbian youth were most likely to be disconnected from their families, schools, and peers. I learned this in 1976, when I did what I believe was the first in-depth national reporting about gay kids in schools. I discovered —and reported—that quite often the kids suffered most at the hands of gay teachers, who were forced to be in the closet themselves and often did not dare reach out to children who must have reminded them of themselves at a young age. Unable to find comfort at schools and often shunned at home, many gay kids dropped out onto the street, where they were exploited by predatory adults.

How that radio program came about is a story in itself. I had gone to Boston for the meeting of the National Association of Independent Schools because I had been asked to be on a panel. I gambled that I could find some interesting people to interview for my weekly program, and I was wrong. The meeting was deadly dull. A few months earlier I had told my newly formed national advisory board that I needed to cover something dramatic and controversial in order to attract national attention. I suggested topics such as child abuse and—because it was in the news in Washington—homosexual teachers. The board was appalled at the idea and advised me to stick to traditional education issues.

All well and good, but there I was in Boston at a boring meeting with an hour of airtime to fill, and soon. So gay teachers it would be, I decided. Because I had no clue about how to begin, I called my good friend Larry, the hippest guy I knew when we were both at Harvard.

"Larry," I said, "I want to do some reporting about gay teachers and am hoping you can help me."

"How did you know?" he asked.

"How did I know what?" I asked in return.

After a few minutes of confusion I figured out that he was gay, and he figured out that I had been unaware until that moment.

Larry introduced me to the underworld of gay men and women. A teacher himself, he knew many closeted gay academics, and soon I was interviewing them.

The kids had it much worse, several teachers told me, and so Larry took me to shelters to meet young gay boys. Though classified as "runaways," most had in fact been thrown away by their families, because being gay was a mark of shame that disgraced the entire family, most often in the eyes of their fathers. To survive, many sold themselves on the street, usually to allegedly straight men, known to the boys as "chicken hawks." The data were depressing. Rates of drug abuse, self-abuse, and suicide were higher in the population of gay and lesbian youth.[13]

The one-hour program we produced, *Gay Kids, Gay Teachers*, received the national attention I was seeking. It was favorably reviewed in the *Washington Post* and a few other national publications, but the review I remember was in a gay newspaper, because the writer paid me a high compliment, noting that he couldn't tell from the broadcast whether I was gay or straight.

My advisory board had been wrong. Covering just classroom education would neither grow our audience nor move people deeply. From here on out, we would define education in the broadest possible terms and try to follow the maxim "Comfort the afflicted. Afflict the comfortable."

How much has changed since 1976 for gay, lesbian, bisexual, and transgender youth? Sadly, not enough. Rather than stepping up efforts to see that those kids are connected to their schools, some educators seem to be turning a blind eye, according to *Educational Exclusion*, a 2016 report from the Gay, Lesbian, and Straight Education Network (GLSEN). "LGBTQ youth's higher likelihood of victimization may put them in greater contact with school authorities and increase their risk of discipline. These youth may be punished even when they are the victims in bullying incidents, including as a result of defensive or preemptive violence."[14]

A RASH OF SUICIDES

What causes young people to decide to end their lives? While every story is different, I think we need to map the terrain that almost all of our adolescents occupy, because that environment may be harmful—and sometimes fatal—for our children. I believe that some of our organizational structures are negative influences on children. A particular concern is the way we isolate our children by age and grade, from kindergarten through senior year of high school.

When I was living in Palo Alto, California, five students from one high school ended their lives violently in less than two years—and more than a few others were prevented from trying, often at the last minute, by observant adults. That was in 2008–10, but, despite the town's best efforts to make whatever changes were needed to keep tragedy away, the problem persists, as *The Atlantic* noted in 2015: "Twelve percent of Palo Alto high-school students surveyed in the 2013–14 school year reported having seriously contemplated suicide in the past 12 months."[15]

And each suicide reverberates for a long, long time. Isabelle Blanchard was the junior class president at Gunn High School when a classmate committed suicide. "I am fifteen years old and I just organized a memorial," she said to her mother, Kathleen, when she got home.

Implicit in her weary statement of fact was the underlying

question "Why?" How could it be that they all lived in a place that inspired jealousy from out-of-towners, where the coolest gadgets and ideas come from, where the optimism is boundless, and where, as Kathleen put it to me somewhat sardonically, "people are working on inventions that will slow aging and probably one day stop death"—and yet also a place where a junior in high school is closely familiar with the funerals of other teens?[16]

Palo Alto is a high-achieving community, and many parents expect their children to do as well as or better than they did. Many kids face the pressures so powerfully depicted in the film *Race to Nowhere*. In one sense that film says to schools and parents, "Back off! You are endangering your children's health."

No argument there, but backing off would not be enough, according to the Youth Development Initiative and some community leaders in Palo Alto. They list forty-one "developmental assets" that, if present, provide the roots and lifelines that are particularly important to those who are in the middle of huge life changes such as adolescence. These assets are both external and internal, but the list makes it clear that it takes a village to raise healthy, grounded children. The list emphasizes "constructive use of time," which may involve creative activities such as music, theater, or other arts; youth programs; religious community activity; and time at home and hanging out with friends "with nothing special to do."

A teacher at the high school the suicide victims attended wrote an open letter to the community in September 2009 about the importance of feeling connected: "There's a basic truth of all our lives that we all sense, even if we can't prove it on a spreadsheet. If we know someone loves us, we have a clue to loving ourselves. If somewhere someone cares about us in such a way as we can't deny, we can care, too. If someone wants to listen to our feelings, we can begin to listen to them, too."

Adults need to help young people get outside of their peer/age group. Adolescence is often defined as the time when youth separate from their parents. They push away because they want to be independent, and they believe—mistakenly—that independence requires the maximum distance between themselves and their parents. That strikes me as a dangerous oversimplification. Real maturity is a healthy balance of independence and interdependence plus enough confidence in yourself so that you are able to form relationships with many others across a range of ages and interests. But how can you form those relationships if you've been told that you're now supposed to be "independent"?

Unfortunately, independence for today's adolescents often turns out to mean that once they turn their backs on their parents, they are left alone with their peers. Since day one at school, they've been segregated by age, never encouraged or required to function beyond that artificial boundary. Schools group children by age for the convenience of the adults who run the system, but I believe that we will have stronger and more resilient children when we encourage and reward cross-age activity as much as possible. We can make cross-age tutoring, group projects, and community service with adults part of the basic curriculum.

Organizing by age may make sense, but *isolating* by age is counterproductive and unnecessary. Telling kids that they need to be "independent" flies in the face of what their hearts tell them— that they want to feel connected. We need to support connections beyond the peer group. However, the way things are now, the typical adolescent is left with his or her peer group, and we all know intuitively, experientially, and from *Lord of the Flies* just how unreliable peers and peer groups can be.

Connecting requires more than knowing children by their first names. Schools must be caring institutions, like that school in Fort Bragg. Schools must be places where kids know they will be not just physically safe but also free to take chances, to own up to not knowing all the answers, and to make mistakes. That's when kids won't mind going to school.

Memory Lane

"If any of these punks give you any trouble at all, just push that button, and we'll take care of things." That was my introduction

to teaching in prison. The tough talker was the assistant warden of the federal penitentiary outside of Petersburg, Virginia, the button in question was smack in the middle of my desk, and the "punks" were twenty men, most of them white and a few African American and Hispanic.

Frankly, my expectations were low. When I'd covered the prison beat in Leavenworth, Kansas, during my year off from college, I learned that most inmates were functionally illiterate, and, although my English class was supposed to be college freshman level, I was prepared to teach basic grammar.

Boy, was I wrong. I discovered that these young men welcomed new ideas and challenges and were eager to participate, analyze, discuss, and argue. What held us back was the lack of material, because the prison library had almost nothing of interest; just lots of Reader's Digest Condensed Books and other discards. So I asked them what they'd like to read, if they had a choice. Soul on Ice, Eldridge Cleaver's book, was the overwhelming choice, and so I bought and smuggled into prison twenty copies. We all knew that I could probably be fired for that, so they were careful not to be caught reading it.

Cleaver's story led to the idea of keeping journals, but that was also illegal, or so they believed. Rather than ask the warden's permission, I used the paper cutter back in my office to make teeny-tiny journals of about forty or fifty pages, each page measuring eight and a half by two inches.[17] I distributed them and indicated that I would be happy to read their journals if they wished. Again, these had to be kept hidden.

Coming into the prison two nights every week taught me one lesson: the guards resented the idea of prisoners going to college. After all, they were criminals and were supposed to be punished, not coddled. In holding that view, the guards—themselves undereducated—mirror American attitudes toward rehabilitation and punishment. The very name of the institution, penitentiary, suggests redemption, but the structure and procedures of those institutions are oriented toward exacting a pound of flesh.

I felt these men would be better served with more educational opportunities, which were available at a nearby community college. My students had been convicted of serious but not violent crimes, generally burglary and theft on a large scale or some other financial crime. They were in a federal institution because their crimes were interstate in nature. So I went to the warden and proposed a "study release" program for a dozen or so of the brightest and most ambitious men in my class. Eventually he grudgingly agreed to allow one student to go to college one day a week, under close supervision. The rules were impossibly strict: no smoking, no alcohol, and no socializing with females. Within a couple of weeks, the young man I had selected was busted for talking to girls, and the study release program was killed—no doubt the warden's plan all along.

I taught there for only eighteen months, but I managed to stay in touch with a couple of the men for some years afterward (and was best man at one's wedding). Those two guys turned out well, but I have no idea what happened to the rest of them.

During my career I also taught in a public high school, at a black college, in a junior high school in Greenwich, Connecticut, and at Harvard (as a teaching assistant). The most focused and determined students were those men in the penitentiary.[18] I've always wondered how those men ended up as criminals. What had gone wrong that led to the misuse of their talent and brains? Was it their environment, or were schools responsible in some way? Had their schools sorted those kids based on their social class or race and missed (or ignored) their talents?

Having schools that ask of each child "How are you intelligent?" will go a long way toward keeping kids on track to become productive citizens. We'll always need prisons, but we needn't be locking up some of our brightest people.

The medical model of schooling (which, as noted in Step Four, I want us to abandon) produces winners and losers. Unable or unwilling to change the fundamental design, many school districts are doing what they can to help the wounded by adopting a more healing approach.

Three Long Island (New York) school districts, East Hampton, Montauk, and Springs, are part of the South Fork Behavioral Health Initiative, a collaboration among the schools, the Family Service League, the closest hospital, and New York State to help improve students' mental health. While the school districts provide some money, the state and county are paying the lion's share. The effort is directly related to teen suicides and a rise in the number of families in crisis.[19]

Providence, Rhode Island, schools have created a partnership with a mental health center that will provide outside mental health counselors to five schools. The goal is to address the deep family issues that keep kids from learning. The services are provided at the schools and paid for by the parents' health insurance.

Schools in the Omaha, Nebraska, area started a similar program in 2014, and school people, who had been clamoring for mental health services for children, are enthusiastic about it. Most of the appointments are off-site at the therapist's office, but a few schools now have on-site therapists.[20]

The point here is that even schools that value every child will need mental health counselors and other services. Children often bring problems from home with them to school, and helping kids work through them is part of the job—and always will be.

Practically speaking, how can educators pay more attention to the social and emotional needs of students? They could set aside a period a day for the school equivalent of a hospital's grand rounds: everyone who teaches Rasheed, Susan, Carlos, or Sharese has the opportunity to talk about how those individual kids are doing—and not just in subject matter mastery.

Rituals help, but only as long as they are meaningful. I've been in schools where the principal led students in morning exhortations, such as "I am somebody!" All chants have the potential to become empty words after a while, so seeking creative ways to infuse meaning and engagement into exercises and routines like this one is key.[21]

If making connections truly matters, adults must provide challenges, along with coaching and other supports. Because failure is inevitable, students must feel secure enough to fall short and try again . . . and again. There's no secret sauce for success, but "Don't judge! Help instead!" is a good motto for adults to follow.[22]

Keep in mind that kids most often express and develop their talent, skills, and grit in activities outside the classroom, in what we incorrectly label "extracurricular" activities. That alone should be sufficient reason for us to restore art, music, drama, and journalism programs, and increase recess.

One great way to build a connected community is to create a team competition within the school. First, assign all students, randomly, to a club/team (Alpha, Beta, Gamma, and Delta, for example) when they enroll. Throughout the year these clubs compete, with so many points for a team when one of its members makes the honor roll, wins a varsity or JV letter, does volunteer work, tutors other students, or earns a part in the play or a position on the board of a student publication. In the spring, each club might put on a play, with the faculty and staff awarding an "Oscar" to the best one. Every semester could end with a field day with all sorts of team activities. The running score could be publicly displayed, and at year's end one club would receive the annual trophy.

In schools run that way, students of all ages and grades get to know each other through real activities, which is the easiest and most natural way. When every first-year student belongs to a club that includes one-quarter of the school's seniors, across-grade hazing by seniors of freshmen is less likely.

Design matters. Planning matters. Be intentional. If you accept the vital importance of connecting, you are ready for Step Six.

STEP SIX
Start Early

Connecting *early* by creating appealing programs for children of preschool age is Step Six in the twelve-step process of transforming the way our children go to school. Here I suggest we follow the model of President Dwight Eisenhower's Interstate Highway System. Ike did *not* build one set of highways for luxury cars and another for cheap ones but instead made sure that *every* interstate highway was wide, safe, and well-constructed, suitable for military vehicles and luxury cars like Cadillacs and Lincolns but, of course, open to Volkswagens and other less expensive cars.

The Interstate Highway System was justified and paid for as part of our national defense effort, and we might be wise to take a similar approach to early childhood education and daycare programs.[1] After all, if we believe that our children are the future and that our nation will always require a strong defense, shouldn't we invest *early* in protecting our future?

I chose the interstate highway model because the record in social programs, including early childhood programs, is clear: when government creates programs just for poor people, it nearly always results in poor programs. Government-funded programs for the disadvantaged, such as Head Start, seem to be constantly scrounging for funds; to reduce staff costs, they often hire people with minimum qualifications; and the hours spent filling in forms and meeting other requirements leaves little time for meeting the needs of children and families, let alone for staff development and "reflection." To satisfy their communities, some programs give hiring preference to locals, qualified or not, leading to the common charge that these programs exist to provide jobs for adults, rather than to support the healthy development of children.

WHEN TO START

What is the right age? Is three too young? That's up to parents. Effective preschool programs such as the Perry Preschool Project and the Chicago Child Parent Centers enroll both three- and four-year-olds. Some say that's critical to success because so many low-income children are already significantly behind by age three.[2]

Opportunities for at-risk low-income children should begin at birth, not when children are already behind at preschool age and later. Former North Carolina governor James B. Hunt Jr. pushed for Early Start when he was in office, but the Republicans who succeeded him have done all they could to erase his legacy. One of his effective programs was the Carolina Abecedarian Project for children from birth to age five.[3]

A critical issue is what happens during the day. Is its focus academic? Beware of a pushed-down curriculum, because it is probably not developmentally appropriate. Linda Johnson, a reader of my blog, wrote to say, "It is my strong belief that a child who is ready for formal education would do better in a class of forty children than an unready child would do in a class of eight. Of course I'm not advocating for large classes, but I am saying that we need to place our priorities where they will do the most good. That place is preschool. Education is critical to the health of our country, and so it's just a matter of time before we see real solutions instead of the nonsense that passes as the present 'reform.'" I hope she's right.

It's also important to figure out who is in charge. Non-educators who are not versed in child development shouldn't be deciding how three- and four-year-olds spend their days. And under no circumstances should those days involve testing.

NO TESTS FOR TODDLERS

Early childhood programs and kindergarten are for growth, exploration, acculturation, and fun. Of course, teachers should be observing children and learning about them, to help them grow, but there's no place for standardized, machine-scored tests in the early years. Unfortunately, many of the people in charge of education place value on what they know how to measure, perhaps because we have failed to articulate what matters to us—what we value. Step Eleven, "Measure What Matters," explores this in detail.

The opposite is happening, unfortunately. In 2012 the National Commission on Excellence and Equity issued a report, *For Each and Every Child*, that endorsed "rigorous" preschool, calling for early childhood education "with an academic focus, to narrow the disparities in readiness when kids reach kindergarten."[4] "Academic focus" and "narrow the disparities" are code phrases easily understood by educators: get those test scores up!

And educators apparently got the message. For example, Michigan's state superintendent wants more testing beyond the federally required tests in grades 3–8.[5] As Sarah Cwiek reported, Brian Whiston told lawmakers from two state House education panels in April 2016 that "students should be tested at least twice a year (with an optional winter test) to get a better sense of academic progress, and inform classroom instruction." And Whiston thinks "age-appropriate" testing needs to start in kindergarten instead of third grade. Frankly, that's insane!

When we institute a test-driven curriculum in early childhood programs, the inevitable result is shallow learning, tense children, and even more anxious parents. Perhaps unsophisticated parents believe that earlier is better, as Erika Christakis argues in *The Importance of Being Little*, but it's the duty of professionals to educate these parents about the importance of play. Not free-form, "do whatever you want" play, but guided play that helps children. "There's a widespread belief that children are merely releasing their energy, like an explosive device, when they play outdoors, not gaining any rewarding benefits from playground play," she writes, but she says this is wrong. Instead, it is the playground where children can learn the most about themselves and their peers.[6]

Christakis writes eloquently about shallow achievement, the superficial learning that allows kids to fill in bubbles with accurate answers. "It's astounding, really, how often well-meaning adults cite naming things—numbers and shapes, colors, and days of the week—as a central learning task for young children. But naming things and understanding them are two different phenomena."[7] Focusing on teaching children a certain amount of predetermined information is, in her wonderful phrase, "simultaneously draconian and insipid," because "what children need rather than tests is challenges."[8]

What matters most, she argues, is the mind of the child, but too many programs concentrate on facts and lists and such. Here's sound advice for parents and grandparents: Don't ask the child "What did you learn today?" or "What did you make today?" Instead say "Tell me about school" or "Tell me what happened today at school."

All of us, but especially educators, need a vocabulary lesson, starting with two adjectives, *academic* and *intellectual*. They aren't synonymous, folks.[9] Lillian Katz draws the distinctions sharply and clearly:

> Academic goals are those concerned with the mastery of small discrete elements of disembodied information, usually related to pre-literacy skills in the early years, and practiced in drills, worksheets, and other kinds of exercises designed to prepare children for the next levels of literacy and numeracy learning. . . .
>
> Intellectual goals and their related activities, on the other hand, are those that address the life of the mind in its fullest sense (e.g., reasoning, predicting, analyzing, questioning, etc.), including a range of aesthetic and moral sensibilities.

If you are looking for a quality early childhood program, listen carefully for the words *academic* and *intellectual*.[10] Run the other way if you hear them used as synonyms.

The debate about whether early education can be life-changing should have ended decades ago. Unfortunately, the opponents won't concede, either because their ideology trumps facts or because they're cheap. Let me quote from the Hamilton Project's 2016 study of the long-term effects of Head Start, the program conservatives love to beat up on:[11]

> A growing body of rigorous evidence suggests that policy interventions aimed at early childhood bear fruit for decades. . . . Across many studies of several programs, preschool attendance among disadvantaged children has been found to positively impact participants. Research has demonstrated strong long-term impacts of random assignment to high-quality preschool programs from the 1960s and 1970s, including Perry Preschool and the Abecedarian program. Head Start, the large-scale federal preschool program, has also been shown to improve post-preschool outcomes, including high school completion and health outcomes.
>
> In this Economic Analysis, we investigate the impact of Head Start on a new set of long-term outcomes. . . .
>
> Consistent with the prior literature, we find that Head Start improves educational outcomes —increasing the probability that participants graduate from high school, attend college, and receive a post-secondary degree, license, or certification.
>
> Overall and particularly among African American participants, we find that Head Start also causes social, emotional, and behavioral development that becomes evident in adulthood measures of self-control, self-esteem, and positive parenting practices.

How many more studies do we need?

Memory Lane

Although this occurred at least twenty years ago, I can still picture a young Hispanic boy, probably four years old, struggling to open a milk carton, the kind where you peel open one corner and push the ends back. I'm sure he knew what an opened carton should look like, but he couldn't seem to figure out the steps. Rather than give up, and determined not to ask for help, he turned it every which way, testing out possibilities. I asked my cameraman to film his struggle, and the ensuing footage—which never aired—was very revealing. It must have taken him seven or eight minutes to figure it out, which he did by trial and error and by looking at open milk cartons on other desks. At one point, an adult offered to help, but he made it clear that this was his struggle. Luckily, it was lunchtime, not a scheduled period like "story time" or "coloring time." He persevered. . . .

Quality programs allow and encourage this sort of learning. Of all the dangerous misconceptions about young children, the one about their supposedly short attentions spans is the most harmful. Engaged children will remain focused for hours on end; disengaged children will flit from activity to activity, often disrupting those around them. Many activities designed for young children are based on this incorrect assumption, and so kids in early childhood education and care programs are made to move from one spot to another, from one activity to another, every twenty minutes or so.

START YOUNG AND STAY YOUNG

In American education today, kindergarten is becoming too much like high school, when the reverse should be happening. High school should be friendlier and less regimented and segmented. Pushing down the first-grade curriculum into kindergarten (and lower) is disastrous for kids, teachers, parents, and society.

"If I had my way, I'd get rid of twelfth grade and spend the money on preschool." The first time I heard this big idea was in a conversation with Zell Miller, the gruff former senator from Georgia, in the fall of 2002. His quote didn't make our documentary, *The Promise of Preschool*, but he basically said he'd swap twelfth grade for free, universal, high-quality preschool.

At the time, Georgia was leading the nation in providing preschool, and it's still near the top of the list. But Georgia and every other state and territory still have twelfth grade. Should they?

Sean Reardon's thoughtful essay in the *New York Times*, "No Rich Child Left Behind," makes a strong case for large investments in early education, which, he says, are the most likely avenue to closing the ever-wider performance gaps between the rich and everyone else.[12] The Stanford professor does not argue that senior year of high school is a waste of time for most kids, so please allow me. States with exit exams generally peg them to a tenth-grade level, which tells you something about official expectations. Across the nation, savvy (and bored) kids are enrolling in college courses while still in high school, if their system allows. In 2012 we profiled one Texas school district on the Mexican border where dozens of students, many of them former high school dropouts who returned to school, finish high school with a substantial number of college credits under their belt.[13] Some actually receive their associate's degrees from the local community college the same day they pick up their high school diplomas!

I conclude from that story, and from the tales of students in other school districts, that a business-as-usual senior year is a waste of time. Thousands of motivated kids refuse to accept that state of affairs, so they enroll in college, and that's commendable. But why not raise the bar in high school and shorten the time? If some students need a twelfth year, fine. But why bore hundreds of thousands of our youth? Why not transform twelfth grade into a systemic variant on early college? High schools could collaborate with neighboring postsecondary educational or career institutions to engage students in dual educational experiences, both on and off the high school campus.[14] This would prepare them for specific educational destinations of their choice after high school, whether it's community college, a four-year college or university, the military, or an apprenticeship in craft trades. Better yet, it would enable the students to glide into post-secondary education.[15] That seamless transition would help eliminate what is currently a waste for many students—an unproductive first year of post-secondary education.

Performance-based graduation requirements—as opposed to seat time—could engage students and allow them to graduate when they demonstrate competency. Maine has abandoned credits based on seat time for core competencies for all students by 2017, and New Hampshire has done away with the 180-day compulsory attendance rule and moved toward competency-based credits.

So, what about former senator Zell Miller's idea to basically swap out twelfth grade for preschool? Is that possible? How much money do we spend on the twelfth grade, and how much of that could actually be diverted to preschool?

When I put the first question to Reardon, he responded, "The country spends in the ballpark of $40 billion to $50 billion per year per grade on public education. There are about four million students per grade in public schools, and average per student spending is approaching $13,000 per pupil." He noted that twelfth graders are more expensive to educate than students in elementary school, but because of dropouts, we have fewer seniors than first and second graders. Let's assume that the higher expenses and fewer students cancel each other out, so we can use his $40–$50 billion number as our spending on twelfth grade.

How much of that could just be shifted over to preschool is harder to figure, because some dollars (such as the money spent on sports) can't be taken from the high school budget. Remember, the team will continue playing, but with a lineup of ninth, tenth, and eleventh graders. The coaches still get paid, the school still needs buses to take the team to away games, and so forth. But, for a back-of-the-envelope figure, let's say that $30 billion would be available for preschool. If we spent it on our 4.64 million four-year-olds, we could spend about $6,400 per child.

Compared to what we're spending now, $6,400 is a lot to spend per child. According to the National Institute for Early Education Research (NIEER),[16] we now spend $4,489 per child enrolled in early education. Things have improved in recent years, according to the latest (2015) NIEER report.

> State-funded pre-K served almost 1.4 million children in 2014–2015, an increase of 37,167 children from the previous year. State spending topped $6.2 billion, an increase of over $553 million, although two-thirds of this increase can be attributed to New York. Spending per child saw the largest increase in a decade, reaching $4,489 per child [an increase of $287, adjusted for inflation]. Six programs in five states met new quality standards benchmarks and two new states, West Virginia and Mississippi, joined the group of states meeting all 10 quality standards benchmarks. However, progress has been unequal and uneven, with some states taking large steps forward and other states moving backward.

Only 29 percent of four-year-olds and just 5 percent of three-year-olds are in state-funded preschool programs, NIEER says.[17] And twenty states now serve less than 10 percent of their four-year-olds.[18] By our not providing preschool, Reardon and others believe, we are hurting our country's long-term chances for prosperity, not to mention shortchanging a lot of our children.[19] As NIEER notes, "At the recent rate of progress it will take decades to serve even 50% of 4-year-olds in state pre-K. Government at every level will need to redouble their efforts and move forward."

By way of contrast, thirteen countries enroll at least 90 percent of their three- and four-year-olds, and the OECD average is 81 percent.[20] Our enrollment, including children in private programs, is just over 50 percent. (The have/have-not split manifests itself early.)

States that have been cutting preschool spending don't have to—if they are willing to think outside the box.[21] They could take a great leap forward, provide free, high-quality, universal preschool for all of our four-year-olds, and rescue our twelfth graders from boredom at the same time.

What's not to like about that?

KINDERGARTEN

Even if your state doesn't provide free quality programs for three- and four-year-olds but does have all-day kindergarten, you can count yourself fortunate, because kindergarten itself is not seen as essential in a number of states.

So if you have the option, which of the following two kinder- garten classes would you want your five-year-old child or grand- child to be in? Option one is a classic kindergarten classroom, rich with tactile art and full of color, energy, and happy noise. Some kids are finger-painting with intense concentration, while others are bubbling over with curiosity and cheer. No mod- ern technology—just chalk and blackboards—is evident at first glance.

The other kindergarten classroom, your second option, is a car- bon copy, with one striking difference: some children are using a mechanical toy to help them learn consonant blends. These kids have small devices (about the size of an adult's hand) that look like a bug, and a three-foot-square chart with consonant blends in different squares (*ist*, *int*, *alt*, and so on). Rather than simply find a certain blend on the chart, the child has to program the bug (actually a small computer) to move to the square with that blend—say, three spaces across and five spaces up. The teacher moves around the room guiding and monitoring the individual learners.

(By the way, the teacher in the second classroom told me that her kids also Skyped with a kindergarten class in Mexico, part of their study of Cinco de Mayo. The thirty-seven-year-veteran had just embraced digital technology in her teaching.)

I'm guessing that, in the digital-free kindergarten, the children will learn consonant blends as a group from the teacher, perhaps in a mix of a game and direct instruction. Is one approach to teach- ing consonant blends superior to the other? I have no clue, but being in the two classrooms raised a question in my mind: what's the right age to introduce digital technology to schoolchildren?

Some would argue that, because most children become familiar with digital technology as toddlers—after all, who hasn't seen very young children manipulating an iPad or tablet?—the schools ought to stay current. Others take the opposite view: "Enough, already! Let's make classrooms tech-free zones where young children can concentrate on human interaction and social skills."

So which kindergarten would you choose? Unfortunately, this is a purely hypothetical question for many, because, depending on where you live, you may not have any choice at all. Believe it or not, six states—Alaska, Idaho, Michigan, New Jersey, New York, and Pennsylvania—do not require school districts to provide any kindergarten at all, according to a report from the New America Education Policy Program. In fact, only eleven states and the District of Columbia actually require schools to provide free full-day kindergarten, even though public education is a state responsibility.[22]

Do the math: in thirty-nine of our fifty states, politicians and other decision-makers have chosen to ignore the fundamental needs of the young. Whether these adults are ignorant, cheap, selfish, or inflexibly ideological is not clear, but what is obvious is that, by failing to provide kindergarten, these decision-makers have decided to keep the playing field tilted in favor of the economically comfortable. It stands to reason that failing to close the opportunity gap is a good way to ensure that the so-called achievement gap will remain wide. Most states require that school districts provide a free half-day kindergarten program, and then allow districts to go full-day if they wish.

A kindergarten in Elwood, New York, canceled its annual play so the five-year-olds could spend more time becoming "college and career ready."[23] That outrageous decision by an interim principal, and the ensuing furor, should not be allowed to obscure another harsh truth about that system: *parents in Elwood have to pay out of their own pockets for the second half of the day.* Sixty of the eighty families have coughed it up, the article says, and one wonders what the other twenty kids are feeling. In fact, at least twelve states make parents pay for the second half of the day (that uneven playing field again).

According to the New America Foundation, somewhere between 23 percent and 42 percent of our kindergarten-age children are not in full-day kindergarten; worse yet, apparently some of those "full-day" programs last only four hours, significantly short of actually being full-day. And budget crises in recent years have led some states and districts to reduce full-day programs to half days. It's not all bad. The study points out that "in recent years some states—including Minnesota, Oklahoma, Washington, and Nevada—have begun to expand the provision of full-day kindergarten."

Perhaps it will take a public shaming of the state political and educational leadership that doesn't care enough to provide free kindergarten programs. These policies are shortsighted and harmful. Kindergarten, done well, is enormously beneficial to young children. It also allows more parents to enter the workforce, which poor families are finding difficult to do because resources for early childhood education and daycare are scarce.

If our Pledge of Allegiance, which all schoolchildren recite every morning, were accurate, it would go something like "One nation, under God, with educational opportunity for some . . . And how would teachers explain that?

I'm guessing that some readers may be thinking, "Okay, incremental reform isn't working. We agree we'll look at each child's strengths and interests, we promise to connect, and we'll begin early. But enough touchy-feely! We want to know what are kids going to do in these wonderful schools you're hell-bent on creating. We want specifics!"

Fair enough. You are ready for Step Seven.

Memory Lane

Over my forty-one-year career I interviewed every sitting U.S. secretary of education, starting with Shirley M. Hufstedler, who gave up a federal judgeship to become our first secretary of education when President Jimmy Carter persuaded Congress to create the department (keeping a campaign promise to the National Education Association).

Of these men and women, by far the most capable and effective was Bill Clinton's secretary of education, former South Carolina governor Richard Riley, a soft-spoken gentleman whose mild manner hid his tough determination. Terrell "Ted" Bell, Ronald Reagan's first secretary, also accomplished a great deal, creating a chart to highlight differences among states in their performance on the National Assessment of Educational Progress. Bell also presided over the launch of the famous A Nation at Risk report, the document that created the first wave of school reform back in 1983.

Bell was succeeded by a lackluster academic, Lauro Cavazos, who was retained as secretary of education by President George H.W. Bush, perhaps because Bush intended to run education from the White House. However, after two years, Cavazos was replaced by Lamar Alexander, a former governor of Tennessee and a genuine education policy wonk who is now a United States senator.

George W. Bush brought a fellow Texan, former Houston superintendent Rod Paige, with him to Washington to serve as his education secretary. Paige, the first and (so far) only traditional public school educator to hold the job, had the unenviable task of enforcing No Child Left Behind, the law that involved the federal government in every aspect of schooling. Paige was followed by Margaret Spellings, an outspoken Republican who seemed more interested in the combat for control of education than in actual ideas, theories, or practices.

Of the nine secretaries I interviewed, the most personable and fun to be around was President Obama's basketball buddy, Arne Duncan, the former CEO of Chicago Public Schools, who might have accomplished great things had he not fallen under the sway of the school reform crowd.[24]

The most transparently ambitious was William J. Bennett, who succeeded Cavazos in President Reagan's second term. The process of making television often reveals a lot about people, and what stands out in my memory are the interviews with Bennett. When the lights were on and the camera was rolling, he was smilingly congenial. Shut the equipment off, however, and a new side—probably the real side—emerged: snarly, unpleasant, and rude to underlings who worked for him or for my production company.

Most presidents did their best to control education from the White House. One exception was Bill Clinton, who trusted Riley, his mentor and, like him, a former governor. Ronald Reagan also left his secretaries, Ted Bell and Bill Bennett, alone, but for a different reason; he was generally uninterested in domestic policy.

For eight years Barack Obama kept a tight grip on education, indicating that he and his White House domestic policy advisors were in fundamental agreement with the policies championed by the school reform crowd, Secretary Duncan, and the Gates, Broad, and Walton foundations.

STEP SEVEN

Expect More

Because children become what they repeatedly do, it's essential that they do different things in school. However, it's equally important that *we* do the right thing, which above all means expecting more from them.

In this chapter I am building on a foundation provided by Aristotle and philosopher Will Durant: "Excellence is an art won by training and habituation: we do not act rightly because we have virtue or excellence, but we rather have these because we have acted rightly; 'these virtues are formed in man by his doing his actions'; we are what we repeatedly do. Excellence, then, is not an act but a habit."[1]

Kicking the habit of school reform demands that we look carefully at the routines of school, because children become what they repeatedly do, just as most live up (or down) to expectations.

If schools demand that students fill in bubbles, color inside the lines, fall into line when ordered to do so, and never ask why or question authority, those children are unlikely to become independent thinkers and doers. Going forward, we must expect and encourage students to dig deeply into subjects and ideas they are curious about. Teachers must then use their students' curiosity—about *The Odyssey*, skydiving, auto mechanics, the French Revolution, or the music of Prince—to ensure that they also master clear writing and thinking, mathematical concepts, and other essentials.

(Habitual behavior at home also matters. Children whose parents allowed them to spend their free time on screens playing video games and texting with friends, who aren't required to pick up their dirty laundry, keep their rooms clean, or help around the house, and who aren't expected to participate in conversations at the dinner table are likely to grow up to be one sort of adult. On the other hand, children whose parents expect them to join them on trips to museums, the library, and the grocery store, who participate in family activities, and who are encouraged to think about the needs of others develop very different habits as adults.)

FAILURE IS ESSENTIAL

It's generally understood that the longer the learning curve, the longer the forgetting curve. That means that students who work something out through trial and error are more likely to retain information than those who are spoon-fed the material. The key word in "trial and error" is the last one, because making mistakes is an essential part of learning. That's right—students must be involved in activities where failure is anticipated as part of the learning process, because failure matters. Independent thinkers, no matter their age, fail . . . and learn from failure. That's not only *not* a bad thing; it's a good thing. In fact, failure is an essential part of the schools we are going to build.

Case in point: if you're at all like me, somewhere in your home you have at least one can of WD-40, because the stuff works wonders. If you teach science, I believe that you ought to have a large WD-40 poster on your classroom wall, not to advertise the product but to teach a basic lesson about learning: *failure is an essential part of succeeding.*

Have you ever wondered why it is called WD-40? The answer is, in a word, failure! In 1953 the three employees of the San Diego–based Rocket Chemical Company were trying to develop a product that would prevent rust, something they could market to the aerospace industry. They tried, failed, and tried again . . . and again . . . and again. Being methodical, they kept careful records. They labeled their first effort Water Displacement #1, or WD-1. After thirty-nine failures, eureka! They had a product, and the product had a name.

Students need to know that adults try and fail and fail and fail—and keep on trying. More than that, they need to *experience* failure.[2] While I am a big fan of both project-based learning and blended learning, I believe the most critical piece of the pedagogical puzzle is what we ought to call *problem-based* learning.

In my experience, many teachers are prone to assign tried-and-true projects where they already know the outcome. Because students, especially older and more capable ones, see through that and don't commit to the work, that approach to project-based learning is suspect. Even blended learning, combining technology and teaching, is a questionable approach if educators embrace technology with the aim of getting students to achieve the adult goals faster or more efficiently. Blending technology and teaching so students can add fractions faster? Bad idea.

Teachers should give students real problems to tackle. Lord knows we have plenty of problems worth tackling that can be given to students. They cannot be intractable ("How can we achieve peace in the Middle East?") or trivial and uninteresting ("What color should classrooms be painted?"). Instead, the problems should be both genuine and manageable. "How does our air quality compare with the air quality at other places in our city, town, or state?" is one example that I will develop in some detail in Step Eight, on technology.

Here's an example of problem-based learning from a good friend of mine, now retired from teaching, about his work with high school juniors and seniors.

> In my social psychology class, I "gave" my students an amount that was $1,000 above the current poverty level and told them that was all they had to live on! First, they had to find an apartment to rent; it became "theirs" when they made an appointment to view it— and then it was no longer available to the rest of the class. They also had to create a budget, shop for food, and design a week of breakfasts, lunches, and dinners

for a family of four. This relatively affluent group of students learned a ton about life in a world they did not know existed. Years later, I learned that this was the experience most students remembered.[3]

Unfortunately, a pedagogy based on discovery and knowledge creation flies in the face of what seems to be happening in most classrooms and schools, where the emphasis seems to be on critical analysis to arrive at the predetermined right answers. Some years back a math teacher in Richmond, Virginia, told me how he used to take his students down to the James River and challenge them to determine how far it was to the opposite shore. He didn't give them a formula; just the challenge. They put their heads together and, he said, eventually discovered the formula, which they then could apply to other situations and problems. They failed and kept on trying, until, like the creators of WD-40, they were successful. Sadly, he said, the new state-mandated curriculum no longer allowed time for field trips and discovery. Now he has to explain the formula and give his students a prescribed number of problems to solve.

The schools we're creating will build on student strengths and interests. While kids will have more control over their learning, that does not mean the adults just say "Whatever" or tell kids to "follow their passion." Most young people aren't likely to have developed a passion yet, and they shouldn't be made to feel deficient. Ask them what they're curious about, and encourage them to explore, experiment, and follow their interests.[4] It's a journey and a process to be celebrated.

PATHWAYS TO FOLLOW

There may be no shortcuts to creating schools that ask "How is each child intelligent?" But there are pathways with good track records that a community can follow. Here are six.

1. Elementary schools could adopt James Comer's approach, meaning that all adults, including parents, receive training in child development and work together to provide a nurturing and supportive environment in school and at home. At the program's height, about 1,150 Comer schools were operating around the nation, giving poor children the supports they need to be successful. Comer, an M.D. and a professor of child psychiatry at Yale, and his schools have been saving children since 1968.

2. Close cousins to the Comer approach are the roughly six thousand schools belonging to the Coalition of Community Schools.[5] This organization has no one model but rather a set of unifying principles. The group uses this analogy to describe itself:

> Most people think of schools today as serving a single purpose: a binary, analog-system of delivery; teachers teach and students learn. Community schools are more akin to smartphones. Schools and communities connect, collaborate, and create. Children and families have an array of supports from community partners right at their school. Communities and schools leverage their shared physical and human assets to help kids succeed.

Noting that 51 percent of students now qualify for free or reduced-price lunch, NEA president Lily Eskelsen Garcia called community schools the "North Star" in an interview with *Chalkbeat* in November 2016:

> You always thought of inner-city schools as the place you have poor children. Now every community has a hefty group of kids whose moms and dads are working two or three jobs just to make the rent and put food on the table.
>
> Community schools would make that school the hub of the neighborhood. The reason they work is because they take care of the whole family, not just the child. There is usually some sort of health service.

I've seen a dentist chair just off the [school] library. They all have a parent resource center. The other thing they always do is beef up the academic program. It's not enough just to stick the dentist chair in the office. More and more, community schools are looking at the International Baccalaureate program. The teachers love it. There's energy there. The parents love it. No one can sell these kids vouchers or a charter school. They're going, "This is where I live. I walk to this school. It's got everything, from the best academic programs to the things that really serve my family like English classes for the moms and dads, counselors, and everyone feels welcome." Those schools become a safe place for everyone who feels marginalized.[6]

3. Elementary schools could adopt Core Knowledge. The Core Knowledge curriculum prescribes roughly half of what every child should study, leaving the rest to the local and state authorities. E.D. Hirsch Jr. recognized back in the 1980s that for all children to have a fair chance at succeeding in life, all must have a common vocabulary of knowledge. All kids must be exposed to the rich curriculum that middle- and upper-class children acquire at home.[7]

Hirsch was a widely unknown English professor at the University of Virginia when he published *Cultural Literacy* in 1987. The book's subtitle—*What Every American Needs to Know*—outraged liberal intellectuals, many of whom, I suspect, may not have bothered to read the book before condemning Hirsch as an elitist. He is anything but. He's a proud small-*d* democrat who believes that knowing lots and lots of things actually levels the playing field for rich and poor.

Hirsch did not stop with *Cultural Literacy*. He created the Core Knowledge Foundation and began issuing curriculum guides, grade by grade: *What Every First Grader Needs to Know*, and so on up the ladder. Before long there were Core Knowledge schools, and the ones I have seen (in several states) were vibrant places where everyone was engaged in learning and discovering. On one visit, I selected kids at random and asked them to read aloud from books I knew they had never seen, books that were either grade-appropriate or one step above. All read flawlessly, probably because students in Core Knowledge schools do a lot of reading. They don't practice taking reading tests because, as Hirsch wisely observed, "if you want children to do well on reading tests, they ought to read a lot."

About eight hundred U.S. schools use the Core Knowledge approach. While that's not even 1 percent of our schools, the number is growing. Perhaps someday Core Knowledge schools will be as ubiquitous as Starbucks.

4. Schools could have a "maker space," and the maker space mentality—students and teachers working together or separately to explore, invent, and create—would underpin the pedagogy. A maker space, sometimes known as a fab lab, can take many shapes; some have the latest and best high-tech equipment (such as 3-D printers), while others aren't so fortunate. What these dynamic new spaces share is a belief in the importance of exploration. Writer Maegan Slowakie-wicz describes it this way: "Maker spaces allow students to take control of their own learning as they take ownership of projects they have not just designed but defined. At the same time, students often appreciate the hands-on use of emerging technologies and a comfortable acquaintance with the kind of experimentation that leads to a completed project. Where maker spaces exist on campus, they provide a physical labora-tory for inquiry-based learning."[8]

5. Schools could embrace project-based learning, as prac-ticed at High Tech High in San Diego and in Expedition-ary Learning schools, a network of over 150 schools.[9] Both approaches provide excellent answers to the question "What should students in our transformed schools be doing?"

Paul Tough, the author of *How Children Succeed*, is a fan of Expeditionary Learning.[10] "The central premise of EL schools is that character is built not through lectures or direct instruction from teachers but through the experience of per-severing as students confront challenging academic work," he wrote in an article in *The Atlantic*. There he also described the schools' inner workings:

> Classrooms at EL schools are by design much more engaging and interactive than classrooms in most other American public schools. They are full of student discussions and group activities large and small; teachers guide the conversation, but they spend considerably less time lecturing than most other public-school teachers do.
>
> EL students complete a lot of rigorous and demanding long-term projects, often going through extensive and repeated revisions based on critiques from teachers and peers. They frequently work on these projects in collaborative groups, and many projects conclude with students giving a presentation in front of the class, the school, or even a community group. In addition, students are responsible, whenever possible, for assessing themselves; two or three times a year, at report-card time, parents or other family members come to the school for meetings known as student-led conferences, in which students as young as five narrate for their parents and teachers their achievements and struggles over the past semester.

However, the best way to fully grasp what Expeditionary Learning entails is to go on an expedition, which is what my former colleague at *PBS NewsHour*, John Tulenko, did. John followed a group of eighth graders in Portland, Maine, over four months as they worked to invent a labor-saving device for the home.[11] It remains one of my favorite *NewsHour* pieces, and I urge you to watch it. It may be the best eight minutes and fifty-one seconds you'll ever spend!

6. High school students could be invited and encouraged to earn college credits, as with early-college high schools; this is a long-overdue change.[12] Everyone who has been paying attention knows that American high schools aren't working; most kids put in the required seat time so they can be with their friends, participate in extracurricular activities, and get that piece of paper. By contrast, when high school students are encouraged to begin their college (or technical) education early, good things happen. We reported on one such program in Texas for *PBS NewsHour*, but this is not unique to south Texas. About 10 percent of high school students are taking college courses in Minnesota, New York, and elsewhere.[13] I would open up early college programs to anyone who's motivated, because it's a win-win all around.

In this approach, senior year will eventually disappear, and education will become seamless. As suggested in Step Six, the savings can be used for quality early childhood care and education programs.

REAL PROJECTS AND BLENDED LEARNING

As I have underscored throughout this book, I am convinced that the very best schools already ask the right question: "How is each child intelligent?" And they follow through and allow students more control over their learning. In these schools, *students* are the workers, and the work they are doing is meaningful. What they actually do—their product—depends upon their ages and stages, but the concept doesn't change. In these schools, teachers are conductors, directors, supervisors, guides or docents. This observation flies in the face of conventional wisdom, which holds that *teachers* are workers whose job is to produce capable *students*. That gets further bastardized when capability is defined by test scores, until we end up thinking that the work of teachers is to add value, which is measured by higher test scores.

Here are two examples of outstanding education that I know firsthand: a twelfth-grade science class in a public high school in Philadelphia, and a journalism class at Palo Alto High School in California.

The Philadelphia twelfth graders were serious workers. Their assignment was to design age-appropriate toys for babies and infants that would amuse them and stimulate their brain development. Stage two of the task: come up with an advertising campaign to sell the toy they designed. That's a serious project with a real product. Science teacher Tim Best designed it in broad strokes, with some clear goals, including learning a great deal about brain development. By twelfth grade at this school, students are accustomed to working together on projects and holding each other accountable, although Best also monitored their progress. Tim Best and other teachers at Science Leadership Academy told me that projects were designed to teach both content and process.

Tim explained, "I learned by memorizing science words, but I don't ask my students to memorize science words. I'd rather them experience the science and learn science by doing science, and, therefore, they're learning science process in addition to science content. And science process, you could argue, is almost more important for the general person who is not going to be a scientist." He added, "Reading chapter two and answering the questions at the end of the chapter is not teaching either science or process."

I think the journalism students at Palo Alto High School must be among the luckiest kids in the world. Their teacher, Esther Wojcicki, and her talented colleagues give them the opportunity to produce meaningful journalism in a number of formats: a newspaper, radio programs, a daily television program, and five magazines.[14] This is real-world work: the print publications are advertiser-supported, and none can come out until the students have the signed advertising contracts in hand. "This is not selling Girl Scout cookies," she told me. "This is how the real world works."

With opportunity comes responsibility. At Palo Alto High, the journalism students hold each other accountable, the faculty is paying attention, and—most powerful of all—their work is public. Among Esther's former students is actor-painter-writer James Franco. Recalling her class, he wrote, "The important pedagogical aspect of working on the paper, that I understood subconsciously then, and that I understand explicitly as a teacher now, is that my work was being seen by a public, and that that changed the work. I wasn't writing for a school grade as much as I was writing for independent readers."

What's essential in all project-based learning is the absence of a "right" answer or "right" product.[15] Project-based learning truly is a journey, one which may also teach the instructor a good deal. Projects that have a predetermined "right answer" are merely recipes, not a journey of discovery. In faux projects, the work quickly loses meaning, and most students do not retain what they were supposed to learn. They may absorb material and regurgitate it successfully on tests, but that's not genuine learning. Good journalism is by definition an inquiry, because journalists are supposed to ask questions they don't know the answers to.

Those students in Philadelphia and Palo Alto are engaged in what's called blended learning, a mix of technology and human teaching. The machines and the teachers are interdependent, truly blended. Think of a chocolate milkshake, as opposed to putting oil and water in the same container.

The popular phrase "learning by doing," is an incomplete thought, a phrase lacking an essential object. *What* the student does is critical. In the schools I described, kids don't get free rein to do whatever they feel like doing. Adults design (or help design) the projects, and they monitor progress. Teachers help students formulate questions and give guidance when they go off track or get discouraged.

"Time on task" is another incomplete phrase. What's the task? Is it meaningful or trivial? Are students memorizing the periodic table and the major rivers of the United States, or are they measuring air or water quality in their neighborhoods and sharing the data with students in other places in order to make sense of it? Many educators make the mistake of focusing on the amount of time students are spending on the assignment (believing that more is better, of course) but fail to think critically about the tasks they are assigning.

The adults in charge of the classrooms I admire were not obsessed with control. Sadly, too many schools focus on regurgitation of information, a process that is encouraged and rewarded by the focus on standardized test scores.

GET OFF THE BANDWAGON!

If students become what they regularly do, should curriculum and instruction be coherent, so that all students are held to the same standards? If so, who sets the rules? The top-down effort by the Obama administration and major foundations to incentivize states to adopt the Common Core was initially successful, but when the Common Core became a political third rail, many of the forty-three states that had adopted it walked away, while others raised standards but eschewed the tainted name.[16] Gone was the school reformers' dream of a coherent system that would allow for clear comparisons across districts, states, and regions.[17]

CHANGE WILL SCARE SOME PEOPLE

There's an important caveat here: schools that give students more control over their learning, stress project-based learning, and expect students to create knowledge instead of spitting back what their teachers have taught will be unrecognizable to the older generation. Can parents and other adults be persuaded to embrace schools that look different from and behave differently than the ones they themselves went to?

Because we all are convinced that we know what school is supposed to be like, the importance of reaching out to outsiders (Step Nine) cannot be overstated. It's also critically important that adults embrace the potential of today's technology. As Step Eight will remind you, today's smartphones have more computing power than the roomful of machines that allowed us to send men to the moon in 1969.

Paradoxically, those who may fight change often bitch and moan about *today's* public schools.

"The college graduates we hire can't even write a clear paragraph."
"Kids today don't read."

"The freshmen coming onto campus today don't know how to ex-press themselves. They're inarticulate."

I heard complaints like that all the time. A few of the speakers blamed technology, but eventually most pointed fingers at teachers and the schools.

I used to just listen—but no more. From now on my response is going to be, "Stop your whining. You need to find out what's really going on. Then, if you really care, do something about it." I will tell them this: if they want to hire literate and thoughtful college graduates, they should get involved in public education. Go to their public schools, starting in elementary school, and find out how much (or how little) writing, reading, and speaking kids are doing—and why.

Anyone wanting to be good at something needs two things: instruction and practice. The only way for kids to learn to write well is by writing, rewriting, and rewriting again. Children become better readers only if they read. They can learn to speak well by speaking often, with some direction, some coaching. It's no different from how children learn to play a musical instrument well or make jump shots consistently: practice, practice, practice. I will suggest the critics ask teachers about reading. How often do students get to read for pleasure? (They should, you know.) And ask them about public speaking. Are children encouraged to speak in public to their classes? Are they taught how to address a group, to make eye contact, and so forth? (They should be, you know.)

When those whiners dig a bit into what goes on in most schools today, they will discover that teachers don't have time to develop speaking skills in their students, don't have time to let kids read for pleasure, and don't have time for rewriting papers. Public education has been quantified, but the only numbers that seem to count are test scores. Therefore, teachers are expected to teach their students how to take and pass tests. (And they know they might lose their jobs if their kids don't fill in the bubbles well enough.)

There's no time, teachers and principals will tell you, for

writing and rewriting, for reading, or for public speaking. A case in point is the school I reported on in the South Bronx, one of New York City's poorest neighborhoods. There the first graders were reading competently and confidently, but the fourth graders couldn't pass the state reading tests. The joy had been squeezed and scared out of them by the incessant test pressure and test prep.[18]

So yes, we are what we repeatedly do, and children become what they repeatedly do. Take that to heart and insist on lots of writing, reading, projects, play, community service, and argumentation in our schools, because "excellence, then, is not an act but a habit."

And so, Mr. and Ms. Citizen, stop complaining. Stop attacking public education and criticizing teachers. If citizens want young people who can write fluently and speak clearly and who are inclined to read for pleasure and elucidation, they must look to the people who tell teachers what to do. Want change? Look to the school board, look to politicians, look to your neighbors. And perhaps in the mirror.

Now let's take the next step, bringing in technology, which in the hands of skilled and flexible teachers has the power to make individualized learning the norm, not the exception.

STEP EIGHT
Embrace Technology (Carefully)

Spoiler alert: this chapter has a clear bottom-line message. It is that technology, no matter how powerful, will *never* completely replace teachers. Wisely used, however, it will make good teachers more effective.

Before the age of the Internet, the schools we need to create for all children could not have existed. No chance! While, in theory, teachers could have asked the essential question about every child—"How is this particular child intelligent?"—the second step, which involves personalized learning pathways for each and every child, was unimaginable. However, that second step is now possible, because the Internet and modern technology enable students to dig deeper and soar higher than ever before. But technology must be embraced with care, and adults will have to learn to give up a large measure of control over children's learning. Neither is guaranteed, and neither one is a slam dunk.

The cliché about idle hands doing the devil's work has been rewritten for an age of smartphones and computers, and now it reads "Idle thumbs do the devil's work." Cute, but wrong, because it is *idle minds* that do the work of the devil. Because technology is ubiquitous among the young, their minds must be engaged productively; if not, lots of bad things are likely to occur.

For too long schools have either resisted technology or, more likely, employed it to process data and increase control. Step Eight calls for what amounts to nearly a 180-degree turn, so that technology, with the guidance of skilled teachers, enables students to have significant control over their learning.

Let's begin with the basics. Both the common #2 pencil and the most tricked-out smartphone are technological tools. Both have commonsense age restrictions. No three- or four-year-old should be handling a sharpened #2 pencil; the appropriate age for a smartphone is arguable, but it exists. Both tools are value-free, meaning that how they are used depends on the user. The individual wielding a pencil can write a love sonnet, a grocery list, or a threatening anonymous letter. The user of a smartphone (which has more computing power than the computers that sent the first man to the moon in 1969) can do all these things, and far more. However, the essential fact remains: *how technology is used depends on the values of the user.*

TERRIBLE TECH: BUY NOW, PLAN LATER

Step Eight will not be a walk in the park, because this step means clashing with education's money train, and that guarantees trouble. Technology, both hardware and software, is big business, and Step Eight will divert money from those vested interests. Right now school districts are spending an estimated $10 billion a year on iPads, Chromebooks, and other hardware. On top of that, they're writing checks for an additional $8 billion for the educational software that is preloaded into the machines.

Because most educators have failed to recognize how technology has transformed learning, I believe that much of that money is being wasted. Unfortunately for students (and creative teachers), many districts are buying prepackaged, computer-based curricula that lead students to predetermined answers. Designed to *control* learning and often advertised as being "Common Core ready," they are catnip to beleaguered school boards under pressure to raise test scores.

Education's decision-makers also have to be wary of supposedly free stuff. The big boys—Google and Amazon—are making offers that schools and teachers will find it difficult to refuse: free tools for writing, editing, and more from Google, and free curriculum materials from Amazon.[1] But nothing is free, so schools must realize that using these materials gives the provider all sorts of information about its users. Google knows me inside and out, and I guess that's okay because I'm on the exit ramp. Should Google, Amazon, Facebook, et alia know everything about your third grader? I'm not so sure about that.

Values come first, technology second, and that's where citizens must hold the feet of educators to the fire. Children swimming in a sea of information need to learn how to sift through the flood so they can distinguish truths from half-truths and fiction. Learning how to formulate tough questions and search for answers should be central to their curriculum, not absorbing and regurgitating facts.

Unfortunately, unsophisticated school districts have tended to buy first and plan later. The poster child for this approach is the Los Angeles public schools, which signed a $1.3 billion contract with Apple and Pearson in 2012, seemingly guaranteeing that 650,000 students would get iPads. However, when the rollout began at forty-seven schools that fall, problems arose immediately.

> Internet connectivity was spotty at some schools, partly because the district's facilities chief was not included in the planning process for upgrading school networks to carry the heavy data demands of so many devices connecting to the Internet. Teachers were ill-trained on how to use the iPads and curriculum, and faculty never widely embraced the tablet, according to the Department of Education report. And many students learned how to bypass the security features and just used the iPads to surf the Internet.[2]

Before it canceled the contract, the Los Angeles school district had spent more than $100 million on 120,000 iPads and 18,000 laptops, teacher training, and technical labor. (In late 2015 the district received a refund of $4.2 million from Apple and $2.2 million in credit from the computer company Lenovo.) The debacle cost Superintendent John Deasy his job and led to an ongoing FBI investigation into whether Deasy and others colluded to make it virtually impossible for vendors other than Apple and Pearson to qualify for the contract. Deasy has denied the allegations.

Los Angeles is not alone, not by a long shot. Unfortunately for students and taxpayers, "buy first, plan later" is a common modus operandi. For example, twenty-six school districts in Texas bought 81,000 iPads and 10,000 other tablets for students in just one year. The *Texas Observer*'s Patrick Michels singled out the Fort Bend Independent School District, which has 70,000 students, and its iAchieve Program.

> [iAchieve] combined a huge investment in new equipment and wireless network upgrades with an all-new set of science lessons and 100 simulated experiments built to run on an all-new app. It was all supposed to take about 18 months. Instead, district administrators canceled the program . . . after months of problems at every turn. The new wireless coverage was spotty; new lessons didn't match district standards; interactive tools never got built; and the superintendent took a contract buyout to leave the district years early.[3]

Disasters abound. Guilford County, North Carolina, first shut down and later canceled its 1-to-1 program when 1,500 of the 15,000 Amplify tablets it had purchased developed problems, including broken screens and overheating battery chargers, within a few weeks. Some Amplify tablets even caught fire.

Many educators bought the company line that technology would make testing more efficient. The valuable publication *Chalkbeat* reported in detail about a 2016 fiasco in Tennessee. *Chalkbeat* reporters obtained about five months' worth of emails revealing that officials knew of the problems but went ahead anyway.

> Tennessee education officials allowed students and teachers to go ahead with a new online testing sys-

tem that had failed repeatedly in classrooms across the state, according to emails obtained by *Chalkbeat*.

After local districts spent millions of dollars on new computers, iPads, and upgraded internet service, teachers and students practiced for months taking the tests using MIST, an online testing system run by North Carolina–based test maker Measurement Inc. They encountered myriad problems: Sometimes, the test questions took three minutes each to load, or wouldn't load at all. At other times, the test wouldn't work on iPads. And in some cases, the system even saved the wrong answers.

When students in McMinnville, a town southeast of Nashville, logged on to take their practice tests, they found some questions already filled in—incorrectly—and that they couldn't change the answers. The unsettling implication: Even if students could take the exam, the scores would not reflect their skills. "That is a HUGE issue to me," Warren County High School assistant principal Penny Shockley wrote to Measurement Inc.

The emails contain numerous alarming reports about practice tests gone awry. They also show that miscommunication between officials with the Tennessee Department of Education and Measurement Inc. made it difficult to fix problems in time for launch.

And they suggest that even as problems continued to emerge as the test date neared, state officials either failed to understand or downplayed the widespread nature of the problems to schools. As a result, district leaders who could have chosen to have students take the test on paper instead moved forward with the online system.[4]

Despite the horror stories, many school districts have kept their feet on the accelerator. Claiming that it had learned from the problems in Los Angeles, the Houston Independent School

District distributed more than 18,000 laptop computers to high schools in 2014, and that same year Baltimore County Schools voted to spend $205 million to equip every student and teacher with a laptop.

Even with a full load of technology, many schools continue to conduct business as usual, with teachers doing most of the talking. According to Stanford's Larry Cuban, "Even in computer-based classes, teacher-centered instruction with a mix of student-centered practice was the norm."[5] In short, the problem goes beyond naiveté. The deeper problem is that those running public education have, for the most part, failed to recognize how technology, and particularly the Internet, have already transformed learning outside of school—just not school-based learning.

It bears repeating: Technology is fundamentally value-free. Just as an old-fashioned pencil and the coolest smartphone can be used to stay in touch with loved ones or to plan terrorist attacks, schools can use computers for "drill and kill" or for exploring new ideas. How our schools are using—and failing to use—technology reveals a great deal about what we value.

Despite having access to all the world's knowledge on their smartphones, most students in most classrooms are expected to learn and then spit back conventional knowledge: state capitals, the periodic table, how a bill becomes law, and the like.[6] More effective than lecturing, however, is providing genuine learning opportunities that engage students in the creation of new knowledge. That sounds grandiose, but it's easier than you might imagine, as I will explain.

THE POWER OF TECHNOLOGY

Can you think of an institution in America—besides our schools—that has not embraced modern technology? In airport restaurants, you order on a tablet. We shop online, and our dry cleaner keeps track of our shirts and skirts from a desktop computer. Cops give traffic tickets electronically, and you now can pick up and drop off your rental car without ever interacting with a live person.

A system of schools in which students are knowledge workers cannot prosper without technology. Sure, students will come to a building somewhere, but in this new system, they will be able to work with peers around the nation and the world. And collaboration among teachers shouldn't be restricted to the building. They can and should be sharing ideas over the Internet and teaching and learning together via Skype.

Today's technologies are occasions for awe, but they are still just tools, like the good old #2 pencil. While much good can come from harnessing technology's potential, harm results when adults ignore technology's potential or fail to accept their adult responsibilities. Some adults are wont to say, "Technology is the kids' world. They're digital natives, and I'm just a tourist." That's inadequate. Young people may be digital natives, but it remains the responsibility of adults to see that they become digital *citizens*.

Unfortunately, right now school systems have few incentives to trust technology, because they don't know how it will affect those test scores that are being used to judge them—and possibly fire them.[7] In my experience, educators understand that they are working in systems that are excessively literal *and* overly reactive. For the most part, administrators don't advance by taking chances, so we should not expect them to take the lead now. Society has been telling them, over and over, that it wants good reading scores; no one says, "We want kids who love to read." So why is anyone surprised when educators use computers to drill kids on reading tests?

Bottom line: schools will never realize the power of technology until we get out from under our current way of holding schools accountable. We need accountability, but what we are now doing is stifling learning and teaching. Hamstringing technology, or harnessing it to try to raise test scores, makes public education worse, not better.

However, our children are growing up in a virtual flood of information. They don't need more regurgitation. They need to understand that just because something is on the Internet, it is not necessarily true, even if they find that same information repeated a dozen times. The challenge for adults is to help students develop what Deborah Meier calls *habits of mind*: What do you know? How do you know what you know?

Technological innovation per se is not sufficient, of course. We need innovations that level the playing field and give all kids—regardless of their parents' income—the opportunity to excel. This matters more than ever. As recently as fifty or sixty years ago, most high school graduates could expect to earn a living doing physical labor, while the rest could look forward to doing mental labor (as an accountant, a bank teller, and so on). Back then only a very small percentage of adults did what we might call creative labor.

Now think about tomorrow. Unless our economy collapses, very few youth now in school will earn a living doing physical labor, and technology is rapidly destroying mental labor jobs by automating accounting, legal research, banking, et cetera. Some adults will do mental labor, but if America prospers, it will probably be because the majority of adults are engaging in creative labor. They have to learn to do this work in school, which means that innovation must become the norm and not the gee-whiz phenomenon it now is. In short, we must close the opportunity gap if we want better educational outcomes for more kids and a competitive economy down the road.

A barrier to innovation is the accounting/accountability mentality. As Suzy Null, a reader of my blog, wrote:

> I think teachers are becoming more like McDonald's workers. They are given precooked products and a specific "recipe" for preparing them. They are expected to follow these orders religiously in order to ensure that everyone gets the same "quality" experience. If they diverge even slightly, they are told that they are negligent and aren't doing their jobs. What's really sad is that the public is so used to mass-produced products and fast food, that they think that uniformity and mass production would be "good" for schools too.

This is happening, I think, because the adults in charge seem to believe that we can test our way out of the mess we are in. More testing is not "innovative," even if the tests themselves are full of bells and whistles.

No one should endorse technology as the innovation that will be education's salvation. What truly matters are the values that drive the uses of technology, and the beliefs of those in charge. Truly innovative programs engage the creativity of kids, expect them to work hard, and know that they will fail but are ready to help when they do. They require cooperation with others, involve the families, and—drumroll, please—spend real money giving poor kids the opportunities that most rich kids take for granted.

That said, you may be surprised to learn that a large majority of our schools and students are on the wrong side of the digital divide. It's not a case of poor kids not having access while rich kids do, because it turns out that a lot of wealthy students must cope with slow, limited access to the Internet.[8] But one aspect of the divide is real and troubling. Simply put, well-off students are more likely to be in control of technology, while poor kids have technology "done to them," in a sense, with computer-based drills and other repetitive activities.

RESPONSIBLE TECHNOLOGY

When technology's powers are ignored by adults and abused by children, death and disaster can be the outcome. Rebecca Sedwick's story should give you pause. The official records note Rebecca Sedwick's death as a suicide. While there's no disputing that the twelve-year-old jumped to her death from an abandoned cement plant in Lakeland, Florida, what happened to her requires new terminology. Perhaps we should call it "peer slaughter" to convey what killed Rebecca, who had been "absolutely terrorized on social media" by fifteen middle school girls for over a year, according to the sheriff of Polk County, Grady Judd.

Preventing tragedies like this requires more than vigilance by parents and educators. Anti-bullying campaigns may help, but unless schools are proactive in their use of technology so that the energies of young people are engaged in meaningful ways, idle minds (and thumbs) will continue to do the devil's work.

The "mean girls" phenomenon is not new, but what's different and frightening today are the weapons at their disposal, an array of apps that allow users to post and send messages anonymously. Rebecca's mother singled out Ask.fm, Kik, and Voxer as three the girls had used to send messages like "You're ugly," "Can u die please?" and "Why are you still alive?"

Rebecca is one of the youngest children to die from the growing number of cyberbullying incidents. About 20 percent of young people have been victimized, according to the Cyberbullying Research Center, a clearinghouse of information on cyberbullying. Around 15 percent of teens admit that they have bullied or ridiculed others on social media, photo-sharing sites, and other websites, according to the center.

"It's now 24-7. It's not just something you can escape after the school day," Sameer Hinduja, co-director of the Cyberbullying Research Center, told the *Orlando Sentinel*.

Rebecca and her mother, Tricia Norman, fought back. Norman told the *New York Times* that she closed down Rebecca's Facebook page and monitored her cellphone use. She changed Rebecca's cellphone number and kept tabs on her social media footprint. Rebecca changed schools, and for a while her life seemed to have turned around. Then she began using the new apps, setting off a new round of cyberbullying. (Apparently her original "offense" was showing interest in a boy that one of the other girls liked.)

"I don't want parents to wait for a tragedy to have those conversations," Cherie Benjoseph, co-founder of the Boca Raton–based KidSafe Foundation, told WPTV. "We're all still pretty naive on many levels. We're all still crossing our fingers and hoping it doesn't happen to our children."

Benjoseph said that Sedwick's suicide should be a wake-up call to all parents, who must demand to know what their kids are really doing online. Keeping computers and phones out of a child's bedroom is another good move, she says, because what teens do

online must not be off-limits to parents. "Our children sometimes lead double lives," she said.

More good advice: Have device-free times at home, especially
at mealtimes. It's difficult to know what's going on in your children's lives if they are always looking at screens. Bedrooms should
be device-free. I know families in which everyone (including the
adults) is required to leave their phones in a basket at the foot of
the stairs when they head upstairs to bed. The phones recharge
downstairs, the humans upstairs. Computers and tablets belong
in common spaces, not in bedrooms. Getting all parents to adopt
sensible policies and practices is unrealistic, particularly in a time
when a lot of parents seem to negotiate every decision with their
children, no matter how young they may be. But even if most
parents were to adopt these practices, schools still need to do the
right thing.

Schools are where most children are, and adults there can set
the tone and—more important—determine what kids do with
their devices. I often hear adults describing today's young people
as "digital natives," usually with a tone of resignation or acceptance: "They are so far ahead of us, but we can turn to them
for help." That kind of thinking smacks of abdication of adult
responsibility. Yes, most young people know more than we adults
do, because the fast-changing world of modern technology is
largely alien to us, wildly different from the one we grew up in.
But being a digital native is not the same as being a digital citizen. Young people have always needed ethical guidance and the
security of rules and boundaries. That's truer now because many
apps allow kids to "go nuclear" without fear of being identified.
Kids who spend hours every day on their devices are unlikely to
develop empathy for others, and it's a lack of empathy that seems
to fuel cyberbullying.

Some experts say that kids spend 90 percent of their tech time
consuming, and perhaps 1 percent doing creative work. If that's
accurate—if they're texting, playing Angry Birds and Grand
Theft Auto, linking up on Facebook and Google Circles, sexting,
and cyberbullying 90 percent of the time—then we adults should
be ashamed.

Unless, of course, we are equally guilty of obsessing over our devices. A central function of schools is what's often called socialization. It might be more useful to call it "developing empathy." As Catherine Steiner-Adair notes in her book *The Big Disconnect*, "Empathy might seem a 'soft' skill when compared to reading, writing, and math, but it is actually a neurological phenomenon as well as a soulful one." She adds, "The development of empathy comes from direct experience."[9] Cathy Davidson of Duke University says much the same thing: "The brain is what it does."[10]

Both are echoing the timeless wisdom, "We are what we repeatedly do." In my experience, the education community uses technology 80–90 percent of the time to control—everything from keeping the school's master schedule and monitoring attendance and grades to tracking teacher performance and imparting the knowledge we believe kids need to have. That's pretty much the opposite of what should be happening.

Because an important purpose of school is to help "grow adults," the creative use of technology—by adults and young people—must be ramped up dramatically. Students ought to be using today's technologies to create knowledge and to find answers to important questions. If they aren't doing that, then those idle brains and thumbs will be doing the devil's work, as those girls in South Florida were doing.

The law is very much on the side of the victims, and school authorities ought to know that they are obligated under federal law to protect young people. I am referring not to anti-bullying legislation, which differs from state to state, but to Title IX of the Education Amendments of 1972, sometimes known as "that damned sports law." Title IX clearly prohibits sexual harassment, and most cyberbullying and other forms of bullying include sexual references. Girls are called "sluts" and "hos," boys are called "fags" and other names. Sexual rumors and comments are frequent. All that violates Title IX.

Title IX also prohibits these behaviors outside the school (for example, when personal computers are used) when the behavior is disruptive to learning or affects a student's ability to partake of the opportunities for learning and in other opportunities provided by the school. In short, schools and school administrators, under Title IX, are obligated to stop sexual cyberbullying. Moreover, they stand to lose federal funding if they do not. Some districts have paid six-figure settlements for their demonstrated failure to protect students from harassment and cyberbullying.[11]

But defensive behavior is not sufficient. Schools today must provide opportunities for young people to create knowledge out of the swirling clouds of information that surround them twenty-four hours a day. You and I were sent to schools because that's where the knowledge was stored—but that was yesterday. Think how different today's world is. Today's young people need guidance in sifting through the flood of information and turning it into knowledge. Because computers seemingly have all the answers, young people need to be able to formulate good questions.

When schools do these things, young people will be learning (or reinforcing) real-world skills that will help them once they move out of school. They'll be working together; they'll be gathering, assimilating, and analyzing data; they'll be learning how to present what they are learning. They will be working with numbers and writing persuasive reports. No doubt some will be speaking publicly about their findings. This is career-track stuff, 180 degrees different from the regurgitation that is the hallmark of most education today.

Another plus is that the hours they spend on projects like these are hours they *cannot* spend consuming technology. And because they are using technology to create, they will not be bored, and will be less likely to use technology's power negatively. Stronger in their own sense of self, they will probably be less likely to feel the need to cyberbully others. Had Rebecca Sedwick's schools taken this approach, she might be alive today.

School critic Cevin Soling believes schools need a complete makeover. In his view, the root cause of destructive behavior is not technology but the nature and design of schools. "The system is a monster and has the capacity for producing monstrous behavior," he wrote. "Mean and apathetic children are created by schools who process children on an assembly line and treat them with very little respect and give them no autonomy over their lives." Bullying, he believes, replicates what they have endured while making them feel powerful, and today's technology is just the most effective tool that's at hand. "Imagine placing a population in a confined environment against their will while also depriving them of the capacity to make choices that affect their lives and to *not* address that when evaluating their behavior."[12]

He is offering his own version of Aristotle and Will Durant: "We are what we repeatedly do." We cannot wish today's powerful technology away or keep it out of our children's hands. It's naive to think that anti-bullying campaigns and posters will be sufficient. Technology can be used for good or ill, and how schools employ it depends in large part on us.

TRANSFORMATION THROUGH TECHNOLOGY

One morning I happened to look out my living room window and noticed there were trash receptacles on all four corners of the intersection our Manhattan apartment overlooks. Probably as a consequence, there's very little garbage on the street and sidewalk. In fact, most intersections in my neighborhood seem to have a trash can on each corner, something I have been aware of (and grateful for) when I walk our Labrador retriever. Later that same day I visited a school in the South Bronx that is just a few miles away, but worlds apart. There I noticed that sidewalks and streets were littered *and* that there weren't very many public trash receptacles—just one per intersection, not the four in my neighborhood.

Now, a couple of casual sightings and an anecdote do not constitute data.[13] But this is a great opportunity for social studies teachers to use technology to enliven their classes, energize their students, and perhaps provide real-life lessons in how cities distribute resources. Working in teams (for efficiency and safety), middle school students could use smartphone cameras to map their neighborhood intersections with photos that answer one question: is there a trash can on the corner? Share the data, not just with classmates but online with other middle school classes around the city. Will patterns emerge? Do well-to-do neighborhoods have many more places for residents to put bags of dog poop and other garbage? And are those streets cleaner?

A more complex project to determine just how often those trash receptacles are emptied could be done with the cooperation of local businesses or apartment doormen. Suppose the students find that this resource (call them "cleanliness opportunities") is unevenly distributed. That raises another question: is that resource distributed by income or according to some other criteria? At this point, students will probably have questions for urban leaders, so that's when they learn how to write properly respectful letters—another valuable exercise. They may discover that some leaders aren't comfortable having established practices scrutinized, which is another lesson and another challenge. But, hey, schools are *supposed* to be preparing youth for life in a democracy. What could be better than actual participation?

These students are not digesting prepared knowledge; rather, they are actually creating knowledge. What's more, they will end up knowing more about their city's sanitation policies than 99 percent of adults.

Here's another example of technology in support of genuine learning. Imagine if every third-grade class in a city had access to an air quality indicator, one of which costs less than $200. Suppose that three or four times each school day the third graders went outside, activated the monitor, and recorded the measurements. After comparing the daily and hourly readings for their playground, they would enter the information into a database that also contained readings from every other school in the city, schools across the state, or schools in a range of places around the world. Now they can compare the air they are breathing with everyone else's! They would need to know how to interpret readings, which would require some basic science research and direct instruction from their teacher. Perhaps they would ask local scientists to come in and talk, but more likely they would Skype with experts from all over the globe. (Bonus: They would also be Skyping with other students and casually learning about different cultures and traditions.)

As they began to understand the patterns—and perhaps be

outraged by what they find—they might feel compelled to write letters or articles for local publications. Perhaps some would create video reports that could be posted on YouTube and maybe even picked up by local television news.

That's for elementary and middle school students. A high school project that would also lead to knowledge creation involves the study and analysis of water. Let me use Texas, which has about four thousand miles of fast-running water, as an example. Suppose every high school within reach of a river owned a water quality monitor (the cost of these instruments vary, but a reliable one can be obtained for about $1,000). Once or twice a week, the science class could go to the water's edge and take measurements of pH, speed, amount of detritus, and so forth. Like those third graders, they would analyze the data, share the results with other high school students around the state, dig deeper when they find anomalies, ask for explanations, and publish the results.

This "curriculum" is about more than trash cans, air, and running water. It's also about democracy, independence, collaboration, and knowledge creation. Projects such as these will teach other lessons besides science: information is power, collaboration produces strength, and social policies have consequences. Students will learn that they themselves are not merely numbers or test scores but sentient, thinking individuals with potential. They matter.

Technology makes all this *possible*. To be clear, I think projects such as these are *imperative* on at least two levels. For one thing, much schoolwork today is hopelessly boring regurgitation, whereas this is real work in uncharted territory. For another, we need our young people to be in the habit of asking questions and searching for answers because we want them to grow up to be productive adults who are engaged in their communities (and vote).

And to circle back to a central theme set forth in Step Four, technology means that our schools *can* ask of each child, "How are you intelligent?"—and then create learning opportunities that allow every child to soar. Technology allows students to have more control over their own learning, without downgrading or minimizing the role of the skilled teacher.

PRACTICAL TECHNOLOGY

Technology can also revolutionize grading and assessment, not just teaching and learning. In the schools we are designing, electronic portfolios should be the instrument of choice. Well-designed electronic portfolios include both in-school and out-of-school illustrations, from work, play, sports, teams, performances, and even lonely poetry writing. Well-constructed portfolios are living documents that illustrate better writing, growth in sophistication, improved multimedia literacy, and information about how students actually use the information from classes to solve daily problems.

Electronic portfolios reflect projects that cross subjects and disciplines and thereby show how one discipline influences others. Whether students are sculpting in a welding class or illustrating a poem with music and art, most of them think visually, tangibly, and engagingly when they actively assess themselves and reflect on those assessments.

Finally, electronic portfolios give students the opportunity to reflect on how soft skills that build on themes such as responsibility, cooperation, inquiry, and negotiation give focus to their achievements and help them compare their work to what others are doing. E-portfolios involve students in constructing their own vision of themselves, what they can learn from each other, and how they respect and celebrate their best teachers in showing off their best work.

ONLY FOOLS RUSH IN

School leadership, including school board members, are besieged with offers of miraculous new technologies that are "guaranteed to raise scores," "aligned with the Common Core," and so forth. Here's an easy rule of thumb for avoiding mistakes: *School systems should not adopt any new technology until a significant percentage of early adopters are enthusiastic about it.* And "significant" means at least 10 percent, in my view. However, early adopters aren't hard to find. They're generally vocal and visible. Leadership should seek them out, listen to their advice, and enlist them in the task of bringing along the reluctant ones. The next steps include creating rewards for trying, celebrating failure, and not punishing the laggards but giving them time instead.

Embracing technology carefully, imaginatively, and effectively makes it much easier to take Step Nine.

STEP NINE

Embrace "Outsiders"
(Enthusiastically)

The problem with the truism "It takes a village to raise a child" is that most villagers have no direct connection to children or to the schools they go to. Only about 25 percent of homes have school-age children, and in some communities that percentage drops into the teens. Even if you include households with grandparents, the percentage probably won't reach 40.[1]

However, people in households with no strong connection to public education hold the future of public schools in their hands. They vote on school budgets, and so their opinions of schools, teachers, and students matter. Not only do older folks vote in greater numbers than younger people, but the gap is increasing. According to the Census Bureau, "the turnout rate among 18- to 24-year-olds fell to 41.2 percent in 2012 from 48.5 percent in 2008. The turnout rates of adults ages 65 and older rose—to 71.9 percent in 2012 from 70.3 percent in 2008."[2]

For these reasons, educators and those connected to schools must develop and adopt strategies to win the support of those without a direct connection to schools. It's not enough for good things to be happening in schools; the "outsiders" need to be supportive. And the best way to make that happen is to get them involved.

It will be difficult for many educators to take this step because they have grown accustomed to a system that says, in effect, "Drop the children and the money at the schoolhouse door, and leave the rest to us." That approach won't work anymore, if it ever did. The outside world, meaning ordinary taxpayers and the business community, may also have trouble adjusting, because they've grown comfortable with being kept at arm's length.[3] But that's what has to change . . . and determined educators can do this pretty easily by meeting the outsiders where they are and involving them in the curriculum of a modern world. Here are a few ways.

- Students can create a photo gallery of the residents of their apartment building or their street and then post portraits on the Web for all to see and talk about.
- Art students can sketch portraits of business store-fronts, or workers and bosses, also to be posted on the Web.
- Utilizing Skype, the school's jazz quintet can perform at community centers simultaneously with the jazz trio from another school in a neighboring county. (That distance should present no problem; significantly long distances can create a sound lag, however.)
- A video team can interview adults in a senior citizen center around a chosen theme (best job, favorite trip, et cetera), to be edited into a short video for the Web. Producing short biographies of ordinary citizens will teach all sorts of valuable skills, including clear writing, teamwork, and meeting deadlines.
- Music and drama students can rehearse and then present their productions at retirement homes and senior centers—but with a twist: involve some of the adults in the process (a small part in the play, a role in selecting the music, and so on).

THE SHARED POETRY PROJECT

Here's an activity that will turn outsiders into strong supporters of public schools. The Shared Poetry Project has multiple goals.

One is to introduce adults who are not connected to the public schools to the young people who attend them, so that the adults will appreciate the value of supporting public education. A second goal is to enable youth to further develop skills that will serve them well throughout their lives:[4]

1. Working together with peers
2. Communicating across generations
3. Specific production skills
4. Making value-based judgments
5. Making difficult editorial choices
6. Meeting real-world professional standards

The team will need a video camera (the one on a smartphone will be fine), a tripod or some other firm support for the camera, paper and transparent tape, and some willing adults.

How it works: A team of students, probably middle schoolers, picks a poem that they all relate to. This is important because they may have to "sell" it to the adults who are going to be asked to perform/recite the poem, on camera. The adults may have to be taught to read with energy and conviction, and having enthusiastic students (now the producers) will help.

Which adults are going to participate? The sole criterion, besides their willingness, is that they do *not* have kids in school. That is, choose outsiders! I ask you to imagine watching this reading of Hamlet's famous soliloquy on YouTube.[5] I've used men and women from my Manhattan neighborhood (plus one celebrity), but you may want to imagine folks from your world:

MRS. ANDREWS IN APARTMENT 9B:

To be, or not to be, that is the question:
Whether 'tis nobler in the mind to suffer
The slings and arrows of outrageous fortune,
Or to take arms against a sea of troubles,
And by opposing end them?

MR. YOUNG FROM THE DRY CLEANERS:

To die, to sleep,
No more; and by a sleep to say we end
The heartache, and the thousand natural shocks
That flesh is heir to . . .

KIMBERLY WONG IN APARTMENT 17C:

. . . 'tis a consummation
Devoutly to be wished. To die, to sleep;
To sleep, perchance to dream . . .

AUGIE RAMOS AT THE DELI:

. . . ay, there's the rub:
For in that sleep of death what dreams may come,
When we have shuffled off this mortal coil,
Must give us pause—there's the respect
That makes calamity of so long life.

ANGELA PACKER AT EQUINOX FITNESS:

For who would bear the whips and scorns of time,
The oppressor's wrong, the proud man's contumely,
The pangs of despised love, the law's delay,
The insolence of office . . .

JACOB EPSTEIN OF THE JEWELRY STORE:

. . . and the spurns
That patient merit of the unworthy takes,
When he himself might his quietus make
With a bare bodkin?

U.S. SENATOR CHARLES SCHUMER (D, NY):

Who would fardels bear,
To grunt and sweat under a weary life,
But that the dread of something after death,
The undiscovered country from whose bourn
No traveller returns, puzzles the will,
And makes us rather bear those ills we have
Than fly to others that we know not of?

CLOTHING STORE OWNER ALICE GOTTESWOLD:

Thus conscience does make cowards of us all,
And thus the native hue of resolution
Is sicklied o'er with the pale cast of thought . . .

RICHIE O'CONNOR, DOORMAN FOR THE APARTMENT
    BUILDING:

. . . and enterprises of great pith and moment,
With this regard their currents turn awry,
And lose the name of action.

Students first print the entire poem in a large font size and identify the obvious verses or couplets.[6] When they are ready to record, they tape the selected verse or couplet to the bottom lip of the camera lens. This way the participants don't have to memorize anything. They will be looking at the camera and their lines at the same time. Although many participants may memorize the words, they will be more relaxed knowing a crutch is there if they need it.

When filming, frame all participants from the shoulders up. Ideally, all of the readers should be sitting or standing in front of a non-distracting, solid-color backdrop. Consistency matters, so frame every adult in the same way. They should look into the camera when reciting their lines. Tell them to continue looking into the camera until the student says "cut." Make sure the audio quality is clear and coherent. As we say in the business, "TV is really just radio with pictures," which means that quality sound is essential. Once completely and fully satisfied with the audio, check it again!

Producers need options, so each adult should be asked to read his/her lines several times.[7] For more choices, have each adult read couplets from different poems. Most adults are not accustomed to performing, and so the student producers will have to gain their confidence, perhaps by giving their own reading of the entire poem and explaining why they like that poem and that poet.

It gets interesting when adults give a lousy reading and have to be coaxed into a second, third, or fourth effort. That's when these twelve-, thirteen-, and fourteen-year-olds who now are directing people old enough to be their parents or grandparents have to learn how to criticize constructively. Because this is sure to happen, it's crucial that the team role-play this situation in advance, in front of classmates, so they can develop strategies for success.

While there are rules such as one couplet per reader, always remember that rules are made to be broken. The producers might decide that the most powerful presentation of the last line of Macbeth's famous soliloquy, "It is a tale told by an idiot, full of sound and fury, signifying nothing," would be a reading by three people:

1. It is a tale told by an idiot . . .
2. full of sound and fury . . .
3. signifying nothing.

To achieve that, however, each individual probably ought to read the entire couplet, which then can be edited to suit.

One rule that cannot be broken is that the readings have to be excellent. No cutting corners and no compromising on quality just to squeeze in an adult whose reading wasn't good enough but who is friends with the principal or somebody important. Only quality matters! Producers have to make all sorts of decisions, always keeping in mind that the goal is the best possible production—in this case, the most emotionally accurate reading of Hamlet's soliloquy by a group of adults who have no connection to schools.[8]

For students, school will be more valuable and interesting, and their enthusiasm will rub off and carry over into other aspects of their school experience. They will be become better and more discerning consumers of education precisely because they are now producers.

The fun—and the rewards—begin when the production is posted on the school's YouTube channel and perhaps broadcast on local news. That's when all of these adults—*chosen because they do not have kids in school*—start talking about the film, sharing the link, and pulling out their smartphones and showing it to friends and customers. They'll be saying, "Did you know what they're doing in school these days? Sure makes me wish I could go to school all over again."

That's one way to turn outsiders into eager insiders. Kids can also produce oral and written histories of people and places in their neighborhood—a sure crowd-pleaser because everyone loves talking about themselves. And this is how our children become confident, productive, and creative adults.

NOTE TO EDUCATORS: PARENTS ARE NOT OUTSIDERS

Unfortunately, adults without school-age children are not the only outsiders. In a public forum professional educators may describe parents as "our greatest asset" and "invaluable partners," but what if you could hear their private conversations or catch them off guard? Or, better yet, what if you simply examined how most schools treat parents? In my experience, most administrators and many teachers hold parents in low regard, and their behavior and policies reflect that. Perhaps that's an inevitable consequence of attempting to elevate education to a high-status profession. "After all, you wouldn't expect a heart surgeon to consult with a child's parents before replacing a ruptured valve and saving the child's life," the thinking goes, as if the work of educating a child were the equivalent of complex surgery.

It seems to me that most schools make parents outsiders in both subtle and not-so-subtle ways. There's back-to-school night once a year, and perhaps a Parent Involvement Committee or Parent Advisory Board that meets occasionally with the principal. Many schools expect parents to hold bake sales, auctions, and fund-raising drives (which can account for a large chunk of a school's budget these days), but that's not treating parents as partners in their children's education. Unfortunately, it's the rare educator who says, "We cannot do a good job of educating your child without you," means it, and then proves it by his or her actions.

Why this negative attitude toward parents? Some educators feel that low-income parents do not have the time or energy to get deeply involved in their children's schooling. But even if their dismissal of parents is rooted in empathy or sympathy, it adds up to the same thing: the exclusion of parents. Unfortunately, however, plenty of administrators and teachers are genuinely disdainful of parents and apt to dismiss them as uncaring, uninvolved, or ignorant. I would characterize their attitude as "Just leave the education to us."

As evidence of parental detachment, these administrators and teachers often cite the low turnout at back-to-school night, concluding from the large number of no-show parents that they don't care. But look carefully at how back-to-school nights are structured: a quick series of show-and-tell presentations by teachers, one-off lectures that make parents feel like visitors or strangers who happened by. The educators will tell the parents to make sure their kids do their homework assignments and don't watch much TV. Why would most parents bother to attend more than once? What's inviting about being talked down to?

What if parents were taught the skills to help their kids become better readers and treated as partners in the education process? No lectures, no Parent Involvement Committees, no window-dressing, but a genuine partnership that required openness and commitment from everyone?[9]

Suppose the root problem is education's failure to recognize that parents want their children to succeed but may not know how to contribute. Suppose the real problem is education's failure to treat parents as assets. Parents can and should be treated as valuable assets and not as outsiders. Teachers who are accustomed to holding parents at arm's length can learn ways to acknowledge that parents are essential. Parents who may have become accustomed to educators saying "Leave the education to us" will have to learn to accept this new role and responsibility.

If you are convinced that outsiders need to be inside the tent, it's time to take Step Ten.

STEP TEN

Embrace Teachers (Respectfully)

Most of the 3.3 million teachers now in classrooms will probably be teaching in the new schools we are determined to create, but with new challenges and opportunities. These experiences will change them and the way they teach. If we do this right, millions of teachers will rediscover why they entered the field in the first place. When they see their students grow and soar, they will become again who they once were, idealistic and socially conscious individuals.

However, embracing teachers is also going to disrupt some institutions and people who work in them. It requires major changes, but since you've come this far in the program, why stop now?

First, let's insist on collaboration. Right now teaching is a closed-door profession, just as it was when I taught high school in the mid-1960s. Most teachers can close their doors and operate as they see fit, with rare visits by colleagues or supervisors. Teachers ought to be able to visit each other's classrooms to learn from each other. That means reducing the number of hours of teaching so that collaboration (including watching each other teach) is possible. At the present time our teachers teach for about twenty-seven hours a week. Contrast that with Finland, where ten to twelve hours is the norm. This sort of observational learning will require hiring more adults, but we can pay for that by scrapping so-called professional development entirely. It's almost universally conceded to be useless, and it's costing as much as $15,000 per teacher per year.

In these new schools, teachers will rarely be asking "what" questions, as in "What is the capital of Missouri?" or "What branch of government originates legislation?" Instead, they will be asking their students "why" and "how" questions. These are big changes.

"HARDER TO BECOME, EASIER TO BE"

Our current education system makes it too easy for just about anyone to become a teacher . . . and far too difficult for most teachers to excel at the task. It's estimated that about 40 percent of teachers leave the field within their first five years on the job. What's not clear is how many of them leave because they failed at the task, how many depart for personal reasons, and how many go because teaching is frustrating work. Among the problems: low pay, low status, poor preparation, not much hope of advancement, lack of professional atmosphere, and (especially but not only for bright women) benighted male administrators.

The basic idea of changing teaching can be reduced to a bumper sticker: "Harder to Become, Easier to Be." But making the needed changes will be neither simple nor easy, because some people and systems actually benefit from today's inefficient approach of weak preparation, inadequate orientation of new employees, an out-of-whack pay structure, a poor rewards system, and excessive (but often unsupportive) supervision. Teacher training institutions, their home universities, school districts, state budgets and budget directors, and others stand to lose something, or at a minimum be significantly changed. Even teachers, accustomed to a certain way of instruction, will face challenges in reinventing themselves.

However, it is important to remember that other changes will also be taking place because educators, policy makers, and school systems have committed to taking the other steps outlined in this book. They will be assessing students differently, they will be engaging their communities, they will be harnessing technology productively, and they will have embraced a vision in which students are the workers and knowledge their product. Changes such as these will make it easier for rookie and veteran teachers alike to remake themselves and to succeed. Making the field of teaching more attractive is essential. These changes should reverse the decline in interest noted earlier and slow the rate of attrition.[1]

WHY TEACHERS LEAVE

I will begin with the bad news.

A Support Problem

Years ago I followed two first grade classes in Washington, D.C.[2] Most first graders understand that reading is the currency of their culture, and so all these children wanted to learn to read. We picked two teachers, a rookie fresh out of ed school trained in the whole-language method of teaching reading, and a veteran who used every tool and technique available.

Johnny Brinson, the veteran, was a treat to watch. He used any method necessary, refusing to fall into either the whole-language camp or the phonics camp. By year's end his first graders were reading with fluency and comprehension.

Across the hall, the young teacher—like rookie teachers everywhere—was on her own, with little or no guidance. We watched as this well-meaning but poorly trained teacher told her children that they were learning to read—even though it was obvious to us that they were merely memorizing a book. We never saw the principal walk into the rookie's classroom. There was no system for her to be mentored by other experienced educators, and no one offered her guidance or a critique. Her students suffered, and so did the rookie teacher. Does any other profession or occupation treat new workers with such disregard?

A Professional Problem

"So, are they quitting because they're fed up with their heavy-handed union bosses?" The hostility of the question took me by surprise. I was explaining to my dinner companion, a veteran lawyer, that about 40 percent of teachers leave the field within five years, and right away he jumped to his anti-union conclusion disguised as a question. I've had similar conversations with hundreds of non-educators over the years, reflecting both misunderstanding and hostility. No, I explained. Unions don't seem to have anything to do with it. Rather, it's most often related to working conditions: class size, discipline policies, and how much control and influence they have over their daily activities.

"It's not money?" he asked, aggressively suspicious.

Not according to surveys, I explained. I described what I'd seen of a teacher's daily work life.

He interrupted, "How can it be a profession if you can't take a leak when you need to?"

While that's not a criterion that social scientists use to define a profession, my cut-to-the-chase acquaintance might be on to something. Can teaching be a true profession if you can't take a bathroom break when nature calls?[3]

Social scientists have no doubt about the status of teaching, according to Richard Ingersoll of the University of Pennsylvania. "We do not refer to teaching as a profession," he told me. "It doesn't have the characteristics of those traditional professions like medicine, academia, dentistry, law, architecture, engineering, et cetera. It doesn't have the pay, the status, the respect, the length of training, so from a scientific viewpoint teaching is not a profession." Ingersoll carefully refers to teaching as an *occupation*, noting that it's the largest occupation of all in the United States, and growing at a faster rate than the student population.

Jennifer Robinson, a teacher educator at Montclair State University in New Jersey, disagrees with Ingersoll. She believes our familiarity with teachers and schools breeds disrespect for teaching. "We don't treat teaching as a profession because we've all gone to school and think we're experts. Most people think, 'Oh, I could do that,' which we would never do with doctors." Robinson suggests that a significant part of our population—including lots of politicians—does not trust teachers. She cites the drumbeat of criticism in the media, blaming teachers for low test scores.

A common criticism is that teachers come from the lowest

rungs of our academic ladder, a charge that Ingersoll says is not true. "About 10 percent of teachers come from institutions like Macalester, Yale, and Penn," he says. "Perhaps 25 percent come from the lowest quartile of colleges," meaning that close to two-thirds of teachers attend the middle ranks of our colleges and universities. At their institutions, however, future teachers tend to rank in the bottom half of their classes.

According to Ingersoll, one hallmark of a profession is longevity, and in that respect teaching does not make the grade. "Teaching has far higher turnover than those traditional professions, lawyers, professors, engineers, architects, doctors, and accountants," Ingersoll reports. "Nurses tend to stick around longer than teachers." When I asked what fields have higher quit rates, he told me, "Prison guards, child care workers, and secretaries."

Perhaps teaching is neither a profession nor an occupation but a calling. Those who teach score high on measures of empathy and concern for others and social progress, as Ingersoll and others have noted. As a reporter and a parent, I have met thousands of teachers whose concern for their students was visible and admirable.

Whether you think of teaching as a profession, occupation, or calling, there's trouble in River City. Large numbers of teachers—49 percent—are dissatisfied to the point of wishing they could change jobs, according to a 2016 report from the Center for Education Policy (CEP).[4] "Listen to Us: Teacher Views and Voices" paints a disturbing picture about how teachers feel about wave after wave of top-down school reform. Almost half (46 percent) of teachers cited state or district policies that get in the way of teaching as a major challenge, and about one-third cited constantly changing demands placed on teachers and students.[5]

Some in the school reform movement seem to want to reduce teaching to mindless factory work. Remember that awful graphic in Davis Guggenheim's film *Waiting for 'Superman'*, where the heads of students are opened up and knowledge is poured in by teachers? That's how some politicians and school reformers understand the role of schools and teachers. The subtext is clear: since it doesn't take much skill to pour from a pitcher, why pay teachers more? Why give them job protection? Just measure how well they pour (using test scores, of course), compare them to other teachers (value-added measures), and then get rid of the ones who don't pour well. Bingo—education is reformed!

Teaching has taken some big hits in recent years, driven in great part by the school reform movement's disingenuous argument that "great teachers" make all the difference. This stance allows them to ignore the clear effects of poverty, poor nutrition, poor health, and substandard housing on a child's achievement. Most parents are not fooled by this. Their respect for their children's teachers and schools remains high, which must frustrate Michelle Rhee, Campbell Brown of The 74, Democrats for Education Reform, and others in that crowd.[6]

To show respect for teaching and teachers, I suggest we consider three actions:

1. Support leaders in education, politics, and business who want schools to ask "How is this child intelligent?" instead of "How intelligent is this child?"
2. Elect school board members who believe in inquiry-based learning, problem solving, effective uses of technology, and deeper learning.
3. Insist on changes in the structure of schools so that teachers have time to watch each other teach and to reflect on their work.[7] Time to collaborate and opportunities to watch colleagues at work are standard operating procedures in Finland and other countries with effective educational systems. (Oh, and so are bathroom breaks.)

Worshiping Test Scores

What makes America's approach different from nearly every other country's is that we use test scores to judge *teachers*, not primarily to assess either students or schools. The people in charge do not trust teachers. That is a major cause of the mess we are in. Years ago we trusted teachers but had no system for verification; today, however, that trust has virtually disappeared, and education is about verifying—using scores on standardized tests to weed out "bad" teachers and reward "good" ones.[8]

Trust without verification doesn't work. Verification without trust is a disaster. Verification without first defining what is *worth* verifying is meaningless. There are three basic options for what needs to be verified in schools: student progress, teacher performance, and school quality.

Mistreatment of teachers in the name of higher test scores is driving some very good teachers out of the classroom and the profession. Exhibit A might be a letter I received, excerpted below, from an experienced teacher in an eastern state.

> Let me tell you what a horrific day I had at work. Okay, so yesterday I had to spend the entire morning proctoring the state science assessment for fifth graders. Today I was called to the office and told I needed to proctor yet another test for the fifth graders, whose results would be used to determine what "track" they will be on in middle school. The test had four subtests. I was told that I had to pick up all the fifth-grade ESL [English as a Second Language] students and get their tests and subtest answer sheets and bring them into another room. None of the classroom teachers knew anything about this test, either.
>
> So my ESL colleague and I took the kids to a separate room and started the test. ESL kids get extended time . . . but while we're giving the test, the noise level outside the room is unbelievable—the assistant principal is yelling to the secretaries because she won't get off her butt to ask them a question but would rather yell from her desk. Talk about disrespect for the ESL kids.
>
> We started at 9:30. The first two parts took until 11:30, then we had to dismiss the kids to their art, music, gym, etc. classes. After those classes they had to come back to us to be tested on math. Oh,

and by the way, we needed calculators for them, but the administrators "forgot" to tell any of the teachers about this. Then *later* we found out the kids were supposed to get a reference sheet about math terms, but the administrators said, "Just give them the test anyway." Then came lunch and recess, and they had to come back again because they *still* weren't done. When we finally finished, it was 2:30. Remember, we started at 9:30.

Tomorrow I have to give them another test. Friday I have to give them *another* test, then they spend the rest of their day finishing up the ESL test on the computer . . . and the computers keep crashing.

I called the ESL person in charge and told them about the proctor who was reading instead of doing his job. She told me that the only reason I was complaining was that I didn't want the proctors there in the first place.

I've called in the union. I don't think they will actually do anything, but this is child abuse, and *my* name is on these tests. And these scores go on *my* evaluation.

Trader Joe's looks better every day.

When I asked this teacher for permission to use parts of her letter, she gave her consent, and added:

The testing mania has caused people to lose their minds and their ability to see that having students sit for hours and hours of testing does *not* enhance their abilities, other than their ability to take a test. Last school year I felt like all I did was teach kids how to game the test.

There is nothing intellectual going on in schools, just taking tests to provide quantifiable data that will be used to judge teachers, schools, and districts, pigeonhole students into tracks, and leave us with a

generation of students who no longer find school fun
but find school a boring, frustrating place to be.

Her experience also made me think of my older daughter's experience teaching Italian in a middle school in Spanish Harlem in
New York City. She had been hired because she's fluent in Italian
and the school wanted the kids to learn a second language (most
kids spoke limited English and Spanglish, but not Spanish). She
energized her eighth graders by challenging them: if they learned
Italian to a certain (high) level, she would treat them to a meal in
an Italian restaurant in midtown Manhattan, where they would
order their meals in Italian! Perhaps because most of her kids had
never ventured outside of Spanish Harlem or been to a fancy restaurant, they rose to the challenge.

However, in mid-May her principal, a fastidious individual
who regularly checked to see that lesson plans were placed at the
right-hand corner of his teachers' desks, came into my daughter's
room and said, loudly and in front of the entire class, "Okay, Ms.
Merrow, that's enough Italian for the year. The tests are coming in three weeks, and I want you to put Italian aside and spend
the time prepping for the math test." She protested, but he over-
rode her, dismissed her concerns, and ordered her to get to it.
She did as directed. Of course, it did not produce better math
scores on the standardized tests, but her students absorbed three
important—albeit unintended—lessons:

1. Italian was irrelevant.
2. Their teacher was equally irrelevant.
3. Only the standardized test mattered.

This administrative idiocy had real-world consequences: one day
after the last test about two-thirds of her students simply stopped
coming to school. The school year had nearly a month to go, but
the kids had absorbed the essential lessons. (So had my daughter,
who resigned at the end of the year.)

My daughter gave up on classroom teaching. How many other
gifted teachers have also moved on for similar reasons? Let's hope

the woman whose letter I shared has persevered. Perhaps her union got involved, or perhaps she shared her story with other teachers, so they could speak as one voice on behalf of students. Odds are, though, that she will choose another profession or will stay in the classroom with her hopes diminished and the fire of her idealism extinguished.

A Complicated, Multidimensional Problem

We know that many new teachers don't last, but why are many veteran teachers leaving the field? Some are aging baby boomers ready for retirement, but we are also losing a lot of experienced teachers who, if all were going well, would be helping our children learn for many more years. The situation is particularly dire in North Carolina, where some counties in that state are experiencing a 35 percent turnover rate. This state could be the canary in the coal mine.[9]

Money is an issue in North Carolina. Teacher pay dropped 16 percent between 2002 and 2012, in inflation-adjusted dollars, to $45,947—well below the national average of $55,418. Once near the national midpoint, North Carolina is now very close to the bottom. Teacher Sharon Boxley moved from North Carolina to Maryland, where she said she was making close to $15,000 more a year. The emphasis on test scores is not unique to North Carolina, Boxley discovered: "I am still in the classroom, but I miss teaching. It's all about testing."

Respect is clearly an issue, as is the human need to feel that one's work has significance. A veteran teacher who left her job in the Chapel Hill–Carrboro system out of frustration with constant testing and other mandates told me, "I was tired of not having a voice. No one listens to teachers." Vivian Connell was another of the teachers on a panel I moderated.[10] Before the session, I explained the ground rules: no opening remarks, all Q&A, and no off-topic speeches. Vivian immediately piped up. "I tend to get carried away," she said, "because I feel passionately about what North Carolina and the Obama administration are doing to public education."

She did in fact get carried away a couple of times, and when she did, I interrupted (nicely, I think). But those who heard what she had to say about the increasing lack of trust of teachers, the government's embrace of "test and punish" strategies, and the system's overreliance on test scores understood her strength of character, passion, and commitment. She told the audience that she had come to believe that her chosen profession was being denigrated by powerful forces bent on destroying public schools, and so she enrolled in law school, graduated with honors, and was admitted to the bar at age forty-nine. She declined a clerkship opportunity in order to spend her energy advocating for public education. A school lost a terrific teacher, but the public interest was much better served by Vivian being an education lawyer.[11]

Penn's Richard Ingersoll, who is, as previously noted, an authority on why teachers leave, is also a former public school teacher. "One of the big reasons I quit was sort of intangible," Ingersoll says. "But it's very real: it's just a lack of respect. Teachers in schools do not call the shots. They have very little say. They're told what to do; it's a very disempowered line of work."

It ought to be obvious that the profession—as I've argued, teaching should indeed be a profession—cannot afford to lose its lifeblood. Instead of making it harder to become a teacher but easier to be one, we seem to be doing the exact opposite, to the peril of us all.

WHAT DO TEACHERS ACTUALLY DO?

If teachers are not "the sage on the stage," "the guide on the side," "the coach," or "the explorer," then what exactly are they?

Common complaints from teachers are that they have to be social workers, surrogate parents, counselors, health care providers, nutritionists and more. Crowded classrooms and other factors mean that teachers are often in the role of referee, which is not what they signed up for. Because of school reform's obsession with accountability, teachers have to be ringmasters, whipping their unruly "animals" so they will jump through the hoops of standardized tests (or the hoops of a curriculum that is handed down from on high and designed to be "teacher-proof"). Someone up there still believes that knowledge is something to be poured into children's heads. I am reminded of John W. Gardner's observation: "All too often, we are giving young people cut flowers when we should be teaching them to grow their own plants."

School reform may also be turning teachers into competitors, not teammates in a shared enterprise. If keeping my job depends on my students' test scores, then the incentive to help colleagues improve becomes practically irrelevant.

My own belief is that most teachers would happily be teaching children to "grow their own plants" if their perspectives were valued. In my experience, many of their supervisors do not have much faith in their teachers. I think of the director of professional development in the Washington, D.C., schools who told me in 2007 that in her opinion 80 percent (no, that's not a misprint) of the teachers in the District of Columbia had neither the skills nor the motivation to be successful teachers.

The schools I admire have strong leadership, a balanced curriculum that includes art and music, and (most often) a strong working relationship with families. Inside these schools you find students and teachers who want to be there. In these schools, the principals protect their teachers, enable them to be coaches and explorers, and hold them accountable for results. Learning is a team sport in these special places, as it should be. The adults in these schools recognize that the (paradoxical) goal of this team sport is to produce strong individuals, because—again quoting John Gardner—"the ultimate goal of the educational system is to shift to the individual the burden of pursing his own education. This will not be a widely shared pursuit until we get over our odd conviction that education is what goes on in school buildings and nowhere else."

And we have to get over our odd conviction that teachers are the problem in education. Such an idea is not merely odd; it's downright destructive of a vital profession.

WHY TEACHERS STAY

Feeling Empowered

What keeps teachers in the classroom? Strong leadership from their principal is essential, particularly if he or she recognizes that the principal's job is to enable teachers, not monitor or play "gotcha" with them. A strong learning community recognizes that effective teaching is at various times a team sport and a solitary activity, because teaching is by nature both collaborative and something done individually. It is necessary for teachers, schools, and districts to work together up to a point. But teaching also requires time spent steeping in the material, the evenings of thought and reading, the slightly eccentric lesson.

Solitude and collaboration complement each other, and to neglect either is to drain teaching of its richer matter. Shael Polakow-Suransky, the dynamic president of Bank Street College of Education, believes that teachers must be engaged in authentic learning communities. That is, if they are to be effective teachers, they must also be active learners. As he says:

> When teachers aren't given the chance to think and learn together, when they don't explore students' work together or share their own work with each other, they stop growing.
>
> When teachers stop growing, learning for children becomes an exercise in compliance. But when educators are actively connected to their colleagues they solve problems, they generate new ideas, and they bring that lively and engaged thinking into their classrooms.

In my ideal school, everyone is there by choice: staff, teachers, and children. Of course, that sounds like a private, independent school, but there are free public schools that fit this description. The late John Sanford, a retired army general hired in 1995 to run the Seattle public schools, got quite a few of these "independent public schools of choice" up and running during his time there. He was able to do this because the local NEA affiliate agreed to waive seniority, allowing each school to hire the teachers that best fit its approach. Sanford's system also put a price tag on the cost of educating each child (special needs kids cost more, for example), and whichever school the child's parents chose then got those dollars.[12]

When the money followed the child and schools were able to choose their teachers, learning flourished. Unfortunately, the Seattle experiment faded away after Sanford was diagnosed with leukemia in 1998, but today there are hundreds of teacher-run public schools around the nation.[13] In these schools, collaboration and teamwork blend with respect for individual needs. Because most of the barriers have been removed at these schools, it's possible to be a great teacher.

Yes, it is doable.

Feeling Supported to *Really* Teach

Good leaders keep good teachers in the field, and bad leaders drive them out. It's almost that simple. In forty-one years of reporting about education, I must have visited at least five thousand classrooms and observed an awful lot of really good teaching. My all-time favorite teacher is George from Maine. To me, George embodies the best in the business, because of what he stood for and how he stood his ground when the going got tough. We met at his public high school in the late 1970s. At the principal's recommendation, I sat in on George's ethics class, which was lively and interesting. Afterward we had a cup of coffee at my request, because I wanted to hear his story. Ethics, he told me, was one of a bunch of elective courses that seniors could choose from for their final semester of high school. He had taught it for the first time one year earlier.

Although the principal had already told me the basic outline of George's story, I asked him to tell me what had happened in his class. He agreed. "I set the bar high because it's an ethics class," he said. "I tell the students that I accept only A or B work. Anything else, they get a grade of incomplete. I make it crystal clear to them that they cannot flunk the class—or even pass with a D or a C." He told me that he did this because he wanted them to approach their lives and careers that way.

How did the kids react? "They're seniors, and so a lot of them blow it off, of course," he told me, "but I make them sign a letter of agreement up front. If they won't sign, they can't take the course." He had cleared this approach with the principal, who agreed to support him. Midway through the semester not even half of the kids were doing A or B work, and so he reminded them of the contract they'd signed. He told me he could see their eyes roll.

With a few weeks left, many were still well under the A/B bar. And that's when it got really interesting, he said. When the guidance counselor spotted all those incompletes on the interim reports, she called those students to her office and told them their diplomas were in jeopardy because no one with an incomplete was allowed to graduate.

Panic ensued, he told me. The students came clamoring to his classroom. "Please just flunk me," some kids begged. They told him that they had enough credits to graduate, so an F wouldn't hurt. "Remember the contract," he responded. "No grade of F, D, or C allowed. Go back and do the work," he advised. Now, remember that George had obtained the principal's approval in advance, probably because he anticipated some problems. But he couldn't have imagined what happened next. One student with an incomplete went home and complained to his father, who just happened to be the chair of the school board. That gentleman made an appointment to see George.

He came in, George recalled, with a mix of bluster and unctuousness. "I'm so proud of my son," George remembers him saying. "My boy has been accepted at Colgate, he was voted most likely to succeed, he's interning this summer at the local bank, and he's spending all his time working on his speech for graduation—he was chosen to be class speaker. He's on track to graduate, so why don't you just give him a D? Or even an F, if that would make you feel better?"

"This is an ethics class," George told the father. "And are you certain that's the ethical lesson you want me to teach your son:

that contracts don't matter, that his word doesn't matter, and that all that really matters is who you know?" Chastened, the father went home. The son did the work.

For me, George and his principal became models for the profession: high standards and expectations; clear rules; choices for students; academic performance as the constant, with time the variable; intellectual courage on George's part; and solid leadership from the principal.

Feeling Respected

The best cure for disrespect from others may be increased self-respect. While the school reform movement often disrespects teachers, the profession has been fighting back, with impressive but limited success. In response to the 1983 report *A Nation at Risk*, the National Board for Professional Teaching Standards was created in 1987.[14] It envisioned a voluntary but rigorous process of training and evaluation that would certify those teachers who measured up as outstanding professionals. Board certification would become the gold standard, education's equivalent of the Good Housekeeping Seal of Approval.

Spearheaded by North Carolina governor James B. Hunt Jr., education professor Linda Darling-Hammond, and teachers union president Albert Shanker, and led by former Ford Foundation executive Jim Kelly, the board developed five propositions that define the teaching profession:

Proposition 1: Teachers are committed to students and their learning.

Proposition 2: Teachers know the subjects they teach and how to teach those subjects to students.

Proposition 3: Teachers are responsible for managing and monitoring student learning.

Proposition 4: Teachers think systematically about their practice and learn from experience.

Proposition 5: Teachers are members of learning communities.

Becoming board certified takes time and hard work but usually means a bump in both prestige and pay.[15] Moreover, studies have demonstrated that students taught by board certified teachers are likely to outperform their peers.[16] To date, more than 112,000 teachers, from all fifty states and the District of Columbia, have achieved board certification.

Feeling Appreciated

Teachers help children and youth grow into accomplished adults. The teachers may feel, hope, and believe they're effective, but how often do they hear or see the fruits of their hard work? How often do adults, their former students, reach out to say thank you?

"Two of her public school teachers, to whom she remains close, saw her potential and helped put her on a path that eventually led her to Harvard." This sentence occurs early in Dale Russakoff's remarkable book *The Prize*, which tells the story of Mark Zuckerberg's $100 million donation to Newark's public schools. The line refers to Patricia Chan, who, after becoming the first in her family to attend college, became a pediatrician and later married Zuckerberg. I recommend the book, but first let's dig into that one sentence.

Two things jump out at me. The first is a familiar story: good teachers change their students' lives. The second is less common, I suspect: Chan has remained close to those teachers. I infer that she reached out to express her gratitude and has continued the connection. Bless her for that.

Have you done that? The fact that you are reading this suggests that you care about education and that it worked well enough for you to stay connected to the field. When you close your eyes and picture the teacher(s) who changed your life for the better, who appears in your mind's eye? I see Mrs. Peterson, my first-grade teacher at Hindley School, and two high school English teachers, William Sullivan and Roland McKinley. Mrs. Peterson taught me to read and made me feel safe, and the two men pushed and prodded and encouraged me to aim higher and write more clearly. I was able to say thank you in person to just one of them, Mrs.

Peterson, and will always regret never having expressed my gratitude to Mr. Sullivan and Mr. McKinley. Have you reached out? I promise that, if you do, your gesture will mean the world to the men and women who taught you so effectively.

I know this from personal experience. When I retired from *PBS NewsHour* and Learning Matters in 2015, I received a few hundred emails. While a few said, "About damn time," most comments were gracious. No response surprised me more than a letter—out of the blue—from a former student of mine at Paul D. Schreiber High School in Port Washington, New York, where I taught English in 1964 and 1965, right after graduating from college.

> Dear John (Mr. Merrow),
>
> You were my high school English teacher at Schreiber, and I was your least successful (at the time) student (much later diagnosed with learning disorders), but of all the teachers I've ever had, you made the most indelible impression. You made every book, poem, and story come alive, approaching each one from open angles and creating lots of room for opinion and broad discussion. You taught me how to think, approach challenge, voice opinion, and appreciate others' points of view, not to mention instilling pretty good grammar and spelling skills!

One student caring enough to reach out and recall what happened in our classroom in the 1960s meant as much to me as any of the stuff that came my way during my forty-one years of reporting. Teachers put up with a lot of bashing from all corners. Everyone who appreciates teachers should make an effort, using social media or other suitable means, to reconnect with the teachers who helped shape their lives. Do that, and you will make their day, week, and year, I promise. And if enough of us do this, perhaps we can begin to turn the tide.

Memory Lane

The best teacher I had outside of school and home was a coach for the St. Louis Cardinals. I've been a baseball fan for as long as I can remember, but I've been only a fan, not a player. In my case fan is short for fantasy, *not* fanatic. *As a kid in the 1950s I spent hours being the hero of imaginary baseball games, throwing an old tennis ball against the barn wall and pretending to be Johnny Logan or Red Schoendienst in the field, Eddie Mathews, Hank Aaron, or Stan Musial at bat. In real life, unfortunately, I was pretty awful, invariably one of the last chosen for pickup games and almost always the right fielder. But I had one glorious moment when I was twenty: an accidental invitation to try out for the St. Louis Cardinals, and a brief—very brief—chance to sit in the Pittsburgh Pirates' dugout during a game.*

In 1961, during my year off from Dartmouth, I was working in Kansas as a reporter-photographer for the Leavenworth Times. *I was restless, enthusiastic, and energetic, and I managed to get myself fired in February 1962, largely for being a pain in the neck.*

Jobless, I was free to do whatever I wanted, so I decided to hitchhike around the country. I took to the road, intending to wend my way south, toward warm weather and, more important, spring training.

I had read Jack Kerouac's On the Road *at least twice and was ready for adventures. Carrying only a sleeping bag and a dark blue flight bag with a Pan Am logo on it, I headed for St. Petersburg, Florida, where I knew I'd find the Cardinals, and Bradenton, where the Braves trained. Along the way I found places to sleep where I could: in fraternity houses, in the jail in West Memphis, Arkansas (my choice, not theirs), and under the stars, snug in my sleeping bag.*

Coming into St. Petersburg toward the end of one afternoon, I asked the driver I had hitched a ride with to drop me as close as he could to Al Lang Field. He did so, and I still remember feeling awestruck, standing outside the park.

I walked right in—no guards, no passes, no questions. My awe turned to confusion because dozens of ballplayers were walking off the field, clad in nondescript, ragtag uniforms that looked more high school than major league. Still on the field standing around home plate, however, were several men in full Cardinal uniforms. Later it occurred to me that they must have been comparing notes on the hopefuls who had just tried out, would-be ballplayers who had paid their own way to St. Pete. That explained their uniforms, as well as what happened next.

Suddenly one of the Cardinals, seemingly one of the coaches, spotted me at the edge of the field. At six feet two inches and 185 pounds, I must have looked like another young hopeful. He walked over and said, "You're too late, kid. I'm sorry."

I had no idea what he was talking about and was too intimidated to ask. He must have taken my silence for shyness, and so he put his hand on my shoulder.

"Where'd you come from, kid?" he asked.

"Kansas," I answered truthfully.

His expression grew sadder. "Jeez, I'm real sorry, but we just finished. It's all over."

I didn't say anything, and after another minute he asked me how I'd gotten to St. Pete. I'd hitched, I told him.

"What position you play?"

"Right field," I answered truthfully, "and third base," I added, not so truthfully—my favorite player, Eddie Mathews, was a third baseman.

"You look like you can hit the long ball," he said. That didn't seem to be a question but an assumption suggested by my athletic build. I wasn't about to tell him the truth.

After another silence, he smiled. "Tell you what, kid," he said. "We've got a game tomorrow with the Pirates. You come here a couple of hours early, and I'll let you hit a few. See what you can do. Whaddya say?"

I was stunned. He was mistaking me for a ballplayer, and he thought I had major league potential! I thanked him and left in a daze. I had just been invited, sort of, to try out for the St. Louis Cardinals. A genuine major league coach had looked at me and concluded that I might be a long-ball hitter! For a few minutes I was eleven or twelve again, in a coiled batting stance like Stan the Man, hitting against Lou Burdette or Warren Spahn.

Slowly I came back down to earth. Not only was I not a major league prospect, I was in a strange city. It was dusk, and I had no place to sleep.

I hitchhiked to Florida Presbyterian (now Eckerd College) and met some guys who agreed to let me crash on the couch in their apartment. At dinner we all laughed at the prospect of my actually trying out the next day— wouldn't it be funny if I held the bat by the wrong end or threw the ball underhand? In fact, I had no intention of embarrassing myself by going through with the charade. But we all decided to watch the Cardinals-Pirates game anyway.

Spring training was relaxed and informal in 1962, not the cash cow it is today. The elderly man taking tickets glanced at my old press card and let me in. He didn't seem to notice when I handed the card back to the next guy, who used it and handed it back to the next guy, until all six of us were in. We sat in the sun for a few innings, but I was feeling cocky and wanted more excitement. I went back to the field entrance and stood near the Pirates' dugout, watching the game and stealing glances into the dugout at more of my heroes. While I was there one of the Pirates left the dugout, crossed in front of me, and went under the stands. He lit a cigarette, and when he took off his cap I saw his nearly bald head and realized that he was Dick Groat, one of the best shortstops in baseball.

I walked over to him and asked for a cigarette. He gave me one, and I told him about my invitation to try out for the Cardinals. Groat was amused, probably because I made fun of that Cardinal coach for having been taken in by my appearance. When he had finished his cigarette, he asked me to tell the story to some of the guys in the dugout. A minute later I found myself sitting on the bench. Bill Mazeroski was there, and so was Roberto Clemente, and I hoped my new college friends could see me. Groat told me to tell the guys my story. I started to, but I never got the chance to finish.

"Who the fuck is that?" a loud, gravelly voice demanded. "Get him the fuck out of here!" It was the tough-talking, cigar-smoking manager of the Pirates, Danny Murtaugh.

I waited for Groat or someone else to speak on my behalf, but no one did. Murtaugh advanced, glowering at me, but then dismissed me with a derisive wave. "Get your ass out of here. This is the big leagues."

I left, but not before hearing Murtaugh say, "What are you clowns up to? If you guys want to win, then pay attention. That kid doesn't even look like a ball player."

Every story should have a hero, the person who teaches an indispensable lesson. It took me a long time to figure out who the hero was. It wasn't Groat, Mazeroski, or any of the other Pirates I'd sat with during my brief major league career. No, the hero was that Cardinal coach. I doubt that he'd seen major league potential in me; instead, he saw a kid with big dreams, and he wasn't going to break my heart simply because I was a few hours late.

I wish now that I knew who he was . . . and that it hadn't taken me so long to appreciate his gesture.

The Chance to Learn

Collaborative learning is at the core of good teaching. One study by Ronald Gallimore found that when teachers in high poverty schools in Los Angeles were given about 150 minutes per month to meet, student learning improved significantly. However, simply providing the time to meet three times a month was not enough. The study identified five keys to effective grade-level learning teams:

- Job-alike teams of three to seven teachers who teach the same grade level, course, or subject. When they shared, they collaborated more effectively.

- Published protocols that guide—but do not prescribe—the teaching team's improvement efforts. A how-to guide that does not say "you must do X" proved to be persuasive.
- Trained peer facilitators to guide their colleagues. Because peer facilitators try out in their classrooms the same lessons as everyone else, they are credibly positioned to model intellectual curiosity, frame the work as an investigation, explain protocol steps, and encourage the group to stick with a problem until it is solved.
- Stability. The same place, compatible colleagues, and enough time combine to raise the comfort level of participating teachers. Teacher teams need at least three hours each month dedicated to instructional inquiry and improvement, while facilitators need about two hours each month to plan ongoing assistance and leadership for teacher teams.
- Perseverance. Whatever goals the teacher learning teams choose, it's critical that they stick with them until their students make progress. Once they saw tangible student gains, teachers were less likely to make an assumption such as "I planned and taught the lesson, but they didn't get it," and more likely to adopt a productive assumption such as "You haven't taught until they've learned."

Memory Lane

Phylicia Rashad was the spark that set us off. The talented actress was traveling around with her favorite high school teacher, a tiny woman who taught Phylicia and her sister, Debbie Allen, in Houston, Texas. After listening to them, I suggested that we create a series about the influential teachers behind famous, accomplished Americans.

"We" was just three of us, John Tulenko, Karena O'Riordan,

and me, and none of us knew any famous people. But we were resourceful. Bill Clinton was campaigning for president in New York the next day, and John went to the rope line with a plan: he wasn't going to let go of Clinton's hand until the candidate gave him the name of his most important teacher. It worked! Soon I was on my way to Arkansas to interview Paul Root, Clinton's high school history teacher, who had since become a university professor.

My older sister had been best friends with the woman who married a brother of President George H.W. Bush. I got her name and number from my sister, called her, and asked her to ask her brother-in-law who his favorite teacher was. Within a week or so, Jodie Bush gave me the name and address of a ninety-year-old retired teacher. We called him and headed for Maine the next day.

At an awards banquet in Chicago that month I found myself sitting next to Edward James Olmos, the brilliant actor who should have received an Academy Award for his performance in Stand and Deliver. *Eddie gave me the name and address of the man who he said had changed his life. That meant a trip to California.*

Around that time I gave a speech in Washington, D.C. The Reverend Jesse Jackson was in the audience, which I learned after the speech when I went to find my wife and discovered the Reverend Jackson sitting next to her. "Great speech," he said.

"What teacher had the most impact on your life?" I replied.

We talked at some length about that teacher, and in fact Jackson later incorporated her story into some of his speeches. Soon I was on my way to South Carolina, where Jackson had grown up. And not long after that I went to Houston to interview Rashad's teacher.

These teachers—women and men, black and white, elementary, junior high, high school, and college—had one thing in common: they had not allowed their young students to do substandard work! Their goals for their students were higher than the kids' own goals, and those higher expectations won out.[17] That was also my experience as a student. I had two high school English teachers who simply would not settle for second-class work from me, because they believed I had some talent.

Whenever I've told this story, every listener has responded with a story about the teacher who looked at him or her and saw not a shapeless lump but a gem to be polished . . . and then made sure the gem did most of the polishing.

SOME ADVICE FOR NEW TEACHERS

Because I spent forty-five years in classrooms (forty-one as a reporter, four as a teacher), I am occasionally asked if I have any advice for new teachers. I do.

First of all, I do *not* say, "Don't smile until Christmas," because that's just plain stupid. Smiles are good. Nor do I say, "Remember that you are their teacher and not their friend," because that equally stupid cliché implies the roles are incompatible. You are teachers first, of course, but friendships sometimes follow, and that's good.

My advice to new teachers has everything to do with their relationships with their new colleagues, the veteran teachers in their school. "Figure out which teachers are generally recognized as being at the top of their profession and seek them out," I say. "Ask them if you can come to them for help when you screw up—because you will screw up, and more than once.

"Then go an extra step," I advise. "Ask those same veterans if they will let you sit in the back of their class during your free period, so you can watch and learn." (Left unsaid is that there's a lot to learn.)

This may be hard advice for some Teach for America corps members to follow, because some of them arrive at their new school on a mission, determined to save the students. But whom do these young idealists think they are saving the kids *from*? While it's not necessarily spoken aloud, the bad guys in that scenario are the veteran teachers and administrators who, by this logic, have not been helping the kids all these years. (And sometimes this savior complex includes stereotypical ideas about the families and communities of their students—also a harmful, dangerous frame of mind.)

Veteran teachers can be your allies. Make the best among them your mentors. You may have to take the first step, because there's now a long history of resentment between (some) rookies and (some) veterans. I always suggest that new teachers take that step, because they have a lot to learn, and—trust me—they won't learn it from other rookies. For those who really want the help, this is the fastest and most reliable pathway.

Memory Lane

I know from experience that teaching is work. In addition to spending forty-one years in the back of classrooms, I was a teacher: in high school for two years, in a black college for two years, in a federal penitentiary for two years, at Harvard as a teaching assistant for one year, and in junior high school for one summer.

But my teaching days ended in the 1970s, and over the next twenty-five years or so, the mantra "Teaching is hard" had become an abstract notion, something I recited but didn't feel in my gut.

That changed one afternoon in 1998 or 1999 in a middle school in Philadelphia, when I volunteered to take over a class of seventh graders . . . and got eaten alive! We were making a documentary about Superintendent David Hornbeck, a devoted and idealistic former minister who was determined to change the public schools.[18] On this day we wanted to see him with teachers, up close and personal. The particular classroom we chose was huge, an open space that housed two classes of seventh graders. I had the brilliant idea of filming Hornbeck talking with both teachers in front of one of the classes. To make that happen, someone needed to take over the other teacher's class, so she could be with the superintendent.

Who better than me, an experienced former teacher? Piece of cake, I thought. After all, it was an English class, and I had been an English teacher. Although I didn't have a lesson plan or a plan of any kind, I was confident I could wing it successfully. The teacher seemed dubious but eventually agreed; after all, she would be in the same room and able to monitor my progress (or lack thereof).

I don't remember much about what I said, but I think I asked the class to tell me what they had been working on. Some of them used the opportunity to diss the teacher and the school, reporting that they weren't doing anything. As I recall, some of the kids began a kind of competition to see who could be the most critical, calling out and getting louder and louder. I tried desperately to quiet them down, using reason. That doesn't work with adolescents who detect the scent of inexperience . . . and maybe panic. I should have taken charge, raised my voice, and said "That's enough! Everyone quiet!" But I didn't do that, perhaps because that would have told the world that I was losing control.

Of course, the rising noise level also sent that message across the room, and the teacher came hustling back. She raised her voice and got the situation under control. Thoroughly chastened, I went back to where I belonged, behind the camera.

Lesson relearned: Teaching is hard work that requires skill, preparation, empathy, a sense of humor, and commitment. I wish those who devote energy to dissing the profession would spend a week teaching. Many, perhaps most, would not survive. It certainly would be illuminating to hear what they'd have to say then.

PRUNING TEACHER TRAINING

"If half of the 1,450 places that train teachers went out of business tomorrow, we'd be better off." The Harvard professor paused. "And, with very few exceptions, it wouldn't matter which half."

His is a widely held view of teacher education: too many institutions doing a lousy job. Most teachers I've met over the years weren't happy with, or proud of, their training, which, they said, didn't prepare them for the real world of teaching.

And so the question is, how do we put half of those institutions out of business?

The federal government thinks that tighter regulation is the answer. After all, cars that come out of an automobile plant can be monitored for quality and dependability, thus allowing judgments about the plant. That's the heart of the regulations issued by the U.S. Department of Education in October 2016: monitor the standardized test scores of students and analyze the institutions their teachers graduated from. Over time, the logic goes, we'll discover that teachers from Teacher Tech or Acme State Teachers College generally don't move the needle on test scores. Eventually those institutions will lose access to federal money and be forced out of business. Problem solved!

Education secretary John B. King Jr. announced the new regulations this way:

> As a nation, there is so much more we can do to help prepare our teachers and create a diverse educator workforce. Prospective teachers need good information to select the right program; school districts need access to the best trained professionals for every opening in every school; and preparation programs need feedback about their graduates' experiences in schools to refine their programs. These regulations will help strengthen teacher preparation so that prospective teachers get off to the best start they can, and preparation programs can meet the needs of students and schools for great educators.

Work on the regulations began in 2011 and reflect former Secretary Arne Duncan's views. "The system we have for training teachers lacks rigor, is out of step with the times, and is given to extreme grade inflation that leaves teachers unprepared and their future students at risk," he wrote in an open letter to the deans of schools of education just before the regulations were issued.

Naturally, some see the department's actions as a continuation of Duncan's discredited "test and punish" approach to teachers. "It is, quite simply, ludicrous to propose evaluating teacher preparation programs based on the performance of the students taught by a program's graduates," American Federation of Teachers president Randi Weingarten said, adding, "It's stunning that the department would evaluate teaching colleges based

on the academic performance of the students of their graduates when ESSA [the Every Student Succeeds Act]—enacted by
large bipartisan majorities in both the House and Senate last
December—prohibited the department from requiring school
districts to do that kind of teacher evaluation."

It's a classic Democratic approach to problem-solving: regulate, regulate, regulate. But the flaw here isn't regulations per se.
Unfortunately, the administration is not attacking the problem,
which is teaching itself, not teacher training.[19]

Even if half of the 1,450 training programs are mediocre or
worse, the *reason* we have that many is the excessive churn in the
field, and churn exists because teaching has become a crummy job.
Teachers leave and have to be replaced, and those replacements
have to be trained somewhere. Because our schools have an annual
churn rate of 8 percent, schools are constantly hiring. Churn creates the market for training institutions. Improve the profession
(higher pay at the outset, more opportunities for collegiality and
cooperation, a greater say in curriculum, and a serious role in the
assessment of students), and the exodus would slow down.

Strengthen training, increase starting pay, and improve working conditions, and teaching might attract more of the so-called
best and brightest. Right now, as noted earlier, it's having trouble
attracting anyone. According to the Learning Policy Institute,
"Between 2009 and 2014, the most recent years of data available,
teacher education enrollments dropped from 691,000 to 451,000,
a 35% reduction. This amounts to a decrease of almost 240,000
professionals on their way to the classroom in the year 2014, as
compared to 2009."

That is the market at work—just not in the way we would like.
Aware of the so-called war on teachers conducted by the administration and the school reform crowd, young people are making
the rational decision to choose other lines of work. However, if
we act to improve the lives of teachers, the market will work. And
if we allow the market to end the constant churn, the need for
more than 1,400 training institutions will evaporate. Programs
would have to compete for students, and many—maybe even
half—would not survive.

Based on what hundreds of teachers told me, most teacher training is neither intellectually challenging nor particularly effective, even though most students earn A's.[20] One forty-year-old career changer told me about his experience at the California institution that trains about 10 percent of the state's teachers:

> The quality of my education in the credential program was dismal. I had just two classes that were led by professors who genuinely added value to my education as a future teacher. The vast majority of other professors were simply collecting a paycheck to add to their own teacher retirement income. More than a few were truly terrible educators and would conduct class with little or no preparation.
>
> The upside to a dismal credential program was that I could work full-time while carrying a full class load, even when I was student teaching. The secret was to just buy narration software, because papers were graded primarily on word count, not content. My advisor for student teaching actually told me that "I have a check list, and as you turn in papers I check them off and put them in this folder."
>
> There is almost no bar to jump over to get into the credential program. You can have a terrible GPA and still get in, just pass the California Basic Educational Skills Test (CBEST).[21] They will take anyone with a BA.

One story is not proof, of course. But what he wrote echoes what veteran teachers often say: because their training was virtually useless, they had to learn to teach on the job or by emulating what they had experienced as students in elementary and high school. Their teacher education program was their ticket-punch, and little more.[22]

We need to raise the bar for entry into the field *and* at the same time make it easier for teachers to succeed. The Obama administration's attempt in its final days to influence teaching and learning is classic school reform stuff. School reformers worship at the altar of test scores, an attitude that grows out of an unwillingness to face the real issues in education—and in society. While it may be well-meaning, it's misguided and, at the end of the day, harmful.

I want to end this step with three tough and very specific questions.

1. *Can teacher training at your local colleges and universities be improved?* It's already happening in a few places. At Arizona State University, would-be teachers spend most of their time in actual public school classrooms (the so-called clinical approach) instead of always being lectured to by college professors. Dean Mari Koerner told me that her new and more demanding curriculum has led some undergraduates to change to another major. "Good riddance" was her private reaction.

Losing a few students who were looking for an easy major is fine, but what happens if a sizable number of students leave, or if many fewer choose the education major because it's too tough? Major changes in enrollment would cause serious economic disruption, which is when that particular rubber would meet the road. And because preparing teachers is a profit center for many universities, which spend far less on training them than they do on preparing lawyers, doctors, and nurses, for example, do not expect strong support for major changes from higher education generally.

We have to raise the bar for entry into teaching. Should schools of education insist on higher test scores? According to the College Board, high school graduates who intended to major in education scored in the bottom third on their SATs, with a combined math and reading score that was 57 points below the national average. However, relying on standardized test scores, given what is known about their unfairness as a measure, would be hypocritical and shortsighted.

Making the job more attractive is the essential first step. We won't be out of the woods until we change aspects of the teacher's job that are belittling and sometimes humiliating.

Teachers can't make or take a phone call when they need to, or answer the call of nature. Rarely do they get to watch their colleagues at work and then share reactions and ideas, which is something most professionals take for granted. All that has to change.

2. *Can your teachers union abandon the trade union model and become a professional union?* In a transformed school district, teachers will have real power over the curriculum and their working conditions. They will be involved in how results are measured, as detailed in Step Eleven.

But book-length union contracts that spell out every move have no place in this new approach. There's been some progress on this. Union leaders have publicly stated that they could craft a slim contract of six to ten pages that lays out essential provisions: due process, some say in hiring, a role in evaluation, a role in developing curriculum and assessments, and other professional issues. As AFT president Randi Weingarten once told me, "There's no need to specify how late a teacher can get there in the morning and how early she can leave in the afternoon." However, writing a model contract may turn out to be the easy part. Who then persuades powerful local unions such as New York City's United Federation of Teachers or the Philadelphia Federation of Teachers to cede power?

3. *Can teacher pay in your district be restructured?* Money talks! If we are going to improve preparation and want to attract more highly-qualified people in teaching, then we have to put our money where our mouths are.

Changing the pay structure is inevitable. It's impossible to argue with a straight face that a teacher's pay should be determined simply by years on the job and graduate credits. Unfortunately, many states, prompted by incentives from the U.S. Department of Education, have adopted statewide approaches that tie student achievement to salaries—also a terrible idea. It can mean even more testing. After all, how will a district set the pay scale for the physical education, art, music, and social studies teachers without testing their students? American students are already the most tested in the world. If teachers' salaries are going to be based on their students' scores, then the so-called best and brightest might just want to teach in Greenwich, Connecticut, instead of the South Bronx in New York City, or in Palo Alto, California, instead of East Palo Alto. Or they might devote even more time to teaching kids how to take tests. Some of them might figure out ways to (wink wink) make sure their kids do well on those tests.

A better idea is to restructure salaries *upward* at the outset—that is, pay new teachers more. A beginning teacher earns a national average starting salary of $30,377, according to the National Association of Colleges and Employers. That compares with $43,635 for computer programmers, $44,668 for accountants, and $45,570 for registered nurses. If starting salaries were higher and the pension system was modernized, teaching would become a more attractive career possibility.

Addressing these tough questions is essential. You don't have to come to closure before moving on, but you have to agree to come to the table and start serious conversations.

STEP ELEVEN
Measure What Matters

Predictably, our addiction to school reform is most visible every spring, during testing season. That's when learning and teaching stop in most schools and test prep begins in earnest. In some schools, as I will explain, it's test prep pretty much all year long. School reform's supporters are obsessed with measurement and testing rules.[1] Districts spend tens of billions of dollars a year buying, preparing for, administering, and grading standardized tests.[2]

That obsessive focus must be overthrown, as I will argue. But even if you are convinced that our current system of measuring achievement is doing far more harm than good, we still have to find better ways of measuring learning. Assessments are necessary to evaluate students and help them learn, as well as to help make judgments about schools and the adults in them.

The maxim "Measure what matters," which could easily be added to my developing line of bumper stickers, is unambiguous: figure out what we care about in education, and develop ways of measuring those skills. Right now most school systems do pretty much the opposite, valuing what's easy (and inexpensive) to measure. A more cynical but defensible interpretation holds that because the school reform crowd endorses and supports "test and punish," with teachers as the target, cheap tests are just fine for that purpose. This policy has poisoned learning by turning it into a "gotcha" game.

A healthier approach calls for "assess to improve," with assessment as a tool to help both students and teachers get better. The contrast between "assess to improve" and "test and punish" could not be more stark.

Whenever anyone talks seriously about changing schools, the elephant in the room is academic achievement: how will we measure academic progress if we abandon these tests, which almost everyone hates? Academic learning must not be understood as the only goal, but its importance cannot be overlooked or dismissed. Yes, the unwarranted emphasis most schools put on costly and time-consuming standardized testing distorts the process of teaching and learning in schools, but the public and parents have the right to know what students are learning. We must have measures of learning—that is, tests—but they must be valid, reliable measures of genuine learning.[3]

The multiple-choice questions on standardized, machine-scored tests are not designed to measure diligence, honesty, tolerance, fairness, and compassion, which are the values and attitudes that parents repeatedly say they want their children to possess. Parents want their kids to be well rounded; to develop the skills they need to continue learning on their own; and to become good citizens, productive workers, and fulfilled human beings. Most employers would probably agree. But how do schools assess those skills and abilities?

The argument of this chapter is that a new system that asks how each child is intelligent must determine what matters most and then—and only then—develop measures to assess progress toward those outcomes. Or, as some advocates express it, measure what we value, instead of valuing what we measure.

TOO MUCH MONEY . . . AND TOO LITTLE

Paradoxically, we spend too much money overall and too little on testing and assessment. Basically, we buy lots of cheap tests and administer them to every student in grades 3 through 10, and sometimes in the grades above and below those. The bill for this comes to tens of billions of dollars a year, according to

FairTest. How much varies widely from state to state. "We find that the 45 states from which we obtained data spend a combined $669 million per year on their primary assessment contracts, or $27 per pupil in grades 3-9, with six testing vendors accounting for 89 percent of this total. Per pupil spending varies significantly across states, with Oregon ($13 per student), Georgia ($14), and California ($16) among the lowest-spending states, and Massachusetts ($64), Delaware ($73), and Hawaii ($105) among the highest spending," wrote Matthew Chingos in a 2012 report.[4]

But to put the highest number, Hawaii's $105, in perspective, consider how much you might spend having your car "assessed" every year. I drive a 2002 Toyota 4Runner (which I bought used in 2010 for $12,000), and the annual tune-up costs about $200. Ironically, I bought the car in California, which spends $16 per child on state assessments—just *8 percent* of what I spend assessing my car's condition!

Testing companies must be laughing all the way to the bank, because they know that there's no good reason to test every child every year. Sampling works in education just as it works in politics and marketing, and school districts could save billions by testing stratified random samples of students every year, then perhaps testing all children every three or four years. Teacher judgments are reliable and valid, and we used to trust them; now we no longer do (another consequence of our addiction to school reform). If we can learn to trust sampling and spend our money on good assessments, we would have better data, teachers and students would have more time for learning, and our students would no longer be the most-tested kids in the world.

QUESTIONABLE QUESTIONS

Experiencing the vapidity of some test questions may help you grasp the problems with testing and understand why American students score lower than their counterparts in most other advanced nations. The first sample problem was offered by the University of Wisconsin–Oshkosh to high school math teachers and was designed to help "close the math achievement gap."

Jack shot a deer that weighed 321 pounds. Tom shot a deer that weighed 289 pounds. How much more did Jack's deer weigh than Tom's deer?

Basic subtraction for high school students?

My second example comes from TeacherVision, part of Pearson, the giant testing company:

Linda is paddling upstream in a canoe. She can travel 2 miles upstream in 45 minutes. After this strenuous exercise she must rest for 15 minutes. While she is resting, the canoe floats downstream ½ mile. How long will it take Linda to travel 8 miles upstream in this manner?

This question's premise is questionable. Will some students be distracted by Linda's cluelessness? Won't they ask themselves how long it will take her to figure out that she should grab hold of a branch while she's resting in order to keep from floating back down the river? What's the not-so-subtle subtext? That girls don't belong in canoes? That girls are dumb?

I found my third sample question on a high school math test in Oregon:

There are 6 snakes in a certain valley. The population doubles every year. In how many years will there be 96 snakes?

a.   2
b.   3
c.   4
d.   8

These three high school math problems require simple numeracy at most. With enough practice—note I did not say critical thinking—just about anyone can solve undemanding problems like these and consequently feel confident of their ability.

School is supposed to be preparation for life, but spending time on problems like these three is like trying to become an excellent basketball player by shooting free throws all day long. To be good at basketball, players must work on all aspects of the game: jump shots, dribbling, throwing chest and bounce passes, positioning for rebounds, running the pick-and-roll, and, occasionally, practicing free throws.

Both basketball and life are about rhythm and motion, teamwork and individual play, offense and defense. Like life, the pace of the game can slow down or become frenetic. Basketball requires thinking fast, shifting roles, and having your teammates' backs. Successful players know when to shoot and when to pass. As in life, failure is part of the game. Even the greatest players miss more than half of their shots, and some (even Michael Jordan!) are cut from their high school teams. And life doesn't give us many free throw opportunities. If school is supposed to be preparation for life, why are American high school students being asked to count on their fingers? This sort of trivial work is the educational equivalent of shooting free throws.

My fourth example is a Common Core National Standards question for eighth graders in New York State. Keep in mind that the Common Core is supposed to introduce "much-needed rigor" to the curriculum.

> Triangle ABC was rotated 90° clockwise. Then it underwent a dilation centered at the origin with a scale factor of 4. Triangle A'B'C' is the resulting image. What parts of A'B'C' are congruent to the corresponding parts of the original triangle? Explain your reasoning.

This problem represents the brave new world of education's Common Core, national standards adopted at one point by nearly every state and the District of Columbia.[5] This new approach exposes students to higher and more rigorous standards. The hope is that the curriculum will challenge and engage students. Reading that prose, are you feeling engaged? Imagine how eighth graders might feel. If the first three problems are the educational equivalent of practicing free throws, then solving problems like this one is akin to spending basketball practice taking trick shots, like hook shots from midcourt—yet another way *not* to become good at the sport.

If schools stick with undemanding curricula and boring questions, our kids will be stuck at the free throw line, practicing something they will rarely be called upon to do in real life. If (under the flag of greater rigor) we ditch those boring questions in favor of triangles and other lifeless questions, schools will turn off the very kids they are trying to reach: the 99 percent who are not destined to become mathematicians.

My fifth example was given to fifteen-year-olds around the world on a test known as PISA (Programme in International Student Assessment):

> Mount Fuji is a famous dormant volcano in Japan. The Gotemba walking trail up Mount Fuji is about 9 kilometers (km) long. Walkers need to return from the 18 km walk by 8 P.M.
>
> Toshi estimates that he can walk up the mountain at 1.5 kilometers per hour on average, and down at twice that speed. These speeds take into account meal breaks and rest times.
>
> Using Toshi's estimated speeds, what is the latest time he can begin his walk so that he can return by 8 P.M.?

Note that this is not a multiple-choice question. To get the correct answer, students had to perform a number of calculations. The correct answer (11 A.M.) was provided by 55 percent of the Shanghai fifteen-year-olds but just 9 percent of the U.S. students.

Ironically, the PISA results revealed that American kids score high in confidence in mathematical ability, despite underperforming their peers in most other countries. I wonder if their misplaced confidence is the result of too many problems like the one about the snakes.

In addition to being more challenging, PISA and other international tests are given to a carefully drawn sample of students.

Administering standardized tests to every student in grades 3 through 8 plus grade 10—which is what current U.S. laws require—is unnecessary and wasteful.[6] Ask yourself who benefits when schools test all kids. Not students, not teachers, and not the general public.

THE ROOTS OF THIS MESS

The current mess didn't just happen. No evil geniuses woke up one morning and schemed to create a flood of machine-scored tests, days and days of test prep (especially for poor kids), and a "test and punish" approach to evaluating teachers. No, we earned our way here. For years teachers were evaluated on the logic of their lesson plans and their manner in class—whether they kept the kids in line, had command of the material, and had lesson plans written out neatly and carefully.

Evaluations occurred once or twice a year, scheduled in advance. Some union contracts even spelled out when and under what circumstances an administrator could enter a teacher's classroom. Savvy teachers kept their special observation-day lesson plan, with all the bells and whistles, ready in a desk drawer. Some teachers gleefully told me that they enlisted their students in a "conspiracy" to dupe the principal. How students performed—how much they learned—was not part of the formula in most public schools. Many state systems did not hold schools accountable, as was clear when National Assessment of Educational Progress (NAEP) results were matched up with performance on state-administered tests.[7] Frustration with this indefensible way of doing business got us into the hole we are in now. I do not advocate for going back to the bad old days.

In the future, however, I believe the focus of our evaluation should be *the school*, followed by students and teachers. Focusing on student achievement first has produced a test-obsessed culture, widespread cheating, and a narrow curriculum. Focusing on teachers—using student test scores to punish and reward—is the worst education policy decision I've observed in my career.

Even the much-criticized No Child Left Behind legislation

got this right. Its fundamental unit of evaluation was the school, which might ultimately be singled out for failing to make "adequate yearly progress" and labeled as "failing" based on the performance of all subgroups in the school.[8] Eventually that morphed into what's now often called "test and punish" and then into blaming teachers, which hit its peak under Race to the Top. Regular people, especially parents, get that schools come first. When they talk about education, they want to know, "Are the schools good?" We can answer that question with a set of multiple measures, not simply by looking at student test scores.

TEACHERS KNOW WHAT'S GOING DOWN

Teachers are well aware that the systems they work in are obsessed with testing. What's more, they are not happy about it. It's worth citing in detail the findings of a 2016 survey of teachers, "Listen to Us: Teacher Views and Voices."[9] On the issue of time devoted to testing, consider these four findings:

- An estimated 37 percent of teachers indicated that they spend one week or less out of the school year preparing students for district-mandated tests, while about 26 percent reported spending more than a month on these activities. For state-mandated tests, 30 percent of teachers estimated devoting less than a week to test prep, and 29 percent estimated spending more than a month. A greater share of teachers in high- and medium-poverty schools than in low-poverty schools reported spending more than a month on test-prep activities for district and state tests.
- A majority of teachers believe they spend too much time preparing students for state-mandated tests (62 percent) and district-mandated tests (51 percent). Very few teachers believed they spent too little time preparing students for district and/or state-mandated tests.
- An overwhelming majority of teachers (81 percent)

believe students spend too much time taking district-
and/or state-mandated tests.
- Many teachers would prefer to cut the frequency and
  length of state- and district-mandated tests rather than
  eliminate them altogether.

Not surprisingly, the students who are worst off economically
spend more time being drilled.[10] High- and medium-poverty
schools spend more than a month on test prep. That's one-eighth
of the school year, but since it all comes at once, it must seem
like an eternity to students and teachers. The sage E.D. Hirsch
Jr. once said to me, "If we want kids to do well on reading tests,
they should be reading, not practicing taking reading tests." Most
teachers know what's going on, but top-down school reform rarely if ever listens to teachers.

MULTIPLE MEASURES

Let's change gears for a minute. Picture the presidents of the
National Education Association and the American Federation of
Teachers, the U.S. secretary of education, and the leaders of the
House and Senate education committees sitting around my dining room table. What are these men and women doing? They
are playing my new parlor game, Multiple Measures.[11] The title
of the game comes from the phrase everybody uses when they're
talking about the most reliable way of evaluating schools, teachers, and students. After all, anybody who knows anything about
education understands that a single measure (i.e., a score on a
standardized test) cannot accurately capture the complexity of
learning. Unfortunately, the conversation usually stops with that
overused phrase, "multiple measures," and most states and school
districts continue to rely heavily on *one* measure: scores on standardized tests.

My game will allow us to get beyond the talk. Get a pile of
index cards. Then invite a few people from differing political
camps who are solution-oriented, or at least willing to engage
in dialogue, to have a cup of coffee and play Multiple Measures.

Distribute pencils and index cards to those education leaders and explain that the challenge is to write *specific* measures on the back of the index cards. Each person must identify three measures. Then put the cards facedown in the middle of the table and mix them up. Finally, turn them over and discuss the measures that have been offered.

With that awesome quintet of union and political leaders mentioned earlier, the specific measures might include test scores, teacher attendance, chronic student absence, participation in Advanced Placement classes, extent of project-based learning, years required to gain tenure, teacher turnover, and who knows what else. A few measures would most likely appear on more than one index card.

Now repeat the process: more cards, turn over, discuss. The rule is that they must keep playing until they have reached agreement on at least five specific measures. (Another vital rule: no shouting!)

The principle behind the game echoes the goal I set forth at the outset of Step Eleven: it's time for us to measure what we value, instead of our current practice of valuing what's easy to measure.

The goals of the game are threefold: general agreement on multiple ways of assessing schooling, a lowered temperature, and a commitment to work together for the benefit of children and society. If these powerful people with competing interests really did sit down to play my game, their focus would shift from measures to goals. Imagine reaching a consensus on the goals of schooling!

But I don't want anyone to think that I am suggesting that these five people, or any small group, should decide what matters when it comes to educating children. What if everyone reading this arranged a game of Multiple Measures in their communities, taking steps to include people from the left, right, and center, men and women, and people of varying ages, races and occupations? It might just break the logjam and chip away at the walls we've built up in our polarized society.

Agreeing on the measures is a big step—but only a first step, because the game's goal is not "gotcha" but making systems better. For example, if teacher attendance is chosen as one of the measures and a particular school scores badly on that metric, the reaction ought to be "Why?" and not "Gotcha!" because the absences could be a symptom of larger problems.

This is not hypothetical, because teacher attendance is a serious problem in many places, particularly in urban schools. As the *Chicago Tribune* reported in November 2016:

> Across the state, 23.5 percent of public school teachers are absent more than 10 days in the school year. That's almost 1 in 4 teachers statewide who aren't in the classroom, according to data made public by the state for the first time in the annual Illinois Report Card, a compilation of data that paints a broad picture of schools. . . . In Chicago Public Schools, teacher absenteeism ranged from a high of about 82 percent of teachers absent more than 10 days to no teachers absent more than 10 days. The district average was 27.5 percent, just above the state average.[12]

Near Chicago, the numbers were also staggering: "North Cook County's Glenview School District 34 showed high absenteeism rates, ranging from about 57 to 83 percent across district schools. That's more than double or triple the state average." The schools with the best attendance rates had the fewest low-income students and the most white students. Again, bear in mind that outcomes like this are symptoms, revealing deeper problems that must be addressed. Punishing these teachers for their absenteeism won't solve the problem.

We know that far too many charter schools are failing to educate their students, generally because the adults in charge at the decision-making level are obsessed with test scores. We also realize that both the for-profit and nonprofit charter sectors include a fair number of money-grubbing operators.[13] Our schools, traditional and charter, test and test and test, but today there are clear signs (particularly the opt-out movement; more on this later) that a critical mass of disgruntled parents and local educators has developed. More people seem to understand that, to close the achievement gap, we must attend to three factors: opportunity, expectations, and leadership (discussed in the next section).[14] But who's willing to play Multiple Measures as the icebreaker to get us to focus on what we value and what we want for our children?

BLATHERING ABOUT THE "ACHIEVEMENT GAP"

Those obsessed with school reform who go on and on about the "achievement gap" are ignoring the real truth that our society has *four* education gaps: opportunity, expectations, leadership, and outcomes.[15]

1. Ours is a land of unequal educational opportunity. The opportunity gap in education is a sad fact.
2. Too many adults have low expectations for some students, particularly students of color or those from low-income families.
3. We also have a leadership gap, born of trivial quarrels among leaders who should be encouraging public dialogue about the purposes of schooling: what we want our children to be able to do, how they can learn those skills, and how those skills can be measured fairly and accurately.
4. The widely publicized outcomes gap—that is, the famed achievement gap—is the inevitable consequence of the first three gaps in opportunity, expectations, and leadership. Focusing almost exclusively on outcomes is counterproductive and is largely responsible for the intimidating task now before us.

Imagine if we discussed the achievement gap in different terms: *In math, Asian Americans outperform whites by more than 15 points. We have to something about that to close the Asian-white achievement gap. So let's eliminate recess, physical education, art, and music for middle- and upper-middle-class white kids and substitute drilling and more drilling until they catch up.* Just imagine the reaction in suburban white America! But replacing recess with drill, eliminating "frills" such as the arts, and turning kindergarten into teaching and testing time is what we're doing to poor nonwhite kids.

"TEST AND PUNISH"

To many in education, testing *students* in order to evaluate, reward, and punish *teachers* is a deeply flawed strategy. For one thing, in any given year half of students are not in the grades being tested that year. For another, beyond the basic subjects in which testing is done, students are studying subjects that aren't tested. However, this approach requires that *all* teachers be evaluated by test scores. And so, bending logic beyond recognition, some teachers are being judged by the scores of students they've never taught! If there's no standardized test for, say, music, then music might as well be dropped from the curriculum. Testing kids in every subject—including art and music—just so their teachers can be rated may strike you as an idiotic notion, but it's the logical outgrowth of federal policy that was developed and enforced during the Obama administration.

Focus on students, argues the president of the National Education Association. Lily Eskelsen Garcia rejects the idea that success is a test score. She believes that we need instead a dashboard of indicators that monitor better measures of success for the whole child—a critical and creative mind, a healthy body, and an ethical character. And we need indicators of each student's opportunities to learn—what programs, services, and resources are available? She wrote:

> Success should be measured throughout the preK-12 system, but a standardized test tells us so little. We want to know which students are succeeding in Advanced Placement and honors programs, where they earn college credit in high school. You can measure that. We want to know which students have certified, experienced teachers and access to the support professionals they need, such as tutors, librarians, school nurses

and counselors. We want to know which students have access to arts and athletic programs. Which middle school students are succeeding in science, technology, engineering, and math tracks that will get them into advanced high school courses, which will get them into a university. You can measure all that, too.

And we want the data broken down by demographic groups, so we can ensure that all types of students have access to these resources. Without this dashboard of information, how would the public know which children are being shortchanged? How would anything change?

Garcia's dashboard and the multiple measures offer a sound plan, but I suggest putting the emphasis on measuring *school quality*. Multiple measures cannot be handed down from on high. We need to trust each community to create the kinds of school programs it wants for its children, instead of the state or federal government making the rules. A community might choose:

- Significant programs in art, drama, journalism, and music
- A community service requirement
- Project-based learning
- Competence in a second language
- At least thirty minutes of recess daily
- Honors recognition for academic excellence
- An emphasis on "blended learning"—the healthy mix of teaching and technology
- Teacher-made tests to regularly measure student progress
- Uniforms for all students
- Economic and racial diversity
- Early college opportunities for advanced students

Give a community one point for each vibrant program it establishes. For argument's sake, let's say a school must get at least

10 points to stay open. However, merely having some or all of these programs would not be enough to earn a passing grade for a school, because every school must also earn points by doing well on the high-stakes test and demonstrating that its graduates are capable of moving on. That's the verification side of the equation.

Give three points if 60 percent of kids score at the "basic" level or above; four points if 75 percent reach that level; and five points if 85 percent or more reach it. The idea is to establish multiple priorities and provide a program that is valuable to the community. A school couldn't just "drill and kill" to pass the test, because it wouldn't earn enough points to stay open. Nor could it just have a host of wonderful programs that make everyone feel good, because passing the state test and preparing graduates for their future are also requirements.

Trust the community to decide what kinds of programs it wants for its children, but look to (a smaller number of) standardized tests and the college/career readiness results for proof that trust in the community is justified—or, in worst cases, is evidence that changes must be made.

I'm advocating that states should focus on verifying the progress of *schools*, not teachers, while the federal government's education policy should return to its roots: gathering data and ensuring the rights of the disadvantaged and the neediest. We need to trust a school's community (of teachers, administrators, and parents) to see that everyone in that school is pulling their weight—and to do something about those who are not.

Still, trust alone is not sufficient, and teachers must be evaluated. Relying on student scores alone is idiotic, as even Bill Gates now acknowledges.[16] It will lead to even more testing, he wrote in the *Washington Post* in April 2013: "In one Midwestern state, for example, a 166-page Physical Education Evaluation Instrument holds teachers accountable for ensuring that students meet state-defined targets for physical education, such as consistently demonstrating 'correct skipping technique with a smooth and effortless rhythm' and 'strike consistently a ball with a paddle to a target area with accuracy and good technique.' I'm not making this up!"[17]

My hope is that Gates now recognizes that the school reform policies and practices he generally supported have done a lot of damage—and that he is willing to put resources behind his words. Later in that same piece he wrote:

> I have talked to many teachers over the past several years, and not one has told me they would be more motivated, or become a better teacher, by competing with other teachers in their school. To the contrary, teachers want an environment based on collaboration, in which they can rely on one another to share lesson plans, get advice and understand what's working well in other classrooms. Surveys by MetLife and other research of teachers back this up.
>
> Teachers also tell me that while compensation is important, so are factors such as high-quality professional development opportunities, a strong school leader, engaged families and the chance to work with like-minded colleagues.

ANOTHER TEST FOR YOU

Here's a one-question test to assess how much you know about standardized testing.

"Standardized" tests are those in which:

a. Everyone is supposed to use a #2 pencil
b. Everyone takes them under the same conditions
c. Some people cheat
d. Everyone has the same amount of time, unless they don't
e. All of the above

The correct answer may well be (e), "All of the above," but let's focus on (c), "Some people cheat." Here some background is in order. We have a cheating problem in our schools, but who are the "some people"? While a handful of students cheat because they are competing to get into top colleges, the more frequent cheaters (or enablers of cheating) are principals, teachers, and administrators whose jobs are on the line because we now judge, reward, and fire them based on student test scores. The situation got out of hand during the years of No Child Left Behind. In Atlanta, the District of Columbia, Austin, Baltimore, Philadelphia, Dayton, and many other places, some adults actually worked together to cheat, even holding "erasure parties" to change student answers from wrong to right.

In school systems, the response has often been to address the symptom of cheating, not its underlying causes. That was the gist of a *Wall Street Journal* report about how schools were beefing up test security, headlined "For School Tests, Measures to Detect Cheating Proliferate."[18] The *Journal* reported that because no school district wants to be "the next Atlanta," where there was massive cheating by some principals and teachers, some school districts are investing heavily in security measures to keep students and teachers from cheating. "School districts from Delaware to Idaho are employing tactics such as hiring anti-cheating consultants, buying software to spot wrongdoers, and requiring testing companies to offer anti-cheating plans when seeking contracts," the paper reported. But the article says nothing about addressing the cause of widespread cheating: the pressure from leadership to produce high test scores.

Public school districts shouldn't be spending time, energy, and money on strategies to prevent cheating. Those resources ought to be devoted to creating a more challenging—not "rigorous"—curriculum that gives students more control over their own learning and engages them in the deeper learning of project-based classes. A more "rigorous" curriculum that focuses on training students to regurgitate information in order to pass tests is a flawed strategy, and all the expensive security measures in the world will not obscure that truth.

A teacher friend of mine chastised me for devoting too much attention to cheating on standardized tests. She wrote in part,

> While I know that the cheating scandals may be considered important, I'm frankly a bit disappointed that

this is the focus because the cheating scandal doesn't really matter in terms of the students and their futures, which should always be the focus of anything related to education. What matters is the lasting damage that is being done to them as a result of the increased pressures being put on the school system over these tests. The lasting damage is the closing of schools with no thoughts as to the repercussions on the community, the constant rotating principals, the removal of teachers connected with the community, the privatization of public schools and property, the fact that schools budgets are getting slashed while the administrative central office expands and gives money to private contractors in huge quantities that accomplish nothing, the constant lack of knowledge about our future in the schools, the increasing class sizes and removal of resources from our neediest schools, etc.

Those test scores mean nothing about how prepared our children are for their futures—whether or not there was cheating.

THE PROVERBIAL CANARY IN THE COAL MINE

The canary in the coal mine—convincing evidence that test-based accountability and test-score obsession are counterproductive—is the Broad Prize for Excellence in Urban Education. Without much publicity, the Broad Foundation did *not* award the $1 million Broad Prize for Excellence in Urban Education in 2015 or 2016. It turns out that the NAEP scores of most of the previous Broad Prize winners (public school districts) have been flat for years. These districts have been living and dying by test scores, and it's not working well enough to impress the foundation's judges. Ben Weider of the website *FiveThirtyEight* deconstructed the issue in a well-reasoned piece, "The Most Important Award in Public Education Struggles to Find Winners."[19] Not long after, the foundation decided to "pause" the award, citing "sluggish" changes in urban schools. As Howard Blume of the *Los Angeles Times* has reported, billionaire philanthropist Eli Broad has shifted his focus to charter schools.[20]

But that's not really *new* news, as the foundation's own pie chart reveals. Since 1999, the foundation has made $589.5 million in education-related grants, and 24 percent of that money, $144 million, has gone directly to public charter schools. No doubt some of the "leadership" and "governance" dollars it gives out have gone to public charter schools as well, which make up 5 percent of all schools. Over that same period, 3 percent of the money, $16 million, went to winners of the Urban Education Broad Prize (mostly for college scholarships).

Eli Broad hoped that urban districts could improve "if given the right models or if political roadblocks" (such as those he believes are presented by teachers unions) "could be overcome," said Jeffrey Henig, professor of political science and education at Teachers College, Columbia University. The suspension of the prize for urban education could signal a "highly public step" toward the view that traditional districts "are incapable of reform," Henig said. Broad seems to have already taken that step in his home city, Los Angeles, where he is backing an effort to greatly expand the charter sector.[21]

Apparently it's pretty simple for the folks administering the Broad Prize in Urban Education: successful school reform boils down to higher test scores. There is no public sign that anyone at the foundation is questioning whether living and dying by test scores is sensible pedagogy that benefits students. There is no public evidence that they've considered what might happen if poor urban students were exposed to a rich curriculum and veteran teachers, essentially the birthright of students in wealthy districts. There's just the dismal conclusion that traditional districts are incapable of reform, and that the way to go is to double down on charter management organizations, despite the truly offensive record of some of them of excluding special-needs children and

driving away students who seem likely to do poorly on standardized tests.[22]

THE SCOREBOARD AND THE GOLDEN GOOSE

In April 2016 scores on the so-called Nation's Report Card
showed that one-quarter of twelfth-graders taking the test performed proficiently or better in math. Only 37 percent of the
students were proficient or above in reading.[23] It turns out that
scores are down five points over the past twenty-three years on
the National Assessment of Educational Progress. The newest
NAEP scores also reveal a widening gap in math and reading
between those who score well and those who do not. That has to
be particularly disappointing to those reformers who go on and
on about closing the achievement gap, because the biggest drop
was among the low performers, who were subjected to the *most*
test prep! Those who said they prepared for state tests "not at all"
scored an average of 291 on the reading test, while those who said
they prepared for state assessments "to a great extent" scored an
average of 282.

Only 37 percent of students scored well enough in both reading
and math to be deemed academically ready for college—roughly
the same percentage as in 2013. Bill Bushaw, the executive director of the National Assessment Governing Board, which man-
ages NAEP, told reporters, "We're not making the academic
progress that we need to so that there's greater preparedness for
post-secondary, for work, for military participation. These numbers aren't going the way we want." Bushaw did not try to explain
why this is happening, nor did he blame the victim, but perhaps
it's time someone pointed out that test-based accountability,
which has meant more drill and test prep and cuts in art, music,
drama, and all sorts of other courses that aren't deemed basic, has
failed miserably—and there are victims.

Students have been the losers, sentenced to mind-numbing
schooling. Teachers who care about their craft have also lost out.
Craven administrators who couldn't or didn't stand up for what
they know about learning have been the losers. Add to the list of

losers the general public, because the drumbeat of bad news has undercut faith in public education.

There are winners as well: the testing companies (particularly Pearson), the academics who've gotten big grants from major foundations to study and evaluate many misguided pursuits, profiteers in the charter school industry, and ideologues and politicians who want to undermine public education. The underlying message of the newest NAEP results is that the emperor has no clothes. But then, we've actually known this for some time.

Testing is a multibillion-dollar industry, a golden goose for Pearson, McGraw-Hill, ETS, and other large corporations, not to mention a large and booming test prep industry. States that are willing to commit to developing coherent assessments with less reliance on fill-in-the-bubble tests will need strong bipartisan leadership, and those leaders should be prepared for an intense lobbying effort from test makers to maintain the status quo.

Change won't be easy. In an effort to reduce the test pressure on their students and teachers, five superintendents in Virginia (representing 25 percent of all students in the state) petitioned their state department of education in 2014 for permission to administer the end-of-year tests in the fall. The goal, according to Fairfax County Superintendent Jack Dale, was to allow kids who passed the first time to experience deeper learning in academic subjects while giving teachers the chance to work closely with those who didn't get over the barrier. The state's answer was an emphatic no.

A polite protest from five superintendents in a single state is hardly akin to Martin Luther nailing his theses to the cathedral door. It's probably closer to Oliver Twist's asking for "more please, sir." Still, it may represent a promising breach in the system.

SURPRISE! STUDENTS UPSET THE APPLECART

At the very beginning of this book I asked you what might derail the testing express, offering four options. Well, the correct answer is D, students and their parents. In 2009 the school reform pack, led by education secretary Arne Duncan's Race to the Top plan, put most of their eggs in the basket labeled "standardized test scores." These scores would be used to reward and punish teachers and principals. Bad teachers and principals—"bad" being defined as those whose students did poorly on the tests—could be fired and replaced, and those who "added value" would be rewarded. It looked to be a foolproof system because federal law requires schools to test 95 percent of students, with sanctions in place for any schools that fell below that vital number. Sure, some teachers and administrators would complain, but the school reformers were certain they'd eventually get with the program because their jobs were on the line.

The grand planners never dreamed that large numbers of *students* might simply refuse to take the tests. But that is precisely what is happening. Led by a few activist teachers and students and with no financial support from teachers unions or private foundations, it was the epitome of a grassroots campaign. What is now a national movement began as more modest local protests in 2010 and 2011 in a number of places, including New York and Colorado. These rump groups of teachers, parents, and a few students connected through social media, largely on Facebook, and eventually through a national organization, United Opt Out (UOO), co-founded by veteran Colorado teacher Peggy Robertson. Many supporters of opting out saw a boycott of standardized tests as a way of slowing down or limiting such testing, which they believed was hurting children. Parents told grim stories about their kids vomiting, not sleeping, and crying all the time during testing season.

However, UOO insists that it is *not* an anti-testing movement. In Robertson's words, "It is a movement to reclaim public schools and to demand that our schools receive equitable funding and a whole and developmentally appropriate education for all children."[24]

Like politics, opting out attracts strange bedfellows. When I reported in 2015 on the opt-out movement in New Jersey for *PBS NewsHour,* I discovered an odd alliance of conservatives and liberals, the former hating what they called government "interference" and the latter objecting to "overtesting" and the use of test scores to punish teachers.[25] A subsequent national survey by two professors at Columbia's Teachers College found that the movement was composed of 52 percent Democrats, 33 percent independents, and 15 percent Republicans.[26] One of the national survey's sixty-five questions asked respondents to pick the two top reasons they participated in opt-out activities. The answers revealed that:

- 36.9 percent said they oppose using students' performance on standardized tests to evaluate teachers.
- 33.8 percent said they believe standardized tests force teachers to "teach to the test" by using drilling and worksheets to promote memorization of test answers rather than more complex, inquiry-based learning strategies.
- 30.4 percent said they oppose the growing role of corporations in schools.
- 26.5 percent said they believe standardized tests take away too much instructional time.
- 25.8 percent said they oppose the Common Core State Standards (CCSS).
- 16 percent said they oppose the privatization of schools, a concern that is closely tied to fears about the growing role of corporations in public schools.

UOO's lack of support from teachers unions and the group's sparsely attended national meetings in Denver in 2014 and Fort Lauderdale in 2015 might have lulled the education establishment into a sense of complacency.[27] But the school reform crowd should have been concerned, because behind the scenes and on social media, the opt-out coalition was growing in numbers, energy, and commitment.

Opting out became a genuine national phenomenon in 2015 when hundreds of thousands of students (some of them in elementary school) refused to take their state-mandated standardized tests. These widespread refusals, and the accompanying publicity, helped propel Congress to finally get rid of No Child Left Behind. However, most professional educators opposed opting out. Their response to parents was direct: *If you let (or make) your kids opt out, you are hurting them. You may think you are helping, but you actually are doing them a disservice. Testing,* they explained, *is in your children's best interests because it tells you where they stand academically.*

Among those campaigning against opting out was Michelle Rhee's successor in Washington, D.C., Kaya Henderson. Valerie Strauss of the *Washington Post* reported on the precipitous drop in scores on the Common Core test known as Partnership for Assessment of Readiness for College and Careers (PARCC) at one of the District of Columbia's top high schools, Woodrow Wilson.

> At Wilson, 68 percent of students who were supposed to take the test did take it, school district data showed. An undetermined number were kids who opted out because they oppose high-stakes testing. Though D.C. Schools Chancellor Kaya Henderson refused about 100 opt-out requests, some students got permission from other administrators to sit out the PARCC, further skewing the overall school results.[28]

Some school districts adopted a punitive "sit and stare" policy, meaning that the opting out kids had to sit at their desks while other students took the tests. The protesters were not allowed to read books; they had to just "sit and stare" for sixty to ninety minutes. This was apparently designed to humiliate the protesters. In some cases, the test booklets and pencils were put on the protesting students' desks, probably with the hope that they would cave in to the pressure.

The poster child for what *not* to do was Dr. Stacey Gross, principal of Ridgefield (Connecticut) High School, where only thirty-five juniors, out of more than four hundred, took the new Common Core tests in 2015. That's right: more than 90 percent of the high school juniors in this wealthy Connecticut town opted out of the test, which was given over several days.[29] In response, Gross decided to punish the protestors by prohibiting learning!

As Dani Blum reported in the *Ridgefield Press*, Gross wrote an email to the parents of the juniors—protestors and test-takers alike—to "reassure" them that during the days in which the tests were being given, the students opting out of the test would be required to go to their regularly scheduled classes, but that "no new learning" would occur in any class where even one junior was absent because he or she was taking the standardized test.[30] That is, while the thirty-five students who toed the line were taking the Common Core tests, teachers would not be covering any new material for the 365 other students, so that the test-takers would not miss anything.

I believe educators like Gross should be identifying useful alternative behaviors that would benefit students who weren't taking the tests. She might have said, "To ensure that students who are taking the test do not fall behind, their teachers will not be covering new material during the testing periods. I've asked those who are opting out to come up with some alternative activities that are educational in nature or somehow contribute to our high school."

Michelle Goodman, who pulled her daughter out of the testing, told the *Ridgefield Press* that the administration's insistence on no new learning was "absolutely ludicrous." "Where are the priorities here, with the students who want to succeed or with the school system who is forcing their policies to the detriment of our children's education?" she asked.

It didn't take long for those who worship test scores to try to corrupt the opt-out movement. In the spring of 2016, principal Brandon Davis of the Cora Kelly School for Math, Science and Technology, a high-poverty school in Alexandria, Virginia, invited his *low-performing* students to opt out. As Emma Brown of the *Washington Post* reported,

> Alexandria school officials said Davis told teachers "to identify students who may not do well on the SOL [Standards of Learning] test, and contact parents of these students regarding their right to refuse SOL testing." The students whose parents were contacted

had scored 425 or below on exams; a 400 is the passing rate.

Helen Lloyd, a spokeswoman for the district, said that teachers told parents only about their right to opt out and about the state law, passed in the spring, which would mean their child's score of zero would not negatively impact the school's accreditation rating. The report does not explain why Davis would instruct teachers to place calls only to parents of students who were on the brink of failing.[31]

Davis, yet another educator who puts test scores above children, was disciplined in some unspecified manner. He also issued the conventional non-apology, saying, "I wish to stress that I did not do anything that I perceived was intentionally wrong at the time."

The established order continues to fight. Florida announced it would refuse to promote any third-graders who opted out of the 2016 state test. It backed off only after parents went to court. And education secretary John King Jr. immediately looked for ways to impose federal penalties on school districts with high opt-out numbers.

The threats didn't seem to scare people. In New York State, where 20 percent of students opted out in 2015, the number opting out increased in 2016 to 22 percent. In just nine states, including New York, an estimated 400,000 students refused to be tested in 2016.

And opting out seems to be working, at least in some places. Because of United Opt Out, some communities have reexamined their testing requirements and schedules, often reducing both.[32] Some districts and states pulled back from their announced intentions to evaluate teachers based largely on student test scores.

The struggle isn't over, because school reformers haven't abandoned their core belief in the primacy of standardized, machine-scored tests as the most reliable way of evaluating teachers.[33] But opting out is the canary in the coal mine, a harbinger of things to come. School reformers are addicted to test scores. Those numbers are their crack cocaine, their oxycodone, their crystal meth.

By refusing to take tests, hundreds of thousands of students are denying the school reform addicts the drug they crave. Students have, perhaps inadvertently, identified the Achilles' heel of the school reform movement: if reformers can't test *everyone*, the entire house of cards crumbles, revealing the emptiness of the enterprise.

Power is shifting, and change is in the air. Of course, student progress must be assessed regularly, but that is best done by trained teachers. As for schools, they can be reliably evaluated by testing a stratified random sample of students. There's simply no need to administer bubble tests to all students every year; the only beneficiaries of that policy are testing companies.

So, no more "test and punish." From here on out, the byword is "assess to improve."

STEP TWELVE

Choose a New Path

We have come a long way. We are convinced we must focus on the educational *and* emotional needs and strengths of individual children. We are committed to free, high-quality early childhood daycare and education programs and to involving the entire village, not just parents and educators. We recognize that technology in the hands of skilled teachers is going to be a major asset, and we're resolved to eschew simple multiple-choice tests in favor of measuring what matters. Raising the bar for entry into the teaching profession, strengthening teacher training, and improving working conditions will make it harder to become a teacher but also easier to be one.

Because you recognize that students become what they regularly do, the schools you are going to help create will be both challenging and interesting. Henceforth, school decisions, especially financial ones, will be transparent in traditional and charter public schools. And you're committed to working to ban for-profit public schools.

Now the bottom-line question: Do those of us who are frustrated with the addiction to school reform have the will and the courage to follow this path? That's hard to say. After all, it will be far easier to keep on doing what we've been doing, even when we know we ought to change. It's more comfortable to work hard on small changes, what David Tyack and Larry Cuban famously called "tinkering toward utopia" in their book of that title—but fiddling and patching, rather than repairing our broken system, is how we became addicted to reform in the first place.

Even though we know in our gut that today's schools are obsolete, the question is whether states, school districts, and individuals will have the courage to do the right thing. Schools are no longer the repository of knowledge they were in the days before the Internet. Today's children swim in a sea of information 24/7. However, information is *not* knowledge. So in this new paradigm schools have new duties and challenges: they must help teach young people how to sift through the flood of information and give them the skills to determine what is true. Teachers have to stop asking so many "What?" questions and instead ask "Why?" and "How?" Formulating more questions and searching creatively for answers is the work that students—knowledge workers— must be doing. We have to build "knowledge factories" for our children, not more schools in the current mold.

We know that, because of technology, the school's longstanding task of socialization has taken on new meaning with our children, digital natives who socialize via thousands of apps. Schools need educ.ators who understand that their job is to transform these digital natives into digital *citizens*. These young digital citizens must use technology to create knowledge, because if they are not encouraged and allowed to do this, many will—out of boredom or malice—use the dazzling variety of tools we call social media to harass and abuse the most vulnerable among them.

If we allow schools to continue as regurgitation factories where students are "products," if we persist in judging teachers based on the test scores of those products, and if we don't insist that schools harness the awesome potential of technology, then we will *always* have schools where the brightest students are bored and the most vulnerable are bullied.

Because we are what we repeatedly do and because we do not want to produce generations of adults who are minimal participants in our democracy (and who do not vote), students must spend their days developing the skills and capabilities that we want them to have as adults. It's a tall order: students must master the basic skills of numeracy, reading, and writing *and* the new basics of speaking persuasively, listening carefully and critically, working collaboratively, and being reflective, all while mastering modern technology.

Many of these new institutions may resemble what the idealists who founded the charter school movement dreamed of: schools where *everyone* is there by choice. In most of these schools, teachers will play an important role in the selection of their colleagues and in assessing student progress. Some schools will be organized around themes, and some will end age segregation and instead allow students to move at their own pace.

While this new paradigm can be seen in a few hundred schools,[1] we have nearly 100,000 public schools. We are a long way from the tipping point. Happily, no one needs to design entirely new curricula to teach decision-making, teamwork, a strong work ethic, communication, and critical thinking. Those skills are fundamental to most extracurricular activities: playing sports, working in theatrical productions, playing in a musical group, and producing the school newspaper, radio or TV program, or yearbook. In those activities, students are clearly the workers, and their work products are tangible.

It bears repeating that *we* have to do the work. Experience has taught us that Washington cannot run public education, we know that the well-organized and well-funded school reform crowd cannot be trusted, and the Trump administration has promised to return power to parents, communities, and states. DIY, America!

This twelve-step approach can cure American business's persistent headache, transform public education, make school much more challenging and relevant for students, and reverse the supposed "rising tide of mediocrity." Perhaps the best way for a school district to start is with a few pilot schools, built on the eight basic principles outlined in Steps Four through Eleven.[2] Creating a system of schools that measures what matters and takes care to ask of each child "How are you intelligent?" will require strong leadership at every level. The larger community must be invested in what happens to other people's children, and that won't happen on its own.

"Freedom to fail" is a new idea for students, who are used to being spoon-fed information that they then regurgitate. *Telling* them that those days are over is one thing; getting them accustomed to this new world of greater responsibility and opportunity won't be easy. School boards and administrators must stick to their guns, because change will be difficult and messy, particularly because every adult grew up in, and was educated by, the old system, the one that sorted them into "winners" and "losers."

The education press will have to get out of the habit of elevating newcomers to heroic status—for a while—and then tearing them down. They must learn to be skeptical from day one. Not cynical, but questioning.

Schools of education and their universities will be challenged as never before, because when teaching becomes an appealing profession that does not lose 40 percent of new teachers within four or five years, ed schools will lose what has been a cash cow for them. Ending churn will dramatically affect the landscape in teacher education—half of the schools of education currently in existence might go out of business. Let's hope that only those that provide value survive. And the teachers they have already turned out will need to be reeducated, because they aren't used to being trusted.

Giant testing companies such as Pearson will lose their huge contracts, as well they should. However, I have no doubt that they will create new instruments and then try to persuade school districts to keep on writing checks. Only if they can help measure what matters should they continue to prosper.

The losers outlined in Step Eleven—students, teachers, and the public—will become winners, and there will be new losers:

1. Those who have been benefiting from failure and mediocrity, that chattering class of critics and scholars who regularly dine out on tales of educational woe or get grants to study trivialities, will discover that their free lunch is over.
2. Jettisoning the medical model that diagnoses weaknesses and claims it can "cure" our children of their "deficits" with drugs, expensive testing and tutoring, or expensive technology will mean pink slips for all those specialists.

Instead we are adopting a health model of schooling that builds on children's strengths—because all children have strengths.

3. The biggest and most deserving losers will be the for-profit charter school chains, including the virtual charters. Nonprofit charter schools that refuse to be transparent about their spending will lose their right to operate.

But what if we ignore the evidence that is right in front of us and do nothing? What if we continue to isolate children by race and economic status, all while blathering about the "achievement gap" and "no excuses" schools? What if we tolerate the continued isolation of schools from the larger society, all the while expecting them to solve myriad problems?

If we do nothing to radically change a system that identifies "winners" and "losers" at an early age; if we do nothing about a system that tests children excessively, labels them permanently, and then uses their test scores to punish educators; if we do nothing about schools that ignore technology's potential but use it instead to control; if we do nothing to transform a system that expects teachers and schools to "do it all," thereby setting them up to fail; then we are dooming generations of children to second-class status. That is not something I can live with or stand for, and I suspect most caring people in the United States feel similarly. Our dangerous, destructive habits have to be kicked.

I hope you are convinced that it's time to choose the future we want for all of our children. And not merely convinced, but ready to act!

A Final Stroll down Memory Lane

"Looking back over my career, I wouldn't change a thing." You did not find that tired cliché in this semi-autobiographical volume, because there's a lot I wish I had done differently. I wish I had reported on the resegregation of our public schools. I regret not

devoting more airtime to celebrating the successes of the hardworking and dedicated teachers I spent time with. I could have called more attention to the distortion of the original idea of charter schools, the creeping influence of big money, some powerful foundations, and the U.S. Department of Education. I regret not doing more to uncover the unsavory and unethical practices of some charter school operators, who deliberately target and get rid of students who seem unlikely to do well on standardized tests or who show signs of independence. Too often we told those stories once and never returned to them. My bad.

In the beginning of my career, Ambassador Walter Annenberg and Leonore Annenberg, through their foundation, and the Ford Foundation generously supported independent journalism, saying, in effect, "Spend this money reporting on public education to the best of your ability." Unfortunately, the polarization that afflicts American society soon poisoned the foundation world, and before long many foundations were trying to influence journalists by offering grants to those who would tell the story the foundation wanted told, and turning down requests from organizations like mine. That made fund-raising tough.

The Great Recession of 2008 nearly destroyed Learning Matters, my nonprofit production company. We went from seventeen employees to eight within a space of a few months, and those who stayed took pay cuts and then endured a pay freeze that lasted for years. From 2008 going forward, I found myself spending more than half of my days seeking funding, precisely at a time when most foundations were actively seeking to influence coverage in support of their particular issue. I did fewer stories, another regret. We limped home, often not quite sure that we'd be able to meet our payroll.

Finally, in mid-2015 I merged Learning Matters with Editorial Projects in Education, the publisher of Education Week, *in hopes that our work would continue. I officially retired that fall after an "exit interview" with Judy Woodruff, a pro if ever there was one.[3]*

What I will never regret is a life spent with teachers and children. Teachers represent, in my view, the best America has to offer, women and men who have chosen to work to shape the future. And children, bless them, are the future: yours, mine, ours.

Acknowledgments

I am indebted to thousands of people for advice and support during my forty-one years of reporting. What follows is my best effort at a list. To those I have inadvertently omitted, my sincere apologies.

Inspirations: Ray Bacchetti, Alison Bernstein, David K. Cohen, James Comer, M.D., Lisa Delpit, Marian Wright Edelman, Sy Fliegel, Patricia Albjerg Graham, Samuel Halperin, E.D. Hirsch Jr., John Holt, Harold "Doc" Howe, Herb Kohl, Jonathan Kozol, the Honorable William E. McAnulty Jr., Deborah Meier, Frank Newman, Diane Ravitch, Fred Rogers, Larry Rosenstock, Albert Shanker, Ted Sizer, I.F. Stone, and David Wald.

At different times and/or in multiple roles: Dick Beattie, Barbara Cervone, Ted Dintersmith, Russ Edgerton, Checker Finn, Ken Fischer, Vartan Gregorian, Linda Darling Hammond, Jim Kelly, David Kirp, Ted Kolderie, Tony Marx, Kent McGuire, Joe Nathan, Arnold Packer, Pasi Sahlberg, Marshall "Mike" Smith, Marc Tucker, and Linda Roberts.

At National Public Radio: Jim Russell, Marcia Witten, Barbara Schelstrate, Barney Quinn, Midge Hart, Wendy Blair, Natalie Iglitz, Rebecca Goldfield, and Jay Kernis.

At *The MacNeil/Lehrer NewsHour*, *The NewsHour with Jim Lehrer*, and *PBS NewsHour*: Linda Winslow, Jim Lehrer, Robin MacNeil, Mike Joseloff, Tim Smith, Murrey Jacobson, Joe Quinlan, Kwame Holman, Judy Woodruff, Les Crystal, Gwen

Ifill, Annette Miller, Mark Shields, Jeff Brown, and Charlayne Hunter-Gault.

At *The Merrow Report*/Learning Matters: John Tulenko, John Heus, David Wald, Donald Devet, Amanda Morales, Cat McGrath, Jane Renaud, Tania Brief, Jessica Windt, Carmen Rojas, Austin Haeberle, Alexis Kessler, Sonia Slutsky, Tira Gray, Hillary Kolos, Sharese Bullock, Bob Frye, Jim Spahr, Anique Halliday, Dien Vo, Valerie Visconti, Colin Mutchler, Edwin Clavijo, Carrie Glasser, Georgia West, Shae Isaacs, Ted Bauer, and Karena O'Riordan; and the Learning Matters Board of Directors, especially Dr. Karen Hein, Esther Wojcicki, Wendy Puriefoy, Josh Kaufman, Virginia Edwards, Adele Pham, and Bob Hughes.

At *Frontline:* David Fanning.

At the Harvard Graduate School of Education: Jay Featherstone, Dick Light, Kathleen McCartney, Howard Gardner, Paul Ylvisaker, Marvin Lazerson, Sandy Jencks, Frank Keppel, Jerry Murphy, Dick Murnane, Dick Chait, Dan Koretz, Kay Merseth, Walter McCann, Rachel Tompkins, Mike Smith, David K. Cohen, Ted Sizer, Harold "Doc" Howe, and Larry Aaronson.

At the Education Writers Association: Lisa Walker, Mike Bowler, Anne Lewis, Jay Mathews, Dale Mezzacappa, Kit Lively, Linda Lenz, Ted Fiske, Stephanie Banchero, Greg Toppo, Richard Colvin, Gene Maeroff, Richard Whitmire, and dozens more colleagues.

At the Institute for Educational Leadership: Mike Usdan, George Kaplan, Ken Fischer, Betty Hale, Harold "Bud" Hodgkinson, Sam Halperin, and Marty Blank.

At the Carnegie Foundation for the Advancement of Teaching: Lee Shulman, Tom Ehrlich, Gay Clyburn, Pat Hutchings, Ann Lieberman, Tony Bryk, and Lisa Wilson.

At Virginia State College: Dr. Joseph Jenkins.

At the American Community Service Network: Rob Shuman.

At South Carolina ETV: Jim Eddins and Polly Kosko.

At the Stanford Graduate School of Education: Linda Darling-Hammond, David Tyack, Gay Hoagland, and Larry Cuban.

At UC Berkeley: David Kirp and Mike Kirst.

At Teachers College, Columbia University: Arthur Levine, Ruth Gottesman, John Rosenwald, Jay Urwitz, Laurie Tisch, John Hyland, Bill Rueckert, John Klingenstein, Arthur Zankel, Scott Fahey, Joe Levine, Susan Fuhrman, and Henry Levin.

At Dartmouth College: Alexander Laing.

At Indiana University: Donald Gray and David Smith.

In Washington, D.C., at the Office/Department of Education, in Congress, and elsewhere: Don Davies, Jack Jennings, Don Bigelow, Bill Smith, Emerson Elliott, Mike Smith, Richard Riley, Patricia Albjerg Graham, and Bernice Sandler.

Ambassador Walter Annenberg, Leonore Annenberg, Wallis Annenberg, and Gail Levin at the Annenberg Foundation; Vartan Gregorian, Avery Russell, Michael Levine, Tony Jackson, David Hamburg, and Susan King at Carnegie Corporation of New York; Harold "Doc" Howe, Ed Meade and Alison Bernstein at the Ford Foundation; Will Miller, Richard Laine, Lucas Held, and Jessica Schwartz at the Wallace Foundation; Bill Pauli at Toyota; Angela Covert and Joel Fleishman at Atlantic Philanthropies; Sophie Sa at the Panasonic Foundation; Ray Bacchetti, Mike Smith, and Barbara Chow at the William and Flora Hewlett Foundation; Anne Petersen at the W.K. Kellogg Foundation; Reed Hastings and Sarah Usdin at the Silicon Valley Community Trust; Tony Cipollone at the Annie E. Casey Foundation; Joan Lipsitz at the Lilly Endowment; Karen Denne at the Eli and Edythe Broad Foundation; Bob Schwartz, Russ Edgerton, and Ellen Burbank at the Pew Charitable Trusts; Marie Groark and Don Shalvey at the Bill and Melinda Gates Foundation; Gisèle Huff at the Jaquelin Hume Foundation; Rick Love at the MetLife Foundation; Dan and Karen Pritzker at the Jay Pritzker Foundation; Larry Tietz at the Tietz Foundation; Anne Wojcicki at the Brin/Wojcicki Foundation; Doug Bodwell at the Corporation for Public Broadcasting and the Annenberg Channel; John Gunn; and John and Anne Doerr.

I want to express my sincere gratitude to The New Press, including editor in chief Diane Wachtell, my careful and thoughtful editor Tara Grove, and Emily Albarillo, my dedicated and hard-working production editor. I also want to thank the New York Public Library, especially President Tony Marx and Melanie Locay, for providing space in the famed Allen Room for me to do research, write, and rewrite.

Above all, I am grateful to my wife and life partner, Joan Lonergan, who has been an honest critic, a patient supporter, and an even better friend. This book would not have been written without her.

Notes

Preface

1. "Voting age population" and "registered voters" are different concepts. The former number is larger because it includes adults who cannot vote because of felony convictions, who have been unable to overcome hurdles placed in their way by a cumbersome registration process, or who have not attempted to register in the first place. As former president Barack Obama noted in his farewell address, the United States makes it harder for its citizens to vote than any other democracy.

2. Nicole Gorman, "New Survey on Civic Knowledge Finds On-Third of Respondents Cannot Name All Three Branches of Government," Education World, September 14, 2016, http://www .educationworld.com/a_news/new-survey-civic-knowledge-finds-one -third-respondents-cannot-name-all-three-branches; Nicole Gorman, "As Independence Day Approaches, We Ask: Should Citizenship Be a 'Third C' After College and Career?," Education World, June 30, 2016, http://www.educationworld.com/a_news/independence -day-approaches-we-ask-should-citizenship-be-%E2%80%98third -c%E2%80%99-after-college-career.

3. They were following Ted Sizer's "less is more" approach, which we documented in The $50 Million Gamble.

4. The sad story is here: http://learningmatters.tv/blog/documen taries/watch-the-50-million-gamble/650.

5. School reform is also often labeled "education reform" and "corporate reform." In the body of the book, I will generally refer to these efforts as, simply, "reform."

6. I am hesitant to use "transform" because that seems to have been adopted by opportunistic "reformers" with a finger in the air. Larry Cuban, now retired from Stanford, nails this here: https://larrycuban

.wordpress.com/2016/05/25/transforming-public-schools-enough -already-with-an-overhyped-word. Frankly, I feel trapped, because I'd like to argue for "transformation" and may do so occasionally in these pages. We aren't putting up new school buildings, but we have to build new schools.

7. Susan Dynarski, "Why American Schools Are Even More Unequal Than We Thought," *New York Times*, August 12, 2016, http:// www.nytimes.com/2016/08/14/upshot/why-american-schools-are-even -more-unequal-than-we-thought.html.

8. However, ending polarization does not necessarily require meeting in the middle. Sometimes one position is correct, or largely correct; some strongly-held convictions are just plain wrong. "Always compromise and meet in the middle" is bad rule to live by.

9. After eight years at NPR I decided to try my hand at television. I spent two years working on a seven-part PBS series that covered every aspect of childhood and adolescence, from abuse and neglect to teenage work. While *Your Children, Our Children* was nominated for the Community Service Emmy, it aired in 1984 just when Ronald Reagan's world view was taking over Washington, and the series didn't change society the way I had hoped it would.

10. You can watch the *NewsHour* coverage here: http://learningmatters .tv/blog/on-pbs-newshour/watch-the-michelle-rhee-series/682.

11. Readers will find occasional trips down memory lane scattered around this book, always italicized.

12. A few school districts, individual schools, and heroic teachers have embraced some of the steps, generally with very positive results. Their inspiring stories may convince you that I am neither tilting at windmills nor arguing for the impossible.

13. An insight about racism attributed to comedian/philosopher Dick Gregory seems relevant: "The disgrace is having a problem that can be solved and a country that refuses to solve it."

Introduction

1. To continue the fantasy, a Lego figure representing France would be neatly turned out, although its clothes would be frayed at the edges, while one from Finland would be sharply dressed and strutting around as if it owned the joint.

2. "Read Donald Trump's Full Inauguration Speech," Yahoo, January 20, 2017, https://www.yahoo.com/news/read-donald-trump-full -inaugural-172850356.html.

3. Educational Finance Branch, U.S. Census Bureau, "Public Edu-

cation Finances: 2013," 29. For more, see National Center for Education Statistics, "Fast Facts," https://nces.ed.gov/fastfacts/display.asp?id=66.

4. "Percentage Difference from National Average Revenue (Cost-Adjusted)," EdBuild.org, http://viz.edbuild.org/maps/2016/cola /resource-inequality/natl-average.html.

5. Lauren Camera and Lindsey Cook, "Title I: Rich School Districts Get Millions Meant for Poor Kids," *U.S. News & World Report*, June 1, 2016. The charts accompanying this excellent article are revealing.

6. Michel Martin, "Education Secretary Says Status Quo in Schools Is 'Unacceptable,'" *All Things Considered*, September 3, 2016.

7. Michael Leachman, Kathleen Masterson, and Marlana Wallace, "After Nearly a Decade, School Investments Still Way Down in Some States," Center on Budget and Policy Priorities, October 20, 2016.

8. However, an interesting case is being argued in a federal court in Michigan, where plaintiffs are claiming that students have a constitutional right to literacy, which was denied them by the schools of Detroit, then controlled by the state of Michigan. See Jennifer Chambers, "State Says Literacy Not a Right in Detroit," *Detroit News*, November 21, 2016.

9. "Learning Matters: First to Worst (2004)," YouTube, posted by Learning Matters, April 21, 2012, http://youtu.be/r5NhiM9ApCw.

10. Private schools enroll less than 10 percent of students, although their numbers increased slightly in recent years from 5.3 million to 5.4 million, according to *The Condition of Education 2016*. The private school share of all U.S. students has grown from 9.6 percent to 9.7 percent. In 2013–14, some 38 percent of all private school students were enrolled in Catholic schools, which accounted for 2.1 million students. Conservative Christian schools enrolled 707,000 students; other affiliated religious schools, 565,000; unaffiliated religious schools, 758,000, and nonsectarian schools, 1.3 million. *The Condition of Education 2016* (Washington, D.C.: U.S. Department of Education, National Center for Education Statistics, May 2016), https://nces.ed.gov/pubs2016 /2016144.pdf.

11. The Sergeant of Lawes in Chaucer's Canterbury Tales comes to mind, seemingly busy but accomplishing little: "Nowher so bisy a man as he ther nas, And yet he semed bisier than he was."

12. The social scientist Lisbeth Schorr published an optimistic study of effective programs, *Within Our Reach*, in 1988. Many years later, she told me, she discovered that most of those programs had shriveled or disappeared. See Lisbeth B. Schorr, "Books," http://www.lisbethschorr .org/books.

13. National Assessment of Educational Progress, "Technology and

Engineering Literacy Assessment," National Center for Education Statistics, 2014. This assessment, given for the first time in 2014, moved beyond multiple-choice questions and instead focused on real-world scenarios. Questions required students to design a healthier habitat for a pet hamster or gerbil, or build safer urban bike lanes.

14. Diane Stark Rentner, Nancy Kober, and Matthew Frizzell, "Listen to Us: Teacher Views and Voices," Center on Education Policy, May 5, 2016.

15. Greg Toppo, "Survey: Nearly Half of Teachers Would Quit Now for Higher-Paying Job," *USA Today*, May 5, 2016.

16. Lisette Partelow and Christina Baumgardner, "Educator Pipeline at Risk," Center for American Progress, September 2016.

17. In the Northeast, for example, more than half of all black students attend schools where 90–100 percent of their classmates are racial minorities; fifty years ago, that figure was 42.7 percent. Economic segregation jumped 30 percent in the country's one hundred largest school districts between 1991 and 2010. See "K-12 Education: Better Use of Information Could Help Agencies Identify Disparities and Address Racial Discrimination," U.S. Government Accountability Office, April 21, 2016.

18. Emma Brown, "On the Anniversary of *Brown v. Board*, New Evidence That U.S. Schools Are Resegregating," *Washington Post*, May 17, 2016. Emphasis added.

19. But not white Americans and African Americans, because school segregation by race has been our unfortunate (and often illegal) modus operandi. Today, more than sixty years after the *Brown v. Board of Education* Supreme Court decision, public schools are more racially identifiable than ever.

20. The National Center for Education Statistics provides a summary, but heartbreaking stories about the grim consequences of bullying appear with depressing frequency. And one in five students reported being bullied in school in 2012–13, the last year for which data were available while I was working on this book. For more, see U.S. Department of Education, "Student Reports of Bullying and Cyber-Bullying," National Center for Education Statistics, April 2015. Another report tells the story of an eleven-year-old girl in Columbus, Ohio, who killed herself in October 2016; see Dean Narisco, "Family, Community Struggles for Answers After 11-Year-Old Fatally Shoots Herself," *Columbus Dispatch*, October 29, 2016. And on December 11, 2014, another Ohio girl, Emilie Olson, "allegedly became the target of mean-spirited social media messages, as well as a fake Instagram account called 'Emilie Olsen is Gay.' One classmate allegedly followed Emilie into the bathroom, handed her a razor and instructed her to 'end her life'"; see Yanan

Wang, "After Years of Alleged Bullying, an Ohio Teen Killed Herself. Is Her School District Responsible?" *Washington Post*, May 23, 2016.

21. While it's upsetting that a few countries outscore our children on international tests, perhaps we ought to be more disturbed about some other numbers: half of America's children get no early education, at least 22 percent live in poverty, and about 25 percent have a chronic health condition such as asthma or obesity. A 2013 report from Share Our Strength documents the extent of, and damage done by, childhood hunger. It found that 60 percent of K–8 teachers say that some of their students "regularly come to school hungry because they aren't getting enough to eat at home." Many educational problems are directly related to childhood poverty, income inequality, and unequal access to health care, nutrition, and affordable housing. But some of the problems in our approach to education *can* be solved by changing the way we school our children. We can create schools that challenge children while giving them opportunities to develop to the fullest. For more, see No Kid Hungry, "Hunger in Our Schools," August 30, 2013.

22. One of the report's authors, Dr. James Harvey, noted, "It went over everyone's head, of course, but the idea of 'educational foundations' was meant to cover a lot of bases besides schools and we wanted to get in the idea that we need to worry about our future as a society and a people, not our future as workers or consumers. But the road to hell . . . !" For more, see National Commission on Excellence in Education, *A Nation at Risk*, U.S. Department of Education, April 1983.

23. Just how influential the Gates Foundation has been is made clear in *Policy Patrons: Philanthropy, Education Reform, and the Politics of Influence* (Cambridge, MA: Harvard Education Press, 2016), by Megan E. Tompkins-Stange, an assistant professor of public policy at the Ford School of Public Policy at the University of Michigan. She had access to top foundation officials at Gates, Broad, Kellogg, and Ford. For more, see Valerie Strauss, "New Book: Obama's Education Department and Gates Foundation Were Closer Than You Thought," *Washington Post*, August 25, 2016.

24. A thorough analysis of the profession's difficulties in attracting and retaining teachers was issued by the Learning Policy Institute in the fall of 2016. See "Understanding Teacher Shortages," Learning Policy Institute, September 15, 2016. A second LPI report examined the issue in more depth. See Anne Podolsky, Tara Kini, Joseph Bishop, and Linda Darling-Hammond, "Solving the Teacher Shortage," Learning Policy Institute, September 15, 2016.

25. Pasi Sahlberg, "Finnish Lessons 2.0," PasiSahlberg.com, January 2015, http://pasisahlberg.com/finnish-lessons/about-finnish-lessons; the key observation, on page 48, is, "High-equity education in Finland is not a result of educational factors alone." The National Center for

Education and the Economy report (Marc S. Tucker, "Standing on the Shoulders of Giants," May 24, 2011, http://ncee.org/wp-content/uploads /2011/05/Standing-on-the-Shoulders-of-Giants-An-American-Agenda -for-Education-Reform.pdf) is indebted to a McKinsey and Company report from September 2007, "How the World's Best-Performing School Systems Come Out on Top."

26. A warning is in order, because even when the reform crowd acknowledges past missteps, it asks for just one more chance to get it right. For example, the American Enterprise Institute talks the talk but then proceeds to put forth the same old stuff: more choice, less regulation and so on: "Although many education reform efforts have fallen flat over the years, there are promising initiatives on the horizon that state leaders would be well-advised to pursue." Andrew P. Kelly, Frederick M. Hess, Katharine B. Stevens, and Michael Q. McShane, "An Education Agenda for the States: Fostering Opportunity from Pre-K Through College," American Enterprise Institute, April 22, 2015, https://www .aei.org/publication/an-education-agenda-for-the-states-fostering -opportunity-from-pre-k-through-college.

27. To be sure, a few reformers have their own political or ideological agendas, such as undercutting teachers unions or expanding charter schools. Their goal—never explicitly stated—is not to improve opportunities for all children but to achieve their own narrow and often self-serving goals.

28. James Harvey, e-mail message to author, May 25, 2016. Harvey, one of the writers of *A Nation at Risk*, told me about this. He now leads the National Superintendents Roundtable. His letter included these thoughts: "This issue of poverty has been ignored, indeed belittled, by the reform crowd. It needs to be addressed. We had this principal from Las Vegas at our meeting in D.C. last October. According to her, 85 percent of her kids are homeless. Schools can't function fully if kids are living in homeless motels, or worrying about gunshots in the community and where their next meal is coming from. I do think the privileged white upper-middle-class leaders who dominate the reform discussion just have no concept of what life is like or where one's priorities lie in a family of four trying to live on $24,000 annually—or even $12,000 annually. Whose responsibility is this? Someone needs to step up to the plate."

Step One: Own the Problem

1. For many years, schools openly sorted students, assigning some to the top track, the rest to lower tracks. This was no secret to students, parents, and others. Elementary schools used names like Bluebirds and Robins, a transparent attempt to cover what they were doing, but in

the upper grades no such efforts were made. Tracks were numbers, 1, 2, 3, and so on, and often the top track was identified as "honors" or "advanced." I know this from my own experience: as a first-year teacher with—literally—no training whatsoever, I was assigned sections of 3s and 4s. My chairman told me that there was no way I would be allowed anywhere near the top kids. I had been hired at the last minute after a spinal injury forced me to drop out of the Peace Corps. Tinkering with tracking has been a common school reform. Schools have responded when social forces put pressure on them to change, perhaps to include more minorities and English-language learners in upper-level history classes, or to see that more girls enrolled in upper-level science and math courses. However, these reformers were not questioning the validity or importance of sorting, merely adjusting the criteria.

2. Alyson Klein, "Graduation Rate Hits Record High of 83.2 Percent: Should Obama Take Credit?" *Education Week*, October 17, 2016.

3. Maureen Magee, "California's Rising High School Graduation Rates Subject of Federal Audit," *San Diego Union-Tribune*, November 30, 2016.

4. "Learning Matters: Failing Forward," YouTube, posted by Learning Matters, April 13, 2012, https://youtu.be/wAOjcs71Qh0.

5. Heather Vogell and Hannah Fresques, "'Alternative' Education: Using Charter Schools to Hide Dropouts and Game the System," *ProPublica*, February 21, 2017, https://www.propublica.org/article/alternative-education-using-charter-schools-hide-dropouts-and-game-system.

6. "Learning Matters: Early College HS in South Texas, Part 1," YouTube, posted by Learning Matters, July 25, 2012, https://youtu.be/jycQiRK8Ngk, and part 2, https://youtu.be/Q-LphKLXvcY.

7. Ian Urbina, "As School Exit Tests Prove Tough, States Ease Standards," *New York Times*, January 11, 2010; Howard Blume, "Graduating with a D? L.A. School Board Expected to Lower Diploma Standard," *Los Angeles Times*, June 9, 2015.

8. Susan Edelman, "High School's New Rules Give Failing Kids Credits Toward Graduation," *New York Post*, October 9, 2011.

9. Pamela Kripke, "Anatomy of a Grievance: Being Asked to Change Students' Grades," *Huffington Post*, June 7, 2011; Susan Edelman, "Staffers Accuse Bronx Principal of Fixing Grades So Students Pass," *New York Post*, November 29, 2015.

10. Robert Pondiscio, "A Wink, a Nod and a Diploma?" *U.S. News & World Report*, August 14, 2015.

11. Molly Bloom, "Retaking Classes Online: 'Awful if Someone Really Wants to Learn,'" *Atlanta Journal-Constitution*, October 17, 2016.

12. "Campbell's Law," *Wikipedia*, last modified November 5, 2016.

13. Here's just one story about spectacular failures in Massachusetts: James Vaznis, "Can Receivership Save a Failing Boston School?" *Boston Globe*, June 20, 2016. For evidence of success, see "Research Findings to Support Effective Educational Policies: A Guide for Policymakers," Wallace Foundation, March 2011.

14. The turnaround specialist program also provided two days of "refresher" training in January. My colleagues David Wald and John Tulenko did most of the heavy lifting on this story. They went to the training session and identified Parker Land as the most promising subject for the story, for openers.

15. The revolving door hasn't stopped. As I was writing this section of the book, Boushall had an interim principal and issued this statement: "Boushall Middle School has begun the process of selecting a new principal. As part of this process, we are inviting all Boushall Middle School parents, students, staff, alumni and community members to provide feedback regarding the skills and attributes they value most."

16. "Deborah Jewell-Sherman: Professor of Practice," Harvard Graduate School of Education, http://www.gse.harvard.edu/faculty/deborah -jewell-sherman. Her biography says: "Dr. Jewell-Sherman is a graduate of Harvard Graduate School of Education's Urban Superintendents Program and has built a reputation over the past decade as one of the most successful urban district superintendents in the country. Prior to joining the Harvard Graduate School of Education's faculty, Dr. Jewell-Sherman served as superintendent of Richmond Public Schools with a track record of success that culminated in her being named Virginia Superintendent of the Year 2009 by the Virginia Association of School Superintendents (VASS). During her appointment, 95 percent of Richmond's lowest performing schools achieved full accreditation under Virginia's Standards of Learning reform legislation. In addition, the district improved from 18 percent to 91.7 percent of all schools meeting this standard as measured by the State Department of Education (2008)."

17. Andy Smarick, "The Turnaround Fallacy," *EducationNext* 10, no. 1 (2010). *Education Next* is a conservative publication with a reputation for fair coverage of issues.

18. U.S. Department of Education, "School Improvement Grants: Implementation and Effectiveness," January 2017, https://ies.ed.gov /ncee/pubs/20174013/pdf/20174013.pdf; Caitlin Emma, "Here's Why $7 Billion Didn't Help America's Worst Schools," *Politico*, November 3, 2015.

19. That phrase was often twisted and paraphrased to read "Public schools are drowning in a rising tide of mediocrity," but the report doesn't specify *schools* or use the word *drowning*. I wrote about this in

2012 in what turned out to be a very popular blog post that is still relevant. See John Merrow, "Drowning in a Rising Tide of . . . ," *Taking Note*, February 23, 2012, http://takingnote.learningmatters.tv/?p=5595.

20. *For Each and Every Child: A Strategy for Education Equity and Excellence*, Equity and Excellence Commission, U.S. Department of Education, February 2, 2013, 14. The commission substituted "schools" for "educational foundations," a common error.

21. Jane Renaud, Cat McGrath, and David Wald, "The Michelle Rhee Series," *Education Week*, October 12, 2010. With her permission, I followed Rhee during her three-plus years in Washington for *PBS NewsHour*. In all, we aired twelve segments. While we aired the views of her critics, we did not uncover the widespread cheating. That was reported—brilliantly—by Jack Gillum, Marisol Bello, and Linda Mathews of *USA Today* after Rhee had resigned. See Jack Gillum and Marisol Bello, "When Standardized Test Scores Soared in D.C., Were the Gains Real?" *USA Today*, March 30, 2011.

In January 2013 the PBS series *Frontline* aired "The Education of Michelle Rhee." Reporting that story was probably the most frustrating experience of my career. We knew about a secret memo that confirmed Rhee was aware of the cheating by adults and yet did nothing about it; however, try as we might, we could not get a copy of the memo. One week *after* the *Frontline* program aired, someone leaked the memo to me. In sum, Rhee got away with it, and thousands of D.C. students were lied to about their progress and probably denied the remedial attention they deserved. See "The Education of Michelle Rhee," PBS, January 1, 2013. The full story of how Rhee and her team manipulated the investigations and covered up the cheating is on my blog: John Merrow, "Michelle Rhee's Reign of Error," *Taking Note*, April 11, 2013, http://takingnote.learningmatters.tv/?p=6232; John Merrow, "A Story About Michelle Rhee That No One Will Print," *Taking Note*, July 31, 2013, http://takingnote.learningmatters.tv/?p=6490.

22. Hall died before her trial could get under way. Eleven other Atlanta educators were convicted and sent to prison. In New York City a successful New York elementary school principal committed suicide after it was discovered that she had forged standardized English exam scores for her third-grade students. Jeanene Worrell-Breeden, forty-nine, jumped in front of a subway train on April 17, 2015, the day the impropriety was reported.

23. John Merrow, "'Tests Great'—'Less Knowing,'" *Merrow Report*, April 27, 2016, https://themerrowreport.com/2016/04/27/tests-great-less-knowing. I reimagined those old Miller Lite Beer commercials when I discussed the results in my blog that week.

24. Liana Heitin, "Reactions to 12th Grade NAEP Declines? Mostly Tempered," *Education Week*, April 29, 2016.

25. For more, see John Merrow, *Choosing Excellence* (Lanham, MD: Scarecrow Press, 2001).

26. That series of programs, "Juvenile Crime, Juvenile Justice," won the George Polk Award. At the award ceremony I got to meet I.F. Stone, one of my heroes.

27. Douglas F. Bodwell was only fifty-five when he succumbed to cancer in February 1998. Doug and I were about the same age and had started in Washington the same year, 1974. I came to know him as the soul of generosity, a good friend to everyone who cared about learning. His death was a great loss in so many ways. As director of education for CPB from 1974 until his death, Doug helped start twenty-two school television series, including *Reading Rainbow, 3-2-1 Contact*, and *Square One TV*, Emmy winners all. He also helped create the Adult Learning Service at PBS, the Learning Link computer network, and the twenty-three-state Satellite Educational Resources Consortium, in addition to being instrumental in the development of the Annenberg Channel.

Step Two: Calculate the Cost of Reform

1. My nonprofit production company, Learning Matters, received funding from the Gates and Broad Foundations, from the Ford, Annenberg, Wallace, Annie E. Casey, Spencer, Carnegie, Lilly, Hewlett, and Brin-Wojcicki Foundations, and from a dozen others. We were also supported by Toyota. In forty-one years, I turned down three grants and returned another when the funders attempted to interfere with my reporting.

2. Annie Em, "Is Public School for Sale? The Cost of KIPP," *Daily Kos*, April 8, 2014.

3. Matthew M. Chingos, "Strength in Numbers: State Spending on K–12 Assessment Systems," Brown Center on Education Policy, Brookings Institution, November 2012.

4. FairTest, e-mail correspondence, September 26, 2016.

5. During that same six-year period, my nonprofit, Learning Matters, received $1.078 million to support our reporting about New Orleans and Washington, D.C.

6. David Wald and John Tulenko, "The Turnaround Specialist Series," *Education Week Video*, November 15, 2005, http://learningmatters.tv/blog/on-pbs-newshour/watch-the-turnaround-specialist-series/1164.

7. As noted above, my nonprofit organization, Learning Matters, received support over the years from dozens of foundations. Two major

foundations cut off support, apparently because they became dissatisfied with our reporting about Michelle Rhee in Washington, D.C.

8. "Percent Difference from National Average Revenue (Cost-Adjusted)," EdBuild.org, 2016, http://viz.edbuild.org/maps/2016 /cola/resource-inequality/natl-average.html. This wonderful website will show you how uneven it is, and how your state and district do.

9. More than 25 percent of that is for Title I programs; another 25 percent goes for child nutrition programs, and 20 percent for special education.

10. National spending on public school students increased in FY2014, after falling for the previous four years, according to the National Center for Education Statistics. Prior to that, spending per student increased steadily each year between 2003–4 and 2007–8, peaking in 2008–9 at $11,621 per student. National spending was $12,131 in FY2014. Among large school districts, Alpine (Utah) spent the least, $5,634 per pupil, while Boston City Schools spent the most, $21,567. The federal government's spending on public elementary and secondary education declined by 4.1 percent in FY2014, to $54.2 billion. Stephen Q. Cornman, "Revenues and Expenditures for Public Elementary and Secondary School Districts: School Year 2013–14," National Center for Education Statistics, February 2017, https://nces.ed.gov/pubsearch /pubsinfo.asp?pubid=2016303.

11. "Taxpayers' Guide to Education Spending 2016," State of New Jersey Department of Education.

12. Most school districts have worked hard to reduce the student-to-administrator ratio ever since President Reagan's secretary of education, William Bennett, went after "the Blob." One exception was Washington, D.C., under Michelle Rhee, from 2007 to 2010. Although she removed about a hundred central office personnel in her first year, the central office was still considerably larger, with more administrators per teachers than any of the districts surrounding D.C. during her tenure. In fact, the surrounding districts reduced their central office staff, while D.C.'s grew. The greatest growth in DCPS over the years has been in the number of central office employees making $100,000 or more per year, from thirty-five when she arrived to ninety-nine when she left.

13. Valerie Strauss, "Guess What Michelle Rhee Charged a School to Speak," *Washington Post*, October 26, 2011.

14. Michael Winerip, "Amid a Federal Education Inquiry, an Unsettling Sight," *New York Times*, February 26, 2012. Rhee founded Students First with great fanfare, announcing on *Oprah* in 2010 that she intended to raise $1 billion and enroll one million members. She fell far short of achieving both goals, raising about $35 million in the first two years.

Membership figures were never announced. She stepped aside in 2014, and the group merged into 50Can, another advocacy group, in 2016.

15. J.D. Vance, *Hillbilly Elegy* (New York: HarperCollins, 2016), 244.

16. Perhaps you are thinking that most Americans believe in helping the neediest. As the Bible (Acts 11:29) has it, "And the disciples, every man according to his ability, determined to send relief." But in 1875 a fellow named Karl Marx copied the Frenchman Louis Blancin's rephrasing: "From each according to his ability, to each according to his need." That gives politicians an out, because nobody interested in a political future wants to echo Marx, even if he was borrowing from the Bible.

17. Jill Barshay, "The Gap Between Rich and Poor Schools Grew 44 Percent over a Decade," *Hechinger Report*, April 6, 2015.

18. Jason Amos, "Below the Surface: New Alliance Report Reveals Nation's Hidden High School Graduation Crisis," Alliance for Excellent Education, April 14, 2015. Nineteen states had at least twenty such schools in 2015. California and New York had 105 and 199 of these schools, respectively, while southern states such as Alabama and Mississippi had more than 50; Georgia had 115.

19. Marian Wang, "Evaluating Charter Schools," *ProPublica*, October 2014–February 2015, series of articles at http://www.propublica.org/series/evaluating-charter-schools.

20. Valerie Strauss, "How Messed Up Is California Charter School Sector? You Won't Believe How Much," *Washington Post*, September 9, 2016.

21. Ibid.

22. Stephen Henderson, "Betsy DeVos and the Twilight of Public Education," *Detroit Free Press*, December 6, 2016.

23. Albert Shanker, State Senator Ember Reichgott, Ted Kolderie, Joe Nathan, Sy Fliegel, and others played major roles at that meeting. All but Shanker, who died in 1997, remain deeply involved.

24. Ember Reichgott Junge, *Zero Chance of Passage: The Pioneering Charter School Story* (Edina, MN: Beaver's Pond Press, 2012).

25. "Learning Matters: Education's Big Gamble—Charter Schools (1997)," YouTube, posted by Learning Matters, April 16, 2012, https://youtu.be/Tlm7y5JdhFU; "Learning Matters: Trailer for New Orleans Charter School Documentary," YouTube, posted by Learning Matters, January 9, 2012, https://youtu.be/ziQ50qH6204.

26. A stunning takedown of the charter industry was provided by John Oliver on his HBO program *Last Week Tonight*. See "Charter Schools: *Last Week Tonight* with John Oliver (HBO)," YouTube, posted by LastWeekTonight, August 21, 2016, https://youtu.be/l_htSPGAY7I.

27. *CMO* is the term for nonprofit public charter schools. EMOs are

set up to make money and represent somewhere around 12 percent of all chartered schools.

28. I do not want to live by a double standard or knowingly hold charter schools to a higher standard. Teachers unions have had corruption issues, and their national leadership hasn't made much of a fuss. The American Medical Association is not upset, not publicly anyway, about Medicaid and Medicare fraud committed by some doctors, and so maybe it's unfair to expect the supporters of charter schools as the last best hope to be raging against the frauds and cheats

29. Arne Duncan, foreword to Richard Whitmire, *The Founders: Inside the Revolution to Invent and Reinvent America's Best Charter Schools* (New York: The 74 Media, Inc., 2016), 13.

30. "Jesse Woodson James (September 5, 1847–April 3, 1882) was an American outlaw, gang leader, bank robber, train robber, and murderer from the state of Missouri and the most famous member of the James-Younger Gang. Already a celebrity when he was alive, he became a legendary figure of the Wild West after his death." See "Jesse James," *Wikipedia*, accessed January 4, 2017.

31. Charter watchers often write about the difference between for-profit charter schools and not-for-profit charter schools. I am wondering whether this may be a distinction without a difference.

32. Marian Wang, "Charter School Power Broker Turns Public Education into Private Profits," *ProPublica*, October 15, 2014.

33. C. Briggs Petway Jr., Roger G. Mills, and Phyllis M. Pearson, "Columbus Schools Audit: 2012–2013," Learning Matters, 2013.

34. He does keep an eye on his teachers, Marian Wang reports: "Mitchell's company has managed the schools' staffs with similar rigor. A strong sense of hierarchy took root as the schools expanded. When a new corporate office was built to house the management company, teachers jokingly began calling it the 'White House.' From the 'White House,' Mitchell and other top administrators could watch teachers in their classrooms via surveillance cameras installed in every classroom, in every school. During a tour of school grounds with this reporter, Mitchell and the school's IT director discussed surveillance software called iSpy. 'We need to call it something else,' Mitchell offered with a chuckle. 'Call it iHelp or something.' Mitchell said the cameras give administrators the ability to observe teachers in action and offer them tips and coaching."

35. Gareth McGrath, "StarNews Files Lawsuit Against Charter Day School Inc.," *StarNews*, September 11, 2014.

36. Baker A. Mitchell, "Transparency—What You May Not Know . . . ," July 7, 2014, http://bakeramitchell.com/2014/07/07 /transparency-what-you-may-not-know.

37. Edward B. Fiske and Helen F. Ladd, "What's Up with Education Policy in North Carolina?" Learning Matters, February 2014.

38. Benjamin Herold, "Cybercharter Students Fall Far Behind on Academic Measures, New Study Says," *Education Week*, November 3, 2015.

39. James Woodworth, "Online Charter School Study, 2015," Center for Research on Education Outcomes, October 27, 2015.

40. For the full series, see Benjamin Herold and Arianna Prothero, "Rewarding Failure: An *Education Week* Investigation of the Cyber Charter Industry," *Education Week*, November 3, 2016.

41. Patrick O'Donnell, "Ohio's Charter Schools Ridiculed at National Conference, Even by National Charter Supporters," Cleveland Plain Dealer, March 2, 2015.

42. Doug Livingston, "Charter Schools Misspend Millions of Ohio Tax Dollars as Efforts to Police Them Are Privatized," *Beacon Journal*, June 3, 2015.

43. Matt Barnum, "Ohio's Charter School Disaster: How Big Profits and Pay-To-Play Operators Have Derailed Reform," The 74 Million, October 1, 2015.

44. He made it clear that he expected states to do his bidding in an interview shortly after he took office. Here's an excerpt:

JOHN MERROW: Do you anticipate using some of this stimulus money, this incentive money to help these national standards emerge?

ARNE DUNCAN: Absolutely.

JOHN MERROW: So states will get money if they do this thing that Duncan wants?

ARNE DUNCAN: If you play by these rules, absolutely right.

For more, see John Merrow, "Duncan Poised to Assert New Power as Education Chief," PBS, March 12, 2009.

45. The Gates Foundation paid McKinsey and Company to assist states with their applications.

46. Edward Cremata, "National Charter School Study, 2013," Center for Research on Education Outcomes, June 24, 2013.

47. Wendy Lecker, "The Hidden Costs of Charter Schools," *Stamford Advocate*, June 28, 2013.

48. "A Misguided Attack on Charter Schools," editorial, *New York Times*, October 13, 2016.

49. Ben Chapman, "Success Academy Charter Schools Revenue Doubles in a Year; CEO Eva Moskowitz's Pay Jumps to $567K," *Daily News*, December 19, 2014.

50. Moskowitz's schools also lose teachers, in droves. The website Glass Door provides testimony to working conditions there: "If you enjoy suspending children, pushing out special needs kids and never feeling appreciated for working 60 hour weeks, this job is for you. Incredible staff turnover leads to miserable schools for adults and kids alike." Or "The school I was at was a sinking ship, teachers were leaving by the dozen and no one was being hired to replace them therefore LT's and AT's were split up, classroom teachers were constantly shifted around, and the children suffered as a result. I had students getting 20's and 30's on exams due to the lack of consistency in the classroom. I was entirely scripted and told to yell at the children and get in their faces. The children were told to sit absolutely still, silent, with their backs straight, and hands locked in their lap. What child can maintain that for an entire school day?" And "I know it made me extremely uncomfortable when 8-year old children were under so much pressure from testing that they were getting nosebleeds and having accidents. You will be micro managed all the time. You will never be trusted to do your job by leadership. Do not work here unless you want to be miserable." See more at "Success Academy Charter Schools," glassdoor.com, accessed January 4, 2017, https://www.glassdoor.com/Reviews/Success-Academy -Charter-Schools-Reviews-E381408_P2.htm.

51. In fairness, some traditional public school districts in New York State are paying their superintendents inflated amounts when computed on a per-student basis. Brookhaven-Comsewogue Union Free School District has about 3,900 students and pays its superintendent $462,000, or $118 per student. Mount Sinai Union Free School District has about 2,600 students and pays its leader $403,000, or $155 per student. And Tuckahoe Union Free School District, with just 1,100 students, pays its superintendent $388,000, or $353 per student.

52. Some African American teachers leave because the system expects them to provide "tough love" to young African American boys, not the positive role model they need but the harsh attention that is supposed to keep them on the straight and narrow. For a persuasive take on this subject, see Christopher Emdin, "Why Black Men Quit Teaching," *New York Times*, August 28, 2016.

53. Stephen Sawchuk and Anthony Rebora, "New Teachers Make Up a Significant Segment of Profession," *Education Week*, October 4, 2016.

54. Darrel Drury and Justin Baer, *The American Public School Teacher: Past, Present, and Future* (Cambridge, MA: Harvard Education Press, 2011).

55. Matthew Ronfeldt, Susanna Loeb, and James Wyckoff, "How Teacher Turnover Harms Student Achievement," National Center for Analysis of Longitudinal Data in Education Research, January 2012.

56. In school year 2000–01, I followed five untrained New York City rookies in a seven-part "serial" for the *NewsHour.* We called it "Making the Grade," although *NewsHour* anchor Jim Lehrer privately referred to it as "the PBS version of *Survivor*" (http://www.pbs.org/newshour/bb /education-july-dec00-morrow_9-19). In the late 1980s I followed two rookies in a Maryland district and observed the same "sink or swim" treatment. That *NewsHour* series is no longer available online.

57. The approach summarized in the slogan "A rising tide lifts all boats" is doomed to fail as long as greed rules in the larger society. And make no mistake, greed is in the saddle. Over the last thirty years, the salary of the typical CEO has increased 127 times faster than workers' salaries. To put this in perspective, the average Fortune 500 chief executive is paid 380 times more than the average worker. In 1982, the ratio stood at 42:1. If we backed away from greed, we would be more open to recognizing the scourge of poverty and the long term threat it poses to our nation. If we were genuinely disgusted by greed and not merely embarrassed by it, our hearts would not be so hard, and our generosity would rise to the surface.

58. That phrasing, "ready to learn," reveals that these people didn't know much about children or learning. Children are born ready to *learn*, because learning is what we humans do. Many young children may not be ready for *school*, but that's an entirely different thing. It's the height of arrogance or ignorance (or both) to equate learning and schooling, and people who do not grasp the distinction should not be setting national goals.

59. There's not one word in any of the eight goals about test scores! And Goal #8 encourages social and emotional growth. I say bravo, but wonder what happened to that noble idea.

Step Three: Don't Pay the Price

1. "Learning Matters: Good School, Bad School," YouTube, posted by Learning Matters, June 7, 2011, https://youtu.be/2HdXHTh3h2o. For the transcript, see John Merrow and Cat McGrath, "Good School/Bad School Transcript," Learning Matters, June 6, 2011, http://learningmatters.tv/transcripts/newshour/GoodSchoolBadSchool.pdf.

2. Charles Taylor Kerchner, "L.A. Board Vote Reveals Charter Politics," *Education Week*, January 13, 2016.

3. It's not possible to determine the amount of funding simply by summing the total of education-related grants because foundations, particularly the Bill and Melinda Gates Foundation, have supported a wide range of education-related activities, including union projects and reporting about education. My organization, Learning Matters, received several grants from the Gates Foundation, including one that supported

our ongoing *NewsHour* coverage of what was going on in Washington, D.C., and New Orleans.

Furthermore, it's not just foundations that are funding school reform. Wealthy hedge fund operators and others have poured money into charter schools, Teach for America, and other "data-driven" efforts. And not every corporation has turned its back on public schools. See Paul Perry and David Callahan, "The 'Big Bet' of a Funder That Hasn't Forgotten Traditional Public Schools," *Inside Philanthropy*, September 7, 2016.

4. See, e.g., Diane Ravitch's blog at https://dianeravitch.net, Mercedes Schneider's blog at https://deutsch29.wordpress.com, and Anthony Cody's blog at http://www.livingindialogue.com.

5. Readers of a certain age and mind-set will recognize that I am stealing from *National Lampoon*, which once devoted an entire issue to that same essential question but asked instead about pornography!

6. "Vergara v. California," *Students Matter*, http://studentsmatter.org/case/vergara; John Fensterwald, "Group Created by Silicon Valley Millionaire Targets Teacher Evaluations in California," *Huffington Post*, July 21, 2015.

7. "Toughest Job in America," Learning Matters, March 15, 1999, http://learningmatters.tv/blog/documentaries/watch-toughest-job-in-america/673.

8. Launa Hall, "This Ed-Reform Trend Is Supposed to Motivate Students. Instead, It Shames Them," *Washington Post*, May 19, 2016. She also writes: "When policymakers mandate tests and buy endlessly looping practice exams to go with them, their image of education is from 30,000 feet. They see populations and sweeping strategies. From up there, it seems reasonable enough to write a list of 32 discrete standards and mandate that every 8-year-old in the state meet them. How else will we know for sure that teaching and learning are happening down there?"

9. An articulate and often painfully funny approach to this can be found on the blog of David Lee Finkle, *Mr. Fitz*, MrFitz.com, http://www.mrfitz.com/the-creator.php.

10. Anthony Cody, "Cui Bono? The Question Rarely Asked, Let Alone Investigated," *Education Week*, April 17, 2012.

Step Four: Ask the Right Question

1. ADD is also called attention deficit hyperactivity disorder, or ADHD. I use the original term in this book. Alan Schwarz's *ADHD Nation* (New York: Scribner, 2016) has a revealing analysis of the history of the condition's naming.

2. John Merrow and John Tulenko, "A.D.D.—A Dubious Diagnosis?"

Education Week, October 13, 1995, http://learningmatters.tv/blog/documentaries/watch-add-a-dubious-diagnosis/640.

3. Alan Schwarz and Sarah Cohen, "A.D.H.D. Seen in 11% of U.S. Children as Diagnoses Rise," *New York Times*, March 31, 2013.

4. Jim Sliwa, "Persistent ADHD Associated with Overly Critical Parents," press release, American Psychological Association, February 8, 2016.

5. Schwarz, *ADHD Nation*, 14.

6. Sue Parry, an activist who has spent more than twenty years educating parents about the perils of medicating young children, told me in an email that she believes school psychologists and counselors bear some responsibility for the ADD epidemic. "I have come to the conclusion that what we really have is a 'system of care' rather than a 'system of education.' Our suggestion is to drastically reduce, if not completely eliminate, the number of non-essential teaching personnel, particularly school psychologists, employed by the public school system. The school psychologists are instrumental if not pivotal in confirming diagnosis such as ADHD, CD, ODD, etc. As you know with the inclusion of ADHD as a disability under IDEA, too many children are being 'identified' (a very harsh word) and found eligible for services. Instead the money should be used for curricula enriched with drama, music, art, better playgrounds. I've seen first-hand when students are given a more exploratory/expressive environment their very severe ADHD symptoms up and disappear. Just like [Dr. Peter] Breggin wrote, 'The schools have provided the mental health professions with the entering wedge for turning a large proportion of children into involuntary psychiatric consumers.'" Sue Parry, e-mail message to author.

7. Richard A. Friedman, "A Natural Fix for A.D.H.D.," *New York Times*, October 31, 2014.

8. No one sued or even threatened to sue, although the program was ignored when broadcasting's major awards were handed out.

9. Samuel Levin and Susan Engel, *A School of Our Own* (New York: The New Press, 2016), 28.

10. Otherwise known as Public Law 94-142, it has been reauthorized five times (1983, 1986, 1990, 1997, and 2004). It is now called IDEA, the Individuals with Disabilities Education Act. A note on the history of terminology: Not long after the law was initially passed, the term *handicapped* was soon cast aside, and *special needs* became the term of choice. Soon *handicapped* became the field's "*h*-word," never to be spoken in public. Word games ensued. Some preferred *exceptional* as the descriptive adjective—and in fact it had been the Council for Exceptional Children in Washington that pushed hardest for passage of legislation in the

1970s. Militants often referred to nondisabled children (and adults) as "temporarily able-bodied," but that did not catch on.

11. Most recently about 14 percent of students were identified and being served, but these services account for at least 21 percent of school spending. Between 1996 and 2005, 40 percent of all new education dollars went to special education, according to Miriam Freedman's new book, *Special Education 2.0: Breaking Taboos to Build a New Education Law* (School Law Pro, 2017).

12. The law and its successors have created other problems, most notably the "lawyering up" of parents determined to force public schools to pay for expensive private school education for their children with special needs. It's not a "cottage industry" for lawyers, the special education attorney Miriam Freedman notes, but a "mansion industry."

13. Freedman, *Special Education 2.0*. In it she asks two important questions: "What if we design schools that *really* focus on teaching and learning for *all* students—general and special education? What if we move beyond tweaking today's broken system to build a 21st century one?"

14. Testing accommodations for students with disabilities are mandated in the newest version of the Elementary and Secondary Education Act, known as the Every Student Succeeds Act. Common accommodations for students with disabilities include extended test-taking time, dictated response, large print, Braille, the use of a sign language interpreter, and assistive technology devices.

15. A nation and its people can be judged by how they treat the least fortunate. In this respect, the United States deserves some credit. Like this country, public schools are a work in progress. It's easy to criticize schools, and often the criticism is warranted, but it's important to stop every once in a while and give ourselves credit for doing the right thing.

16. Richard K. Davis, "CEO Survey Results," Business Council, May 2013, 7.

17. Of course, "business" is not monolithic in its goals and interests. At the national meeting where the study referenced above was made public, I happened to be sitting next to Amazon founder Jeff Bezos, whose company's innovations have cut thousands of jobs. As the list of what business supposedly wants was presented, Bezos muttered to no one in particular, "What about getting to work on time!"

18. Some examples include Robin Hood, Teach for America, and Success Academy. See "Programs," Robin Hood, http://www.robinhood .org/programs; "#71 Teach for America," *Forbes*, http://www.forbes .com/companies/teach-for-america; Carl Campanile, "Charter School Network Lands $25M Donation From Hedge Fund," *New York Post*, April 12, 2016; Eliza Shapiro, "Success Academy Announces $8.5M. Donation," *Politico*, July 30, 2015.

19. Colonial leaders including John Adams, James Monroe, Robert Livingston, Benjamin Franklin, and Oliver Wolcott knew that education mattered. They most likely learned to read, write, and calculate at what were called "dame schools," generally in the homes of elderly women who tutored children for a fee. Others may have learned in private schools, which were more expensive and rarer, in Sunday school, or at home, taught by a parent.

There were few public schools in early America, most of them one-room grammar schools, even though the Land Ordinance of 1785 specified that the western territories were to be divided into townships made up of 640-acre sections, one of which was to be set aside "for the maintenance of public schools."

The first system of publicly funded schools emerged in Massachusetts in the 1840s, but the state had passed a law in 1827 requiring towns with more than 500 families to have a public high school.

While education mattered to early Americans, it was for boys, and it was a local matter. As we know, the words *education* and *school* do not appear in the original U.S. Constitution or in the Bill of Rights.

Slave owners clearly knew that education was important, and most owners did all they could to prevent their "property" from learning to read and write.

For nearly two hundred years, the federal government had scant involvement in primary and secondary education, largely restricting itself to collecting data through its Office of Education, which was established in 1867 (the same year that Howard University was founded). Washington played an important role in the development of higher education, notably through the two Morrill Acts that established the land grant colleges and universities and historically black colleges and universities.

Step Five: Make Connections

1. Erika Christakis, *The Importance of Being Little: What Preschoolers Really Need from Grownups* (New York: Viking Press, 2016), 4.

2. Angela Duckworth, Education Writers Association meeting, Boston, May 2016.

3. Carol Dweck, *Mindset: The New Psychology of Growth* (New York: Penguin Random House, 2006).

4. The concept of social and emotional learning was popularized by *New York Times* science reporter Daniel Goleman. See Daniel Goleman, *Emotional Intelligence: Why It Can Matter More Than IQ* (New York: Bantam Books, 2005).

5. "Social and Emotional Learning: A Short History," Edutopia, October 6, 2011.

6. Politicians looking for an appealing school photo op often went to a Comer school. The list includes Bill Clinton, Barack Obama, and both Bushes. That didn't stop them from embracing widespread testing, however.

7. "Comer School Development Program," PBS, http://www.pbs .org/makingschoolswork/sbs/csp.

8. When reporting a school story, I liked to watch the principal greet students arriving on school buses. Often he or she seemed to greet every kid by name, and I could tell from the kids' reactions that it meant a lot to them to be known by name. This was, a principal told me, "part of my job." That got me wondering: was there an upper limit to the number of names a principal could retain? One principal told me that she knew all four hundred of her students by sight and generally could come up with first names. But another principal of a school with four hundred students said that he knew only "the good kids and the bad kids," but not the ones in the middle. That man needs to be in a smaller school! Rule of thumb #1: Schools should be small enough so that the principal can know every child's name. Rule of thumb #2: Anyone who is not interested in knowing students by name shouldn't be a school principal.

9. John Tulenko and Carrie Glasser, "Lessons of War," Learning Matters, April 5, 2007, http://learningmatters.tv/blog/on-pbs-newshour /watch-lessons-of-war/46.

10. One of my brothers had a mental breakdown when he was twenty-one. Because of that experience, I have been alternately fascinated and repelled by our national attitude toward mental illness.

11. We put that on the air, although we sent all the stations an advance warning notice and we put a disclaimer on the air at the beginning of the program. As it happened, many stations aired my program in the afternoons. After all, it was called *Options in Education*, and what could be more wholesome than that? Most NPR stations back then were affiliated with a college or university, and a college president in Texas happened to be riding in his car, listening to "his" station, when all of a sudden he heard some girl talking about blow jobs. Lesson learned: tough issues may *not* get you thrown off the air, but curse words and descriptions of explicit sex definitely will.

12. I would not be allowed such access today, but I am virtually certain that if I were, I would meet today's versions of Lisa, Mary, and Roy in every public mental health facility.

13. Neal A. Palmer, Emily A. Greytak, and Joseph G. Kosciw, "Educational Exclusion: Drop Out, Push Out, and the School-to-Prison Pipeline Among LGBTQ Youth," GLSEN, June 2, 2016.

14. Ibid.

15. Hanna Rosin, "The Silicon Valley Suicides," *The Atlantic*, December 2015.

16. Ibid.

17. At Virginia State College, the historically black institution where I was teaching during the day.

18. Ellen Condliffe Lagemann has written a thoughtful, persuasive book about the value of providing educational opportunities for incarcerated men and women. See her *Liberating Minds: The Case for College in Prison* (New York: The New Press, 2017).

19. Christine Sampson, "$175K for South Fork Mental Health Services," *East Hampton Star*, March 31, 2015; Christine Sampson, "Hotlines Not Enough to Fight Suicide Epidemic," *East Hampton Star*, June 4, 2015.

20. Erin Duffy, "Mental Health Program Goes Extra Mile to Get Kids Help," *Omaha World-Herald*, December 6, 2015.

21. The charter school chain known as Rocketship pays careful attention to its outdoor morning rituals. These include music and dancing, shout-outs to children who've done something noteworthy, and asking parents to say hello to newcomers.

22. People are trying to teach and measure grit or buying into a formula like "10,000 hours." Not smart.

Step Six: Start Early

1. What to call these programs is open for debate. They're usually called early childhood education or preschool, but both terms put too much emphasis on formal learning, a danger in real life, as I will explain. Others call them early childhood education and care (ECEC), but I suggest we call them early childhood care and education, because the acronym ECCE is Latin for "behold!"

When I was working on this chapter, I read of the death of Bettye Caldwell, whom the *New York Times* called "a prekindergarten apostle." At Syracuse University in the 1960s, Caldwell did the ground-breaking research on the effects of poverty on young children that led to Head Start. She preferred the term *educare*.

2. Betty Hart and Todd R. Risley, "The Early Catastrophe," American Federation of Teachers, Spring 2013.

3. Lori Hil, "The Amazing Benefits of Early Education," Early Education Central, http://www.earlyeducationcentral.com/educational/early-education-matters.

4. *For Each and Every Child: A Strategy for Education Equity and Excellence*, Equity and Excellence Commission, U.S. Department of Education, February 2, 2013, 28.

5. Sarah Cwiek, "State Superintendent: Student Assessments Should Happen More Often, Start Younger," Michigan Radio, April 20, 2016.

6. Erika Christakis, *The Importance of Being Little: What Preschoolers Really Need from Grownups* (New York: Viking Press, 2016), 109.

7. Ibid., 95.

8. Ibid., 106, 107.

9. Lillian G. Katz, "Lively Minds: Distinctions Between Academic Versus Intellectual Goals for Young Children," *Defending the Early Years*, April 9, 2015, https://deyproject.files.wordpress.com/2015/04/dey-lively-minds-4-8-15.pdf, 4.

10. I also recommend shunning educators who encourage "rigor" and the importance of a "rigorous" curriculum. Merriam-Webster defines rigor thusly: "1 a (1) : harsh inflexibility in opinion, temper, or judgment : severity (2) : the quality of being unyielding or inflexible : strictness (3) : severity of life : austerity b : an act or instance of strictness, severity, or cruelty. 2 : a tremor caused by a chill." Some educators now say there's also an "educational definition," but they're just covering their asses.

11. Lauren Bauer and Diane Whitmore Schanzenbach, "The Long-Term Impact of the Head Start Program," Hamilton Project, August 19, 2016.

12. Sean F. Reardon, "No Rich Child Left Behind," *New York Times*, April 27, 2013.

13. Cat McGrath and Jeremy Levine, "Early College HS in South Texas," *Education Week*, July 4, 2012, http://learningmatters.tv/blog/on-pbs-newshour/watch-early-college.

14. Service learning is now required for high school graduation in some school districts, including some in Chicago. The hours are minimal because many students need paying jobs, which these are not. See "Service Learning: Mission and Goals," Chicago Public Schools, accessed January 4, 2017, http://www.servicelearning.cps.k12.il.us. The Jobs for the Future Early College High School model blends secondary and postsecondary curricula; similar models in career and occupational fields are sponsored by industry and by unions.

15. Should two years of college be free, as several candidates urged during the prolonged 2016 presidential campaign? Sorry, but there's no free lunch. What I'd support is two years of post-high-school education or training in return for two years of national service, which could be in the military, tough-to-staff schools, the Civilian Conservation Corps, the Peace Corps, or some other organization that seeks to improve our society.

16. W. Steven Barnett, "The State of Preschool, 2015," National Institute for Early Education Research, May 2016. This report comes

out annually, so please go to the NIEER.org website for the most recent data.

17. Ibid. "Across all public programs—Pre-K general and special education enrollments plus federally funded Head Start—41 percent of 4-year-olds and 16 percent of 3-year-olds were served. Since 2010, total enrollment in these programs at age 4 has risen by just one percentage point and enrollment at age 3 by one percentage point as well."

18. The "Hall of Shame" includes many western states: Washington, Oregon, Montana, Idaho, Wyoming, North and South Dakota, Minnesota, Nevada, Utah, Arizona, Hawaii, and Alaska. Also on the list are Vermont, Rhode Island, Massachusetts, Indiana, Ohio, Missouri, and Mississippi.

19. Other countries do a better job, including France, whose programs we profiled. See "The Promise of Preschool," *Learning Matters*, October 4, 2002, http://learningmatters.tv/blog/documentaries/watch -the-promise-of-preschool/9946.

20. France, Israel, New Zealand, Belgium, Denmark, Italy, Iceland, United Kingdom, Spain, Norway, Germany, Sweden, and the Netherlands. For preschool and kindergarten enrollment in the United States, see "Preschool and Kindergarten Enrollment," National Center for Education Statistics, May 2016, http://nces.ed.gov/programs/coe /indicator_cfa.asp.

21. Including two of our most populous states, Texas and Florida. The latter spends less than $3,000 per child.

22. CJ Libassi, "Raising Arizona: Lessons for the Nation from a State's Experience with Full-Day Kindergarten," *New America*, February 24, 2014.

23. James Ford, "Kindergarten Play Canceled So Students Can Focus on 'College' and 'Career,'" WPIX, April 28, 2014.

24. While I met John King, Duncan's successor, several times, he had not yet become secretary of education by the time I retired, and I never formally interviewed him.

Step Seven: Expect More

1. I am quoting Will Durant's (1885–1981) 1926 work, *The Story of Philosophy* (New York: Pocket Books, 1991), 76. Durant was expanding upon an observation of Aristotle's, and the quote within the quote is from Aristotle's *Ethics*. The observation is particularly appropriate for children and the schools they go to.

2. The civil rights icon James Meredith agrees. "The right to fail is just as important as the right to succeed: children must be encouraged to experiment and to learn from their intellectual mistakes and failures

without punishment. They must be free to be children." See Valerie Strauss, "Civil Rights Icon James Meredith: 'We Are in a Dark Age of American Public Education,'" *Washington Post*, June 1, 2016.

3. Richard C. Clarke, e-mail correspondence with the author, April 23, 2015.

4. Angela Duckworth, "Graduating and Looking for Your Passion? Just Be Patient," *New York Times*, June 4, 2016. She writes: "Rather than ask 'What do I want to be when I grow up?,' ask 'In what way do I wish the world were different? What problem can I help solve?' This puts the focus where it should be—on how you can serve other people."

5. For more information, see the "Coalition for Community Schools: Overview," Institute for Educational Leadership, accessed January 4, 2017, http://www.communityschools.org/about/overview.aspx. Full disclosure: I serve on the board of the Institute for Educational Leadership, the umbrella organization that houses the coalition.

6. Nicholas Garcia, "New Federal Education Laws Can Reestablish Respect for Teachers, Union Chief Says," *Chalkbeat*, November 7, 2016.

7. I find it revealing that Comer and Hirsch are not professional educators. Perhaps education is too important to be left to educators, after all. Don was the classic mild-mannered professor of English at the University of Virginia when he had his epiphany. Full disclosure: I consider both men to be my friends, although our friendship grew out of my admiration for their programs, which I came to know as a reporter.

8. Maegan Slowakiewicz, "All About Makerspaces," Corbett Inc., April 14, 2015, http://www.corbettinc.com/blog/?p=2726; "What's a Makerspace?," Makerspace.com, accessed January 4, 2017, http://spaces .makerspace.com.

9. High Tech High began as a single high school in 2000 but now encompasses four elementary schools, four middle schools, five high schools, and a teacher-training institution. Founder Larry Rosenstock is an American hero, in my book. See *Most Likely to Succeed*, documentary film, directed by Greg Whiteley (2015; El Dorado Hills: One Potato Productions), DVD.

"Learning by doing" is too glib a description of Expeditionary Learning, now called EL Learning. Here are its ten principles, with some descriptive phrases:

1. The Primacy of Self-Discovery
2. The Having of Wonderful Ideas
3. The Responsibility for Learning (personal and collective)
4. Empathy and Caring: Learning is fostered best in communities where students' and teachers' ideas are respected and where there is mutual trust.
5. Success and Failure: All students need to be successful if they

are to build the confidence and capacity to take risks and meet increasingly difficult challenges. But it is also important for students to learn from their failures, to persevere when things are hard, and to learn to turn disabilities into opportunities.

6. Collaboration and Competition (integrate them)

7. Diversity and Inclusion

8. The Natural World: A direct and respectful relationship with the natural world refreshes the human spirit and teaches the important ideas of recurring cycles and cause and effect.

9. Solitude and Reflection: Students and teachers need time alone to explore their own thoughts, make their own connections, and create their own ideas. They also need to exchange their reflections with other students and with adults.

10. Service and Compassion: We are crew, not passengers.

The ten design principles reflect the values of the founder of Outward Bound, Kurt Hahn. For more information, see "EL Education," http:// eleducation.org.

10. Paul Tough, "How Kids Learn Resilience," *The Atlantic*, June 2016.

11. John Tulenko, "Maine School Engages Kids with Relevant Problem-Solving Challenges," *PBS NewsHour*, May 6, 2103; John Tulenko and David Wald, "Teachers Embrace 'Deep Learning,' Translating Lessons into Practical Skills," Learning Matters, January 30, 2013.

12. "Reinventing High Schools for Postsecondary Success," Jobs for the Future, accessed January 4, 2017, http://www.jff.org/initiatives/early -college-designs.

13. Kimberly Mobley, "Exemplary Concurrent Enrollment Now Stretches from Coast to Coast: 15 Programs Awarded NACEP Accreditation," National Alliance of Concurrent Enrollment Partnerships, May 2, 2016.

14. "Esther Wojcicki," *Wikipedia*, accessed January 4, 2017.

15. Projects can have wrong answers, of course. In the example of designing toys based on neuroscience, students might get the science wrong, or they might design something that an infant or toddler could not manipulate. Other answers might be impractical or inappropriate, such as an advertising campaign for the toy that featured sexy naked people draped over sports cars, and the class discussion of that campaign would be a major teachable moment. Process matters a great deal. Students get to try their ideas with each other (and their teacher) during the project. Falling short is a huge part of the learning process.

16. Ashley Jochim and Patrick McGuinn, "The Politics of the Common Core Assessments," *Education Next*, August 3, 2016. The number of states participating in either the Smarter Balanced or PARCC Common

Core tests dropped from a high of forty-five in 2010 to twenty in 2016. Some of the opposition came from the SAT and the ACT testing organizations, which stood to lose a substantial amount of money if schools dropped them in favor of the Common Core tests.

17. Coherence created *from the bottom up* with the participation of teachers, students, and the community would probably go a long way toward making the teaching profession more appealing, and that could lower the attrition rate in the teaching profession. But should that happen, schools of education would find themselves with a lot of empty seats, meaning goodbye to higher education's golden goose.

18. Cat McGrath and David Wald, "Good School, Bad School," http://learningmatters.tv/blog/on-pbs-newshour/watch-good-school-bad-school/7162.

Step Eight: Embrace Technology (Carefully)

1. I wrote and edited this book on Google Docs, an invaluable tool. For more on Amazon, see Meg Conlan, "What Does Amazon Inspire Mean for Education?," *EdTech*, July 19, 2016.

2. Tod Newcombe, "What Went Wrong with L.A. Unified's iPad Program?," GovTech, May 14, 2015.

3. Patrick Michels, "The High Cost of iPad-mania in Public Schools," *Texas Observer*, November 5, 2013, http://www.texasobserver.org/run-school-ipad-program.

4. Grace Tatter, "Emails Reveal Months of Missteps Leading Up to Tennessee's Disastrous Online Testing Debut," *Chalkbeat*, June 28, 2016' experiences with technology, see Molly Hensley-Clancy's fine article, "Baltimore's Challenge: Buy Tablets For 100,000 Kids, And Don't Mess It Up," *Buzzfeed*, June 22, 2015, https://www.buzzfeed.com/mollyhensleyclancy/the-plan-to-buy-100000-baltimore-kids-a-tablet.

5. *Inside the Black Box of Classroom Practice: Change Without Reform in American Education* (Boston: Harvard University Press, 2013), 33. He also addresses this issue frequently on his blog, https://larrycuban.wordpress.com.

6. After writing this, I came across these lines: "The problem was, the nature of most of our classes meant that you could learn the material well enough to get good grades without ever really engaging with it in any meaningful way. We would learn the periodic table—something I now know to be elegant and fascinating—by memorizing the abbreviations and their places in the boxes. So you could sail by on a test without ever knowing how the periodic table might save lives, or how you would use it to go about designing an experiment to find a new element. So the friends who were getting straight A's were doing it without

ever becoming passionate about their work or about learning itself." Sam wrote those words based on his own high school experiences. See Samuel Levin and Susan Engel, *A School of Our Own* (New York: The New Press, 2016).

7. As long as adult jobs and student promotions and graduations are determined by test scores, there will be cheating. Some adults will look the other way as students use wireless devices to share answers, for example. After the tests are turned in, some adults may use an older technology, the pencil eraser, to change scores.

8. My colleagues and I were surprised to discover this during our reporting for what became my final film for PBS. See John Merrow, *School Sleuth: The Case of the Wired Classroom*, PBS, October 1, 2015.

9. Catherine Steiner-Adair and Teresa H. Barker, *The Big Disconnect: Protecting Childhood and Family Relationships in the Digital Age* (New York: Harper Collins, 2014).

10. Cathy N. Davidson, *Now You See It: How Technology and Brain Science Will Transform Schools and Business for the 21st Century* (New York: Penguin Books, 2012).

11. Money talks. Understanding the legal and financial ramifications of all forms of bullying is one of the best incentives to get schools involved in developing specific programs for students, families, administrators, teachers, staff, including the janitors. Self-interest is a powerful incentive, as are the threats of federal involvement and individual lawsuits. Together, these should motivate schools to proactively develop strong prevention programs—to let everyone know that "we don't tolerate bullying here, because we're better than that."

12. Cevin Soling, comment on *The Merrow Report*, September 19, 2013, https://themerrowreport.com/2013/09/19/a-heartbreaking-and -preventable-death. Other excellent work on bullying includes Emily Bazelon, *Sticks and Stones: Defeating the Culture of Bullying and Rediscovering the Power of Character and Empathy* (New York: Random House, 2014), and Elizabeth Kandel Englander, *Bullying and Cyberbullying: What Every Educator Needs to Know* (Cambridge, MA: Harvard Education Press, 2013).

13. The MacArthur Foundation supports a lot of great research on the uses of technology in school settings.

Step Nine: Embrace "Outsiders" (Enthusiastically)

1. Another 1 percent (of all Americans) are public school teachers, who also have a personal stake in the success of schools.

2. Paul Taylor and Mark Hugo Lopez, "Six Take-Aways from the Census Bureau's Voting Report," Pew Research Center, May 8, 2013.

3. I'll wager many readers can remember when a firefighter came to class and talked about the job, or maybe it was a police officer. In younger grades, teachers often ask parents to come and talk about their jobs. That's a common way of "connecting with the community," in edu-speak. In many school districts, businesses are invited to "adopt" a school and donate stuff they don't need. My children's elementary school had lots of pretty useless crap lying around, the largess of some neighborhood businesses. Do those strategies work? As the lawyers say, asked and answered.

4. Oh, and there's a third goal that other former English teachers will appreciate: creating a network of shared poetry for all to enjoy.

5. Here's a list of poems that I think will work for this project:

"Where the Sidewalk Ends," Shel Silverstein
"How Do I Love Thee? (Sonnet 43)," Elizabeth Barrett Browning
"The Road Not Taken," Robert Frost
"Do Not Go Gentle into That Good Night," Dylan Thomas
"I Know Why the Caged Bird Sings," Maya Angelou
"If," Rudyard Kipling
"The Tiger," William Blake
"As Soon as Fred Gets Out of Bed," Jack Prelutsky
"The Rose That Grew from Concrete," Tupac Shakur
"America," Claude McKay
"The Pig," Roald Dahl
"The Waking," Theodore Roethke
"The Lanyard," Billy Collins
"anyone lived in a pretty how town," ee cummings
"Anthem for Doomed Youth," Wilfred Owen
"The Llama," Ogden Nash
"The Remains," Mark Strand
"Shall I Compare Thee to a Summer's Day," William Shakespeare
"When I have fears that I may cease to be," John Keats
"To Be or Not to Be" (from *Hamlet*), William Shakespeare
"A Boat Beneath a Sunny Sky," Lewis Carroll
"A Nation's Strength," Ralph Waldo Emerson
"I Am a Rock," Paul Simon
"Whatif," Shel Silverstein
"Still I Rise," Maya Angelou
"Messy Room," Shel Silverstein
"I Wandered Lonely as a Cloud," William Wordsworth
"O Captain! My Captain!," Walt Whitman
"All the World's a Stage" (from *As You Like It*), William Shakespeare
"Poem for the Musical Stomp," Janee J. Baugher
"An Opera House," Amy Lowell

"Listening," Amy Lowell
"Jabberwocky," Lewis Carroll
"A Lower East Side Poem," Miguel Pinero
"At the Blue Note," Pablo Medina

6. Don't be a slave to the line breaks of a poem, but pay attention instead to the thought and idea breaks. The lines that participants recite should make sense, standing alone. And students should be prepared to talk with the adults about the poem and its meanings. That is, they will be teaching.

7. Readers are going to screw up. Do *not* be tempted to compile the errors into a "just for laughs" reel to show others. That attitude will get out, as will the film, and your project and your reputation are toast. The only person you should tease or make fun of is yourself!

8. As they search for talent, and as they edit on their computers, I am sure that some of these young producers will start to take some chances, let their imaginations run free. Perhaps they will have the dry cleaner saying "Out, damned spot." Or the local watch repair guy reciting "To-morrow, and to-morrow, and to-morrow, creeps in this petty pace from day to day, to the last syllable of recorded time . . ." The credit roll at the end could have still images of the adults with their names on the screen (if they want to be identified by name). Or the kids could ask adults to identify themselves and their place of business. The team of producers also might want to turn the camera on themselves and say, "We're students at ZZ school, and we produced this video."

9. For an example, see my report for the *NewsHour*, "Turning Parents into Teachers to Fight the 'Summer Slide' in Reading," *PBS NewsHour*, August 22, 2014.

Step Ten: Embrace Teachers (Respectfully)

1. Lisette Partelow and Christina Baumgardner, "Educator Pipeline at Risk," Center for American Progress, September 2015; Lelb Sutcher, Linda Darling-Hamond, and Desiree Carver-Thomas, "A Coming Crisis in Teaching? Teacher Supply, Demand, and Shortages in the U.S.," Learning Policy Institute, September 15, 2016.

2. Washington has one of the highest turnover rates in the nation. Mark Simon, "Is Teacher Churn Undermining Education Reform in D.C.?," *Washington Post*, June 15, 2012. Simon writes: "55 percent of new teachers leave in their first *two years*, according to an analysis by DCPS budget watchdog Mary Levy. Eighty percent are gone by the end of their sixth year. That means that most of the teachers brought in during the past five years are no longer there. By comparison, in Montgomery County just 11.5 percent leave by the end of their second year, and

30 percent by the end of year five. DCPS has become a teacher turnover factory."

3. The question of whether teaching is a profession or an occupation is something of a red herring. The real issue is the degree of autonomy that teachers have within the school bureaucracy. When they have the time and ability to collaborate, and when they have significant influence over what is taught and how progress is assessed, then labels do not matter, and arguing about status is a waste of time.

4. Diane Stark Rentner, Nancy Kober, and Matthew Frizzell, "Listen to Us: Teacher Views and Voices," Center on Education Policy, May 5, 2015.

5. Ibid., 5.

6. DFER is the principal vehicle for corporate reformers and supporters of test-based accountability. Its leadership and key supporters include Whitney Tilson, Shavar Jefferies, Joe Williams, Barbara O'Brien, and Andrew Rotherham. As the opt-out movement picked up steam, Rotherham reassured *U.S. News and World Report* readers in July 2016 that all would be well and that school reform would survive. For more, see Andrew J. Rotherham, "Democrats Aren't Done with Education," *U.S. News and World Report,* July 20, 2016.

7. I think schools should also create opportunities and incentive for teachers to make home visits. My colleague Anne Henderson, a keen observer of education, told me that teacher turnover in Sacramento significantly decreased after teachers made relationship-building home visits with low-income families. She said teachers told her things like, "I never felt before that I could make a difference in my students' lives, but now I know how to make a real connection to families and collaborate with them to improve their children's learning. I was going to leave teaching because I felt so hopeless."

8. The Obama administration put its money on *assessing teachers,* using standardized test scores as the essential measure. A requirement for Race to the Top dollars was a test-based system of teacher accountability.

9. "Teacher Town Hall: 2014 Emerging Issues Forum," YouTube, posted by Institute for Emerging Issues, February 24, 2014, https://youtu.be/WrhST79USXU.

10. Ibid.

11. Life is unfair. A month after that panel, Vivian went to her doctor to find out why one leg was giving her trouble. She wrote about it on her blog: "On March 12th, 2014, I learned that I have ALS, better known as Lou Gehrig's disease, and that over the next 2–10 years—most likely 3–5 years—my motor neurons will gradually stop working and I will lose the use of my limbs, then become unable to breathe and swallow,

and then cease to be." She never asked for sympathy, just that we do the right thing: "As my students have heard me say, regardless of what we each believe about our ability to 'Change the World,' we all DO change it: we each make it a little better or a little worse. I have tried to live with a determination to be on the right side of history and, when I could muster the strength, the generous side of kindness. I certainly have won some and lost some—I am not the gentlest or most patient soul—but I hope I have made the world a bit better, and I have a very short bucket list. I wish you all the courage to aspire to your highest ideals and the blessing of facing the end of your days with as few regrets as I have." Sadly, Vivian Connell died in August 2016. I wrote about her on my blog: "Vivian Connell, RIP," *The Merrow Report*, August 23, 2016, https://themerrowreport.com/2016/08/23/vivian-connell-rip.

12. "A Tale of Two Cities," Learning Matters, 1999, https://youtu.be/W7DiicWqiG0.

13. Barnett Berry, Ann Byrd, and Alan Wieder, *Teacherpreneurs: Innovative Teachers Who Lead But Don't Leave* (Hoboken, NJ: Jossey-Bass, 2013).

14. "About Us," National Board for Professional Teaching Standards, accessed January, 4, 2017, http://www.nbpts.org.

15. "Get Started," National Board for Professional Teaching Standards, accessed January, 4, 2017, http://boardcertifiedteachers.org/get-started/value-for-teachers.

16. Richard Klein, "Two New Studies Add to the Evidence Base on Board-Certified Teachers' Impact on Student Achievement," National Board for Professional Teaching Standards, accessed January 4, 2017, http://www.nbpts.org/newsroom/two-new-studies-add-evidence-base-board-certified-teachers-impact-student-achievement.

17. The series, which aired as part of a monthly "magazine" program on PBS, *The Merrow Report*, is in the Learning Matters archive, which now belongs to Editorial Projects in Education.

18. John Merrow, "Toughest Job in America," *Education Week*, March 15, 1999, http://learningmatters.tv/blog/documentaries/watch-toughest-job-in-america/673.

19. This, readers will recall, is the M.O. of school reformers: attack symptoms!

20. Cory Koedel, "Grade Inflation for Education Majors and Low Standards for Teachers," American Enterprise Institute, August 22, 2011. Koedel writes: "Students who take education classes at universities receive significantly higher grades than students who take classes in every other academic discipline. The higher grades cannot be explained

by observable differences in student quality between education majors and other students, nor can they be explained by the fact that education classes are typically smaller than classes in other academic departments. The remaining reasonable explanation is that the higher grades in education classes are the result of low grading standards."

21. The California Basic Educational Skills Test (CBEST) is a standardized test administered throughout the states of California and Oregon for individuals who want to teach at public schools and gain a credential. The test is designed to provide information about basic proficiency in reading, mathematics, and writing.

22. Darrel Drury and Justin Baer, eds., *The American Public School Teacher: Past, Present and Future* (Cambridge, MA: Harvard Education Press, 2011).

Step Eleven: Measure What Matters

1. The single best source of information about testing and resistance to over-testing is the National Center for Fair and Open Testing, better known as FairTest. FairTest regularly publishes a free scorecard of developments that you can subscribe to. It's a small nonprofit, however, so I hope readers will consider contributing. Over the years, I've found FairTest to be an honest and honorable advocate, and, trust me, not all advocates can be trusted.

2. Matthew M. Chingos, "Strength in Numbers: State Spending on K–12 Assessment Systems," Brookings Institution, November 2012.

3. Validity and reliability are fundamental building blocks. A valid test measures what it's supposed to measure, and a reliable test can be counted on to always measure what it's designed to measure.

4. Chingos, "Strength in Numbers."

5. States have been abandoning the Common Core in droves, usually for political reasons.

6. John Merrow, "The Adventures of Sampleman," *Taking Note*, December 1, 2014, http://takingnote.learningmatters.tv/?p=7377. I had some fun with this when I created a comic strip, "The Adventures of Sampleman." In the first (and last) installment, Education Secretary Arne Duncan visits the doctor for his annual physical.

7. This contrasted with the furor that arose when Reagan's secretary of education, T.H. "Ted" Bell, created his wall chart that compared states by their SAT scores, without indicating how many students in each state actually took the SAT, or the incidence of poverty. In the early versions, Oklahoma ranked very high . . . because so few students there took the SAT. Bell adjusted the approach but did not back off.

8. I realize that the law never used the word *failing*, but that's what it signaled.

9. Diane Stark Rentner, Nancy Kober, and Matthew Frizzell, "Listen to Us: Teacher Views and Voices," Center on Education Policy, May 5, 2016, 5–6.

10. Ibid.

11. It's a faux game, of course, but I'll copyright it (Multiple Measures©), to be sure.

12. Diane Rado, "Almost 1 in 4 Illinois Teachers Miss 10-Plus Days of School Year," *Chicago Tribune*, November 7, 2016.

13. Defenders of charter schools sometimes respond with the equivalent of "Yeah, but public schools are worse." Well, at least someone is watching the store, and those who steal from traditional public schools often get caught, while most charter schools are not financially transparent. Here's a case in point, two crooks in Detroit: "2 Ex-Detroit Principals Sentenced in $2.7 Million School Fraud Case," CBS News, September 7, 2016.

14. Regarding the expectation gap: At NBC's 2012 "Education Nation" Mitt Romney said he once asked some Massachusetts teachers if they could tell which children were likely to succeed and, if so, how. He said the teachers told him that they could easily identify the likely dropouts just by noting which parents came to back-to-school night. If parents showed up, those kids were likely to do well. If no parents bothered to attend, then those kids were probably going to be failing students. That was tantamount to saying that what they did as teachers didn't make a difference, and I found the governor's lack of reaction striking. If some teachers said that to me and I was in a leadership position, I would have gotten upset. I would have told them that we have come to a fork in the road here. "We have to figure out how to change your attitude, or you have to find work elsewhere, because we cannot have teachers who accept that reality. We need teachers who will redouble their efforts to change that kid's trajectory, and if there are things you need from me to enable you to make that difference, tell me now." Think about it: What those teachers were telling Governor Romney was that, as far as they were concerned, schools and teaching don't make a difference!

15. I wrote about our affection gap in Step Three.

16. Bill Gates, "A Fairer Way to Evaluate Teachers," *Washington Post*, April 3, 2013.

17. He wasn't. For more information on Ohio's education standards, see "Physical Education," Ohio Department of Education, accessed Jan-

uary 4, 2017, http://education.ohio.gov/Topics/Ohios-Learning-Stan dards/Physical-Education.

18. Cameron McWhirter and Caroline Porter, "For School Tests, Measures to Detect Cheating Proliferate," *Wall Street Journal*, September 26, 2014.

19. Ben Wieder, "The Most Important Award in Public Education Struggles to Find Winners," *FiveThirtyEight*, September 22, 2014.

20. Howard Blume, "Broad Foundation Suspends $1-Million Prize for Urban School Districts," *Los Angeles Times*, February 8, 2015.

21. He has also created the annual Broad Prize for the outstanding Charter Management Organization, worth $250,000.

22. Daniel J. Losen, Michael A. Keith II, Cheri L. Hodson, and Tia E. Martinez, "Charter Schools, Civil Rights and School Discipline," Civil Rights Project, March 2016.

23. Jennifer C. Kerr, "Math Scores Slip, Reading Flat for Nation's 12-Graders," Associated Press, April 27, 2016.

24. Peggy Robertson, "My Comment on PBS NewsHour's Opt Out Coverage," *Garn Press*, June 1, 2015, http://garnpress.com/2015/peggy-robertson-my-comment-on-pbs-newshours-opt-out-coverage; Peggy Robertson, "I Refuse to Administer the PARCC: A Letter to the Citizens of Colorado," *Corave*, September 21, 2014, http://corave.k12newsnetwork.com/2014/09/21/i-refuse-to-administer-the-parcc-a-letter-to-the-citizens-of-colorado. In the open letter, she writes:

> By funneling all of our tax dollars to corporations for curriculum, tests and technology to implement the test, we have ignored the elephant standing in the middle of the room—the number of homeless school children in Colorado, which has more than tripled in the last decade. The poverty rate of black children stands at approximately 40 percent while the poverty rate of Latino children is approximately 30 percent. Colorado also has the third fastest growing rate of childhood poverty in the nation. We know quite clearly that children who have quality nutrition, healthcare, as well as access to books via libraries with certified librarians, and all the other resources provided to children in particular zip codes, actually, have done quite well on standardized tests in the past. Yet, we continue to ignore this fact, and we continue to feed our children living in poverty only tests.

25. John Merrow, "Why Some Students Are Refusing to Take the

Common Core Test," *PBS NewsHour*, March 11, 2015; John Merrow, "Mending School: An Annotated Poem by John Merrow," *Learning Matters*, http://learningmatters.tv/images/blog/FINALMENDING .jpg. In my version of the famous poem "Mending Wall," I imagined Robert Frost as a supporter of the opt-out movement.

26. Oren Pizmony-Levy and Nancy Green Saraisky, "What's Driving the Opt-Out Movement? The Belief That High-Stakes Testing Promotes Rote Learning and Is Unfair to Teachers, a TC Survey Finds," Teachers College at Columbia University, August 2016.

27. Robertson told me that the unions had spurned requests for support early on. Now, she said in 2015, UOO isn't particularly interested.

28. Valerie Strauss, "How Can Anyone Take Standardized Test Scores Seriously When Stuff Like This Happens?" *Washington Post*, September 4, 2016.

29. Apparently, they had reached their limit on testing, finally. One student explained to a reporter: "I find this time of the year to be just as stressful as before APs," Kristin Li said. "Now that APs are over, I've simply shifted my focus to SATs and ACTs. On top of that, I'm studying for my national registry exams to become a certified EMT, I'm becoming increasingly involved in my school clubs, and I dance four to five days a week. I can't speak for everyone, but my life is just as busy as it was earlier in the year." Dani Blum, "More Skip New Standardized Tests," *Ridgefield Press*, June 2, 2014.

30. John Merrow, "'Sit and Stare' to Prepare for Democracy?," *Taking Note*, June 18, 2014, http://takingnote.learningmatters.tv/?p=7039, note 6.

31. "School Informed Parents of Low-Performing Students They could Opt Out of State Tests," *Washington Post*, September 8, 2016.

32. The challenge, as school districts cut back on bubble testing, is to determine what students and teachers will do with all the free time. "More direct instruction" is the worst possible choice, in my view. Today's technologies offer remarkable opportunities for exploration and creation, but if educators just swap computers for textbooks, the enterprise is doomed. As we showed *in School Sleuth: The Case of the Wired Classroom*," nothing is impossible . . . but only if educators are willing to take risks.

33. In the 2014–15 school year Robertson refused to administer the Common Core test known as PARCC to her students in Aurora, Colorado. She was suspended and eventually resigned.

Step Twelve: Choose a New Path

1. For an inspiring example of what's possible, go to http://hechingerreport.org/statewide-school-reform-gains-fans-concerns-letting-students-learn-pace. I suggest you read the article and watch the video.

2. If I were a young man, I know I would be building a team to open a charter school. I've even got a name: the HAYI Charter School. Pronounced "hi ya," the initials stand for "How Are You Intelligent?" Since I'm no longer young, I hope some readers will do it instead.

3. John Merrow, "Wisdom from Four Decades of Education Reporting," PBS, October 15, 2015. As you will see, she got me to promise to write this book!

Index of Names

About the Author

John Merrow recently retired as education correspondent for *PBS NewsHour*. He has won the George Polk Award, two George Foster Peabody Awards, and the McGraw Prize in Education. His books include *The Influence of Teachers*, *Declining by Degrees*, and *Choosing Excellence* and he blogs regularly at *The Merrow Report*. He lives with his wife, Joan Lonergan, in New York City.

Celebrating 25 Years of Independent Publishing

Thank you for reading this book published by The New Press. The New Press is a nonprofit, public interest publisher celebrating its twenty-fifth anniversary in 2017. New Press books and authors play a crucial role in sparking conversations about the key political and social issues of our day.

We hope you enjoyed this book and that you will stay in touch with The New Press. Here are a few ways to stay up to date with our books, events, and the issues we cover:

- Sign up at www.thenewpress.com/subscribe to receive updates on New Press authors and issues and to be notified about local events
- Like us on Facebook: www.facebook.com/newpress books
- Follow us on Twitter: www.twitter.com/thenewpress

Please consider buying New Press books for yourself; for friends and family; and to donate to schools, libraries, community centers, prison libraries, and other organizations involved with the issues our authors write about.

The New Press is a 501(c)(3) nonprofit organization. You can also support our work with a tax-deductible gift by visiting www.thenewpress.com/donate.